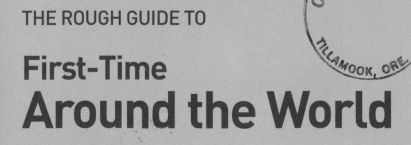

THE ROUGH GUIDE TO

First-Time
Around the World

written and researched by

Doug Lansky

**ROUGH
GUIDES**

roughguides.com

Contents

Introduction to

First-Time
Around the World

The world is flat. Or so the thinking went, until someone actually went off to circumnavigate it. You may not make such a colossal discovery during your own global journey, but what awaits you "out there" is something only you can find: your very own adventure. Beyond your part of the planet lie mountain ranges with echo-bending canyons, tangled jungles, deserts that stretch into sanguine sunsets and yellow savannah veiling lions, wildebeest and springbok. There are retina-burning white beaches tapering off into gin-clear waters that serve as a playground for dolphins, turtles and manta rays. Not to mention over six thousand languages, countless botanical wonders, architectural masterpieces and geological anomalies. All that is already out there. The decision to find it is yours. Who knows, you may just find a best friend, even the love of your life, along the way.

My own plan was to walk out the front door, head to Florida and try to hitchhike on yachts to South America – all on a budget stretched tighter than an aging Hollywood forehead. Without getting into details, my yacht-hitching scheme only got me as far as the Virgin Islands. And the only reason I made it that far was because I flew there. (Turned out I was trying to hitch south during hurricane season, when all the boats were headed north or into safe harbors.) This start, however rocky, did launch me on a two-and-a-half-year trip that forever changed my life. And not just because it ended with a car accident in Bangkok, which left me in the unfortunate position of having a broken ankle and amebic dysentery – a tragic combination of constantly having to go to the loo, and never being able to get there quickly enough. I ended up traveling for another seven years as a travel columnist, meeting my Swedish wife, and then living in five countries for over the next twelve years.

ABOVE TEMPLE OF HEAVEN, BEIJING; COUNTY GALWAY, IRELAND; MATTERHORN, SWITZERLAND
OPPOSITE HMONG MINORITY PEOPLE, VIETNAM

MEETING LOCALS

It's hard to pick up a travel magazine, brochure or guidebook without seeing an exotic cast of faces. The unspoken message seems to be that this is who you'll meet in these countries. The people you're far more likely to encounter, however, are other travelers. And the local people you'll mostly come in contact with are vendors, taxi drivers, guides and hotel clerks – people serving you. To make more genuine contacts takes some effort, but is perhaps the single most important aspect of enriching travel. Volunteering or working in a place is one of the most traditional methods. You can also use the web. Get in touch with local organizations (eg if you're a fencer, get in touch with the local fencing clubs and attend practice when you are in different cities) or find out about Couchsurfing opportunities. But even if you're just looking to take a picture of someone, a thoughtful approach might lead to a more meaningful connection.

Before I get ahead of myself, though, I just want to assure you this book is not going to try to persuade you to travel, nor make grandiose assertions that stomping around the planet with a coated-nylon pack will somehow fulfill whatever may be missing from your life. Travel is an urge best cultivated from within. In fact, one of the biggest favors you can do for yourself is to **travel if and when you're ready**, not when someone else thinks you should. The more eager you are to open yourself up to life on the road, the more willing you are to embrace the unknown rather than sign up for a pre-packaged, air-conditioned experience, the more likely you are to reap real rewards.

Believe it or not, nearly anyone can get around the world in one piece (or in my case, two), and I'd be lying if I told you that you needed this book to come back alive. However, the downside to blindly winging it is that you'll make **mistakes**, some potentially dangerous, many costly and some just plain embarrassing. By the time you get through the first section of this book, you should be savvy enough to chart an itinerary for your trip and avoid nearly all the snares that await you. With a glimpse of

WORLD FACT FILE

- **World population** over 6.8 billion
- **Circumference of the earth** 40,000km
- **Height of Mount Everest** 8850m/29,035ft
- **Depth of the Mariana Trench, Western Pacific Ocean** 10,924m/35,840ft
- **Highest temperature** El Azizia, Libya 136°F/58°C
- **Lowest temperature** Vostok, Antarctica -126°F/-88°C
- **Tourism** The World Tourism Organization's most recent figures show there were 940 million international tourist arrivals, which generated $930 billion and accounted for five percent of the world's GDP. More than six percent of all jobs worldwide are supported by the travel and tourism industry.
- **Worldwide**, according to UNHCR, there are now 42.5 million refugees (15.2 million displaced, 26.4 million internally displaced, and 895,000 in the process of seeking asylum).

life on the road, a feel for the essentials, and by addressing a number of travel's most testing issues ahead of time, you'll be well on your way.

The **regional profiles** in the second part of the book tell you what it costs to get around, how long it'll take to cross the various landmasses and if there are any rail, bus or air passes you may wish to buy ahead of time to make things cheaper and more convenient. You'll notice we took some liberties in dividing up the world into eight regions: North America, for instance, normally includes Mexico, but because of popular overland routes, a shared language and its latitude, Mexico has been placed in the Central America and the Caribbean section. The regional **maps** are meant to provide ballpark estimates of the times of overland travel on common routes. They are by no means instructing you to take such routes (it's always better to find your own way), nor are they completely accurate, since delays do occur, particularly in less-developed regions.

Of course, you'll want more specific information eventually, either from websites or publications listed in the **Directory** section at the end of this book or from your guidebook once you arrive. But at this point, much more information than what you'll find provided here will bog down your planning process instead of helping it along. And remember that there's such a thing as too much planning. One of the greatest thrills of travel is trying to make your way between two points by the least travelled, most arduous route, chancing rides and roads and climates as you go.

TIME AND SPACE

One thing that travelers often forget to mentally prepare for is the different conception of **time and space** on the road. With buses that don't leave until they're full, boats that wait at the harbour for the captain to return from his family holiday, and mechanical problems that require spare parts sent by cargo ship from Australia, the hardcore traveler's mantra "no watches, no calendars, no worries" begins to seem like a healthy response to seeing your carefully planned itinerary fly out the window. Your **personal space**, on the other hand, is likely to shrink, whether you're speaking with someone who insists on standing almost nose-to-nose during the conversation or you're packed into a six-person minivan with seventeen other passengers.

Plan for twice as much transport time as you think you need, try to grab a seat near a window so you can control the fresh-air supply – and make sure you've got something to read.

things to enrich your journey

Adventure and cultural insights can be found almost anywhere. How you decide to travel (your mindset) and what you decide to do is far more important than where you decide to go and what you intend to see. Thinking in terms of "doing" rather than "seeing" will enhance that most vital, often elusive, dimension to your travels: depth.

1

1 PARTICIPATE IN A FESTIVAL

Don a costume and join a Brazilian samba school, get sauced at a tomato-throwing melee or covered in colored dye at Holi .
Holi festival, India

2 LEARN A LANGUAGE

Break the ice by speaking Mongolian or bargaining in Hindi. Private and group lessons are a bargain in many countries.
Studying Spanish, Guatemala

3 GO ON A SAFARI

Get out of the minivan and view the wildlife on foot, from a canoe, or even from the back of an elephant.
Lake Nakuru National Park, Kenya

4 BARGAIN AT THE MARKET

Practice your language skills, meet some locals and get a good price all at the same time.
Sham Shui Po Market, Hong Kong

5 TAKE A LITERARY JOURNEY

Connect the sites from your favorite foreign book or follow in the footsteps of an author.
Hotel El Muniria where William Burroughs wrote *Naked Lunch*, Tangier, Morocco

6 RIDE A BICYCLE

They're available for rent in almost every city and a great way to explore places off the tourist trail.
Mountain biking in the Făgăraş Mountains, Romania

7 GO UNDERGROUND

With the right equipment and a guide, the subterranean world is ripe for exploration.
Gruta de las Maravillas, Andalucia, Spain

8 CHECK OUT A SPORTING EVENT

Don the local team's colors and make a few new friends.
Estadio Olimpico Atahualpa, Quito, Ecuador

9 FIND YOUR OWN PRIVATE, DESOLATE BEACH

Find a hammock with your name on it and stay still until you've recharged your wanderlust.
Ko Wua Talap, Ang Thong Marine Park, Thailand

10 PICK UP SOME LOCAL TRENDS

It could be learning a new skill or you might just spot a hat, shirt or shoes from a traditional outfit that you could incorporate into your wardrobe.
Tango, Buenos Aires, Argentina

11 TAKE A TRADITIONAL BATH OR HAMMAM

Don't forget the traditional scrub and massage as well.

Gellert Baths, Budapest, Hungary

12 TRY THE STREET FOOD

Even if you get unlucky, gastrointestinal setbacks can usually be treated in a few hours if you know what to do.

Night market, Cambodia

13 WAKE UP EARLY

See the sights before the crowds arrive.

Safari, Tanzania

14 LOSE YOUR GUIDEBOOK

Wander the backstreets of a city.

Amman, Jordan

15 TAKE A COOKERY COURSE

Even if you just learn to make one great dish, your friends and relatives will be grateful for years.

Thai cooking course, Chiang Mai, Thailand

16 RAFT THE RAPIDS

For an instant shot of adrenaline.

Trancura river, Chile

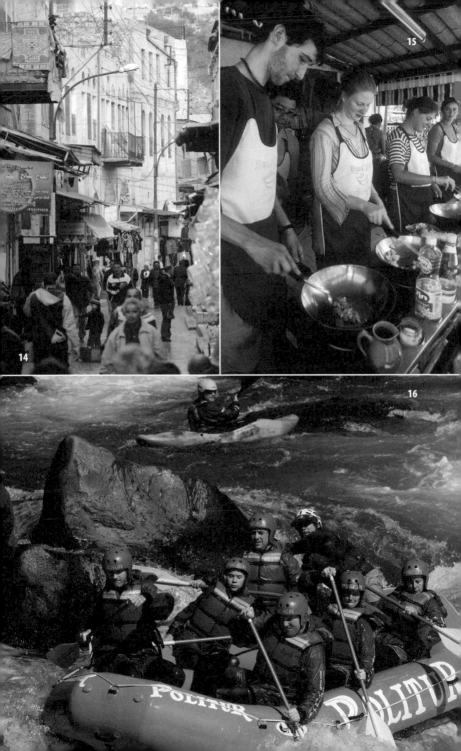

20

21

22

17 CLIMB A MOUNTAIN
Walk one of some classic trekking routes or take a mountaineering course and scale a peak.
Trekking to Everest, Nepal

18 SPEND A FEW DAYS IN THE JUNGLE
Hire a guide to learn about animals and plants – and to help you find your way back.
Monteverde Cloud Forest, Costa Rica

19 SAMPLE THE LOCAL FIREWATER
Leave the backpacker bubble and take a seat beside a local.
Japanese whisky bar, Tokyo, Japan

20 PUT YOUR LOCKS IN THE HANDS OF A LOCAL BARBER
Some consider this more nerve-racking than bungee-jumping.
Hair braiding, Bali, Indonesia

21 SPEND THE NIGHT SOMEWHERE UNUSUAL
The underwater hotel in Florida, a cave hostel in Turkey, Sweden's ice hotel, a pit dwelling in Tunisia… There are plenty to choose from.
Matmata, Tunisia

22 HEAD UNDERWATER
Even if you can't dive – a mask and snorkel are often sufficient and can be even better for exploring.
Hanauma Bay, Honolulu, Hawaii

23 MEET LOCALS WHO SHARE YOUR INTERESTS

Check the web to find the local clubs or where people show up to play.

Reggae concert, Negril, Jamaica

24 TRY OUT A NEW SPORT

One you've always been curious about or one you've never seen.

Kitesurfing, Lake Wakatipu, New Zealand

First-Time Around the World

The big adventure

1

FAQ

Q: I've just got three months. Is that too short to travel around the world?

Well, since the actual flight time to circumnavigate the planet is about 40 hours, no it's not, but it is too short to try to see most of it. As long as you don't attempt to visit too many destinations, you're fine. In fact, you'll likely have a far more enriching trip than someone who travels for twice as long but tries to see four times as much (see p.35).

Q: I've got $5000 (£3150) saved up. Will that get me around the world?

No problem. You can find great deals on round-the-world tickets for about a third of that price (see p.47), or hitchhike on yachts (see p.53) for free. The more important question is what kind of trip do you want to take and how long do you want it to last? To figure out a daily budget that fits your comfort level, and to learn which countries offer the best value, turn to the "Costs and savings" chapter (see p.71), where you'll find some budgeting tips.

Q: I've got a smart phone. How do I use it while traveling without it costing me a small fortune?

You're going to have to make some adjustments to your mobile usage. Exactly what depends on how long you're staying in one spot and what you're willing to spend for the convenience of constant connectivity. If you're spending a couple of weeks or more in one place, it can be worth your while to pick up a local SIM card (or a cheap phone with one if your SIM is locked in). Otherwise, you'll probably want to shut off data roaming until you find a wi-fi hotspot (see p.164).

1

Q: How do you know where to sleep each night, what to see during the day, and how to get around?

Carry a guidebook – or a digital version of one. It will cover all the sights in each town, with a short review of the best affordable accommodation, often accompanied by a helpful map (although getting a bit lost now and then is a healthy way to travel). In peak season, you may want to book accommodation a day or two ahead of time, easily done on the internet from wherever you are staying, since just about every remote hostel around the planet has a high-speed connection these days. If you want to think even less, just wander into the tourist office, conveniently located in train and bus stations or in the center of town, tell them your budget, and they'll call around and make a booking for you, draw it on a free map and tell you how to get there.

Q: I can mispronounce about five words of French and less than that in Spanish. Can I manage traveling around the world speaking English?

Better than your digestive tract will manage only eating at *McDonald's*. Learning the local language (see p.98) would enrich your experience and make it easier to understand your new environment and to meet locals, but even the least gifted linguist can pick up "please", "thank you", "excuse me", "how much?" and "no, that's my backpack you're smelling" in about twenty minutes – about the time it takes to make the final descent before you touch down in the new country. If you must use English, lose the slang, keep your speech slow and basic, and don't take a puzzled look as a sign to speak louder. Plus, you can even get an offline app (see p.291) that will let you speak into your phone in English and it will spit out your phrase in any language.

Q: Are there some basic precautions that can help me travel safer?

Quite a few. You can make yourself less of a target for pickpockets/muggers (see p.170), you can learn how to avoid unsafe neighborhoods in each city (see p.172) and you can inform the right people when you head off the beaten path (see p.178). It's also a good idea to register with the State/Foreign Office (p.45) and keep an eye on local alerts for violence/terrorism. And solo women travelers should be aware of special safety strategies (see p.67).

Q: What about travelers' diarrhea? What should I expect?

You should expect to get it. But if you get it checked out quickly (simple microscope analysis) you can typically get some meds at any clinic and you should be feeling fine within an hour or two. Don't "ride it out" – total waste of a couple of days. Surprisingly, more travelers get the shits when eating from buffets (yes, even in nice hotel restaurants) than simple, cheap restaurants because so many people work with the food and all it takes is one set of unwashed hands.

1

Q: Is taking time off going to ruin my career?
It might delay that promotion, but there's a better chance it will improve your career prospects, and make it easier to land a new job. That gap in your CV (résumé) isn't going to make you look like a drop-out stoner unless you walk into your first post-trip job interview with the same dreadlocks, nose piercing and tattered shirt you only washed twice while crossing India. Most prospective employers will find your journey an interesting topic of conversation (one you should be prepared to talk about); it's likely to be either something that they've done or a dream they wished they had fulfilled. Make sure you've worked out a few life-lessons from your trip and how they might apply to the job at hand. Or consider looking for employment that might fit well with your travel experience (such as wine sales if you worked on the grape harvest in France one season, or a job at a newspaper if you honed your photography skills and put together a solid portfolio from your travels). If you're particularly concerned, you might see if you can plan some work-related education into your trip – such as learning a language, taking a writing course or attending cooking school (see p.97). That also shows prospective employers you were cerebrally engaged during your trip and viewed it as a continuation of your education.

Q: I'm thinking of going with my best friend. Is that a good idea?
It's a tough decision. And if doesn't seem like one, that's probably because you haven't fully considered what you're getting into. Make sure you think through the potential pitfalls and how to minimize them (see p.66).

Q: C'mon, do I really need travel insurance?
Only if you get really sick. Or injured. Or sued for some driving accident. In short, yes. But unless you get insurance that fits your travel plans, it won't do much good. Which means you shouldn't necessarily sign up for that convenient policy your travel agent pushes across the desk or the convenient "click here for insurance" button when you buy your ticket online. If you plan to trek in the Himalayas but your policy doesn't cover you for trekking (and you get injured), it's a policy payment down the drain and you've still got an enormous bill to cover. Oddly, insurance companies rarely cover the exact same things, so you have to dig a little deeper to find out (see p.109).

Q: I want to make my journey alone, but I'm worried about several things… about feeling alone, about foreign diseases, about getting injured overseas, about getting everything stolen.
There are hundreds of thousands of travelers out there right now making solo journeys and most of them had just as many concerns as you do.

1

What experienced travelers do differently

This entire book is filled with lessons learned, but here are the seven most noticeable things that have changed in the way I travel after having spent ten years on the road in over 120 countries. I've noticed many of my most experienced traveling colleagues have developed similar habits.

- I am no longer that interested in traveling someplace simply to see something, so going to a new city just to have a look around now holds much less appeal. These days, my motivation for travel is what I'm going to do when I get there: hike a specific trail, volunteer with an interesting project, try my hand at some new thing, or get to do one of my favorite activities (such as kitesurfing) in a new spot.
- I'm more comfortable with a small pack. For some reason I thought I needed more stuff – you know – just in case. The more you travel, the more you realize you can find virtually anything you need on the road.
- I don't need to conquer as much territory. I used to think, for example, that a month in New Zealand was loads of time, and I'd start trying to figure out how much ground I could cover in that time. Now I'm happy (and realize I get more out of it) if I visit fewer places, stay longer in each one and try more of the local things in each spot.
- I plan the stops during the trip, even look forward to them. If I travel quickly for a bit, I know I'll get sensory overload and appreciate the travel less. I count on this now and decide on some interesting places to stay put for a while.
- I take more pictures of the details along the way (road signs, toilets, meals, doorways) and fewer postcards and posed shots.
- I always find out the approximate price for any taxi ride, then make sure I'm getting in the right type of taxi and that we've agreed on the price (or meter) before getting in. Even in the most developed nations (like Sweden) getting in the wrong taxi will cost you dearly.
- I'm less worried about the micro savings. I realized I don't sit around after a trip and think, oh, I should have walked an extra three kilometres for that slightly cheaper bakery that day I was hanging out in Rome. It's good to be frugal, but I'm better at not letting the tiny expenditures dictate my entire trip.

Doug Lansky

Loneliness can be a problem, particularly at the beginning of a trip and during some meals, but you'll find your stride and start meeting other travelers before long. For tips on coping with this, learn how to manage the "culture shock" of your new surrounds (see p.159). For advice on how to handle injuries, diseases and other survival issues, it's not a bad idea to pack a little emergency kit and manual such as *The Rough Guide to Travel Survival* (book or iPhone app version), which will run you through what to do in the event that everything gets stolen, how to get rescued if you get lost in the wilderness and how to treat the most common travel medical emergencies.

Q: I hear a lot about "attractions", "must-sees" and "wonders". Is it tourist-bureau hype or is there something to it?
A bit of both. When the hype lasts long enough, it seems to become legend, or even fact. The classic is the "Wonders of the World" lists (see p.28). Truth is there's no such thing as a "must-see" and you'll have a far

more enriching trip if you personalize your journey (see p.43) and don't construct it around seeing the major attractions.

Q: Is there one thing I'm likely going to forget?

Earplugs. Hostels and cheap hotels are often located next to busy streets and nightclubs. Some buses and trains have minimal ventilation and you'll need to keep the windows open, which lets in plenty of air but more decibels than you'd care for. And don't forget about the snoring roommate – there's typically one assigned to every dormitory room. There are a few more things you'll want to bring; see our clothes pack list (p.122), toiletry pack list (p.125) and medical pack list (p.128) to make sure you don't forget anything.

Q: Should I register with my government before I leave?

Not a bad idea. If there's any terrorism or a natural disaster, you'll be first on the list to get help from the embassy. Plus you'll get important updates as you go. It's easy to sign up (see p.45) and it's all free.

Q: What new technology is available to help me travel safer?

A well-informed and well-prepared traveler is the best form of safety, but there are two interesting tech-gadgets (see p.166) that some may find appealing. Rather, your worried parents may find appealing. These wallet-sized items pair with your smartphone and tap into the global satellite network to send out text messages (sorry, no photos yet) to your friends and family (by email or via Facebook/Twitter) from any ocean, desert or mountain top. If you enable a function, they can even follow you on an online map. Best of all, if you get into trouble, they can send out an SOS. However, it's another gadget you have to keep charged, worry about and learn how to use. And the interface on both items leaves room for improvement.

2

Initial planning

Deciding where to go, how to get there, what to do and how long to stay is a lot easier than it sounds. In this chapter, the planning process is dissected into small, easy-to-chew pieces that will get you under way, from choosing which treks and courses to consider to avoiding troublesome weather or catching festivals you won't want to miss.

How do you calculate how much time you need for your trip?

With 196 countries stretched around the planet's 47,000-kilometre girth, it would take several lifetimes to see it all and do it all. Almost everywhere you go, you'll meet travelers who will tell you about amazing places you won't have time to visit. The truth is, you won't know how long you'll want to go for until you get out there. Your best defence, therefore, is to try to carve out as much time as you can for your trip beforehand, since it's easier to come back early than try to push back deadlines once you're on the move.

If you already know how long you've got, you should be thinking about the pace of your trip. How many countries, cities, festivals, courses, jobs and so on should you try to tackle in that amount of time? While it may not be a scientific formula, a good guideline is this: don't plan more than four **major activities** per month in advance. (Sorry, visiting India does not count as a single activity. Nor does visiting a region. But things like a two-day cooking class, short stay with a relative, a few days exploring a major city and a hiking trip do.) If you plan to see, say, Paris and Rome in June, that doesn't mean you just see these two cities. It means you get to make up the rest of your plans on the move as you travel between them. This approach allows for ample flexibility, plus any transport delays you may encounter.

Should you see the world on a tight budget?

Independent budget travel isn't for everyone – especially if you're not thrilled about riding on buses that use the horn as a turn signal, greeting *and* emergency brake. Or using toilet paper better suited for removing barnacles from the underside of harboured yachts. Or spending the occasional night in a place that considers the urine stain on the mattress all the decoration the room needs. If this little sample didn't faze you (much), you're in luck. The **cultural and social pay off** of budget travel is enormous, the experience invaluable and it's unlikely to bankrupt you, or your parents.

This book is primarily designed for the independent budget traveler because… well, they're the ones who need the most information. If you're not planning to travel on the cheap, you'll still get plenty of essential information and itinerary ideas from the following pages, but you should be aware that a thick wallet has a tendency to insulate you from the very culture you're trying to experience. Also, you may have to limit your time on the road, or knock off a bank. A year of air-conditioned tours, meals served on real tablecloths and comfortable hotel rooms could set you back $100,000/£63,000, whereas it can be done for as little as $10,000/£6300. Or, with a few tips from Chapter 5, for even less than that.

2

If the length of your trip is largely dictated by budget, check out Chapter 5 to help calculate your time on the road and maximize the funds you have (rough budget estimate: $20–75/£13–47 a day not including major transport costs). However, you don't necessarily need to let your initial funds shorten your trip. Chapter 6 covers jobs and volunteer projects, so you can leave home with minimal funds or stretch your trip for years.

A year off has a nice ring to it. Besides, most round-the-world tickets (see p.47) are designed with that as an upper limit. It almost seems like this is the length of time society and the travel industry has deemed appropriate. Much shorter and you may get accused by "hardcore" travelers of not getting a real taste of the road. Much longer and people back home may start to think you've completely lost it. Even if you have to be back in a year, better to tell people (and yourself) that you're returning when you're ready. It's not worth keeping going just to reach an imaginary time limit, or cutting your trip short just when you find a great travel job or fall in love.

Where should you go? (not where you might think)

Since no traveler can do it all, the tendency is to head for the "best" places. What are the best places? It feels like a natural question, but you're better off refraining from asking it as you gather information about your upcoming trip, because it isn't going to reveal much useful information. Ninety percent of your travel experience will be made up of the people you meet, the weather, spontaneous adventures and little cultural discoveries you make along the way. It goes the other way as well: a bad experience is colored with random mishaps ranging from bus breakdowns to bed bugs to boring travel companions. I'm not a big fan of Bangkok, for example, but my perspective includes the fact that I was run over by a car and spent time in the hospital there. I know others who love it. Besides, what may seem awful at the time may, in retrospect, prove to be the most life-changing event of your journey.

The only person to ask where you should go is yourself. Grab a pencil, take a look at the four points below, and start jotting down places, sights and activities that sound appealing. You can figure out how to connect them later. You can also get some ideas from the sample round-the-world itineraries in Chapter 3 (see p.51).

Go where you speak the language

No, not English. A second language. (Although an English-speaking country is a fine place to start your travels. Think of travel like learning to ski… hit the "easier" places first and work your way up to the lands with more cultural and logistical challenges.) Even if you can just read a menu and a few street signs, you're off to a good start. You can begin to interact with a country in a real, independent way. And once you start using a language, once you start looking around and trying to decipher the words or communicate where you need to go, the learning curve becomes nearly vertical.

Go where you have family or friends

Don't be afraid to look up that childhood pen pal in Ghana or your third cousin once removed in Hungary. To cover your bets, bring along some kind of document or a snapshot to help bridge any language gaps. With a little luck, you'll find you've got yourself a cultural guide. You'll almost certainly get a free place to stay and, if nothing else, an inside look at the way they live, from food and interior decor to bowling and strip clubs – whatever, in fact, your relatives happen to do for fun. If you're still at university, take the opportunity to get involved with **international groups**. Students visiting your campus from other countries for a year (or several years) are typically members of an international club, and tend to want to make friends with locals. Hanging out with club members is a nice way to start traveling while still at home and, better yet, you'll have some new friends to visit (and maybe free places to stay) during your trip.

Go somewhere you've longed to see

A little wanderlust goes a long way. If you've read about a place, heard other people talk about it for ages, or had some sort of childhood fascination with it, that's not a bad reason to go. At the very worst, it's a decent starting point (many of the travelers who end up in Timbuktu are there because they like the sound of it).

Is it ethical to visit oppressed countries?

Should you go to Uganda and allow your tourist dollars to fuel a government that has not managed to put a stop to warlord Joseph Kony? Are you lending legitimacy to a Chinese-occupied Tibet with even a quick visit to Lhasa?

A limited **influx of tourist money** might make those in power realize that they could make more by catering to tourists' desires with a free society. It might also deter them from taking action; they could argue that tourists are coming anyway. Some say boycott visiting. Nobel Laureate and spiritual leader His Holiness the Dalai Lama is encouraging visitors to Tibet. In both cases, some money goes to the oppressed, some goes to the oppressors. Should you decide to visit one of these places, while you're there you can help a little, or rather, you can minimize the damage. You can steer clear of government-run tour agencies, hotels and shops, so that more of your money buys bread instead of bullets.

To some extent, your real **impact** depends on what you do afterwards. Your visit in and of itself may not help the causes of the oppressed, but what you learn about them and pass on to others can. The Dalai Lama is counting on visitors' tales to fight the giant Chinese propaganda machine. You can give money or volunteer your time to various good causes, such as Amnesty International. You can write to your local representative and insist on more political pressure to not do business with those in power. Even a "Free Tibet" bumper sticker on your car is a step in the right direction.

Can you do these things without visiting the country? Of course. But if you plan to raise your voice in protest, it can be helpful to get a first-hand look.

But where should you **draw the line?** You don't like the death penalty in the USA? Maybe you shouldn't spend your tourist dollars there either (or shouldn't go to the states where it's permitted). Historically, Australia hasn't been kind to Aboriginals. The Brazilians are wiping out the Amazonian rainforest. The Turks, Iraqis, Armenians, Iranians and Azerbaijanis have it in for the Kurds. The Norwegians and Japanese are hunting whales. The more you think about traveling ethically, the trickier it gets. Just about every country on the planet has dozens of skeletons in the closet if you choose to look closely enough. And once you start down that path, it's hard to know where to stop. It becomes a very personal decision, with few whites and blacks, just a vast collection of greys. The best thing to do is arm yourself with as much information as possible, and pass on what you learn to others.

Best way to figure out where to go: follow your interests

The concept is simple enough: instead of thinking about what you'd like to see, think about **what you'd like to do**. Approach the trip as a chance to collect unique experiences, not postcards. If you're a golfer, you might pursue the sport to its roots with a round at the Old Course in St Andrews in Scotland. Or try a twist, and stop for a game of sand golf in the United Arab Emirates. There's even ice golf in Finland, where you can play with a bright orange ball, tee it up on an ice cube you hack out of the fairway and putt on icy "whites". If you like to cook, you may take a pastry course at the world-famous Cordon Bleu school in Paris or try a day of curry preparation at the *Oriental Hotel* in Bangkok. The more original your approach, the more memorable your experience is likely to be.

"Wonders of the World"

Nothing seems to attract visitors like a Wonder of the World. And, once you start traveling, these Wonders seem to be everywhere. You may start to wonder yourself which wonders are actually Wonders (not to mention UNESCO World Heritage Sites, a status currently conferred on 878 places in 145 countries).

Only one of the Seven Ancient Wonders remains intact today: the Great Pyramids. The list, first referenced in the *History of Herodotus* in the fifth century BC and then by chief librarian Callimachus of Cyrene (305–240 BC), proved to be such a public relations success that historians, writers and architects have been trying to create updated versions ever since. Not surprisingly, they can't quite reach consensus. Some assert, for instance, that the ancient list was flawed because the Greeks were unaware of such marvels as the Great Wall of China, and have filled in the gaps with a list of "forgotten wonders". Today, several lists of geological anomalies and man-made structures have also emerged, each with its own merits. With so many attractions touting their particular wonder, this round-up may provide some perspective to the PR you're bound to encounter.

Seven Wonders of the Ancient World

- The Pyramids of Giza, Egypt
- The Hanging Gardens of Babylon, Iraq
- The Statue of Zeus at Olympia, Greece
- The Temple of Artemis at Ephesus, Turkey
- The Mausoleum at Halicarnassus, Greece
- The Colossus of Rhodes, Greece
- The Lighthouse of Alexandria, Egypt

Natural wonders

- Angel Falls, Venezuela
- The Bay of Fundy in Nova Scotia, Canada
- The Grand Canyon in Arizona, USA
- The Great Barrier Reef, Australia
- Iguaçu/Iguazú Falls, Brazil/Argentina
- Krakatoa Island, Indonesia
- Mount Everest, Nepal/Tibet
- Mount Fuji, Japan
- Mount Kilimanjaro, Tanzania
- Niagara Falls, USA/Canada
- Paricutín Volcano, Mexico
- Uluru (Ayer's Rock), Australia
- Victoria Falls, Zambia/Zimbabwe

2

Forgotten wonders

- Abu Simbel Temple, Egypt
- Angkor Wat, Cambodia
- The Aztec Temple in Tenochtitlán (Mexico City), Mexico
- The Banaue Rice Terraces, Philippines
- Borobudur Temple in Java, Indonesia
- The Colosseum in Rome, Italy
- The Great Wall of China
- The Inca city of Machu Picchu, Peru
- The Leaning Tower of Pisa, Italy
- Mayan Temples of Tikal, Guatemala
- Moai Statues in Rapa Nui, Easter Island
- Mont-Saint-Michel in Normandy, France
- The Old City of Jerusalem, Israel
- The Parthenon in Athens, Greece
- The rock-carved city of Petra, Jordan
- The Shwedagon Pagoda, Burma (Myanmar)
- Stonehenge, England
- Taj Mahal in Agra, India
- The Temple of the Inscriptions in Palenque, Mexico
- The Throne Hall of Persepolis, Iran

Modern wonders

- The Channel Tunnel between England and France
- The Clock Tower (Big Ben) in London, England
- The CN Tower in Toronto, Canada
- The Eiffel Tower in Paris, France
- The Empire State Building in New York, USA
- Gateway Arch in St Louis, USA
- Golden Gate Bridge in San Francisco, USA
- The High Dam in Aswan, Egypt
- The Hoover Dam in Arizona/Nevada, USA
- Itaipú Dam, Brazil/Paraguay
- The Kremlin in Moscow, Russia
- The Millau Bridge over the River Tarn, France
- Mount Rushmore National Memorial in South Dakota, USA
- The Panama Canal, Panama
- Petronas Towers in Kuala Lumpur, Malaysia
- Statue of Cristo Redentor in Rio de Janeiro, Brazil
- The Statue of Liberty in New York, USA
- The Suez Canal, Egypt
- Sydney Opera House, Australia

2

What the hell happened to the "adventure" in adventure travel?

These days, with 70-year-olds waiting for hip replacements signing up for "adventure tours", it's hard to know exactly what the term means.

An **adventure** used to involve exploring uncharted waters and lands with hidden dangers. It meant not knowing where it would end up or how or if. Similarly, safari (borrowed from Swahili, originally meaning "a trip") was once used to describe a hunting expedition in Africa and now encapsulates taking pictures of animals from a bouncing minivan, then relaxing by the pool with a dry martini.

"Adventure travel" is typically applied to whitewater rafting, bungee-jumping, trekking and getting spun about in jet boats, especially when these activities take place in foreign countries. The fact is, they're completely **packaged activities** with an outcome nearly as predictable as a fairground ride, rendering them closer to the X Games than what any explorer would dub an adventure. Does that mean you should avoid them? No. A little adrenaline is healthy and good fun. Does that mean there are no "real" adventures left? No. Just make sure you understand which kind you're signing up for. Come to think of it, if you need to sign up for the adventure, that's a pretty good indication of what kind it is.

The trick to timing your trip right

On a long trip you can't be everywhere at just the **ideal time**. And it's not worth trying. Usually, if it's too hot inland, you can head for the coast. And if it's too hot on the coast you can move to higher elevations, where temperatures are milder. If there are monsoon rains in one place, an overnight train or bus can usually take you to the coast that's getting all the sun. This only requires one thing: flexibility. In general, you'll find your timing is great for 75 percent of your trip and you'll take a few hits for the other 25 percent. What you need to investigate, therefore, is not the ideal time to be in each location, but if there are any dates to absolutely **avoid** (see opposite). Much of this depends on what you plan to do. Vienna in January may be chilly but fine for city exploring, especially if you plan to be inside museums and churches, whereas a bike trip around Austria would probably be punishing at that time of year. If you plan to hitch sections of your journey on yachts, make sure you check out the seasonal schedule; same for rough overland trips that could get snowed under or rained out. Likewise, you'll want to know if there are any dates not to miss. If you're applying for a seasonal job, there's usually a tight window. And it's a pity to unwittingly arrive in Venice a day after Carnevale has ended: you're stuck with the crowds but have missed the event (see box, pp.36–38).

How (and why) to beat the travel seasons

Tourist season is climatically favorable, but plagued with crowds and, as a result, more expensive. The advantages of traveling out of season are numerous: low-cost and less-crowded flights, better chances of finding a room at the cheapest hostels, shorter queues at museums, less need for reservations, and – best of all – fewer visitors to distract you from the culture you came to observe. However, you may be looking at some hidden expenses. Some of the cheapest hotels shut down in the off-season, so you may be forced into nicer digs. If it's cold enough to rattle your teeth loose at night, expect to pay extra for a room with heat. If you've arrived in the hot and sweaty season, be prepared to pay more for air conditioning. Sure, you can combat these with a good sleeping bag or a cold, wet sarong wrap, but you might not always be in the mood. As a general rule, the best times to visit are often at the beginning and end of the tourist cycles, the so-called **shoulder seasons**, when you get most of the good weather without the crowds.

A planning must: figuring out when NOT to go

The regions listed below don't necessarily share a common weather pattern, so it's difficult to broadly apply monsoon or dry-season dates. Consult the "Regional profiles" section at the end of this book for more information, plus country guidebooks or specific books on weather (such as *The Rough Guide to Weather*).

- **Africa** March–June: rains in eastern Africa can soak a safari and make roads muddy and impassable. May–June & Oct: northern parts of Africa experience prolonged sandstorms. May–Nov: rains in western Africa bog down roads and render Sahara transit difficult. Christmas season: southern African coastal resorts and safaris fill up with locals.
- **Australia/New Zealand** June–July: freezing nights in the Outback.

Stuck in a typhoon

I can't even remember how many typhoons passed through while I was working in Hong Kong.

The most common local response to a typhoon warning is to shop. The stores might close while the storm passes, so people gather up food, flashlight batteries, that sort of stuff. The bread gets picked clean by the end of the day, but it's far from panic shopping. There's enough advance notice to keep things calm. You just pick up enough to get you by for a few days. Besides, you probably won't be going anywhere since the airport and the public transport to and from it are shut down during the worst of the storm.

When you're picking up some food, it's probably not a bad idea to get some Scotch tape as well. They say if you make a giant X across the window with it, it minimizes the danger of shattering. More commonly, though, the driving rain eventually seeps through the window – or bleeds through – so your things might get wet if you put them in the wrong spot.

The stronger typhoons are serious – flying trees and the like – but if you're inside you're fine. In fact, many places have typhoon parties with cheap beer and offers to "Come weather the storm here". If things officially close down due to weather, it becomes a designated typhoon shelter and everyone already inside is allowed to keep on partying.

Where I lived, when the eye of the storm passed over, everyone ran out to body surf. It was the only time we had big enough swells to do it.

Ron Gluckman, correspondent
(Ⓦwww.gluckman.com)

2

Average temperatures and rainfall

	Jan	Feb	Mar	Apr	May	Jun	Jul	Aug	Sep	Oct	Nov	Dec
Auckland, New Zealand												
Av daily max (°C)	23	23	22	19	17	14	13	14	16	17	19	21
Rainfall (mm)	79	94	81	97	127	137	145	117	102	102	89	79
Bali, Indonesia												
Av daily max (°C)	28	28	28	28	27	27	26	26	27	27	28	28
Rainfall (mm)	394	311	208	115	79	67	57	31	43	95	176	268
Bangkok, Thailand												
Av daily max (°C)	32	33	34	35	34	33	32	32	32	31	31	31
Rainfall (mm)	8	20	36	58	198	160	160	175	305	206	66	5
Beijing, China												
Av daily max (°C)	1	4	11	21	27	31	31	30	26	20	9	3
Rainfall (mm)	4	5	8	17	35	78	243	141	58	16	11	3
Cairo, Egypt												
Av daily max (°C)	18	21	24	28	33	35	36	35	32	30	26	20
Rainfall (mm)	5	5	5	3	3	0	0	0	0	0	3	5
Cape Town, South Africa												
Av daily max (°C)	26	26	25	22	19	18	17	18	18	21	23	24
Rainfall (mm)	15	8	18	48	79	84	89	66	43	31	18	10
Caracas, Venezuela												
Av daily max (°C)	24	25	26	27	27	26	26	26	27	26	25	26
Rainfall (mm)	23	10	15	33	79	102	109	109	107	109	94	46
Copenhagen, Denmark												
Av daily max (°C)	2	2	5	10	16	19	22	21	18	12	7	4
Rainfall (mm)	49	39	32	38	43	47	71	66	62	59	48	49
Damascus, Syria												
Av daily max (°C)	12	14	18	24	29	33	36	37	33	27	19	13
Rainfall (mm)	43	43	8	13	3	0	0	0	18	10	41	41
Hong Kong, China												
Av daily max (°C)	18	17	19	24	28	29	31	31	29	27	23	20
Rainfall (mm)	33	46	74	137	292	394	381	367	257	114	43	31
Istanbul, Turkey												
Av daily max (°C)	8	9	11	16	21	25	28	28	24	20	15	11
Rainfall (mm)	109	92	72	46	38	34	34	30	58	81	103	119
Kathmandu, Nepal												
Av daily max (°C)	18	19	25	28	30	29	29	28	28	27	23	19
Rainfall (mm)	15	41	23	58	122	246	373	345	155	38	8	3
Kingston, Jamaica												
Av daily max (°C)	30	30	30	31	31	32	32	32	32	31	31	31
Rainfall (mm)	23	15	23	31	102	89	89	91	99	180	74	36
London, England												
Av daily max (°C)	6	7	10	13	17	20	22	21	19	14	10	7
Rainfall (mm)	54	40	37	37	46	45	57	59	49	57	64	48

	Jan	Feb	Mar	Apr	May	Jun	Jul	Aug	Sep	Oct	Nov	Dec
Marrakesh, Morocco												
Av daily max (°C)	18	20	23	26	29	33	38	38	33	28	23	19
Rainfall (mm)	25	28	33	31	15	8	3	3	10	23	31	31
Mexico City, Mexico												
Av daily max (°C)	28	29	37	41	40	33	33	33	32	31	29	28
Rainfall (mm)	13	5	10	20	53	119	170	152	130	51	18	8
Moscow, Russia												
Av daily max (°C)	-9	-6	0	10	19	21	23	22	16	9	2	-5
Rainfall (mm)	39	38	36	37	53	58	88	71	58	45	47	54
Mumbai, India												
Av daily max (°C)	28	28	30	32	33	32	29	29	29	32	32	31
Rainfall (mm)	2.5	2.5	2.5	0	18	485	617	340	264	64	13	2.5
Nairobi, Kenya												
Av daily max (°C)	25	26	25	24	22	21	21	21	24	24	23	23
Rainfall (mm)	38	64	125	211	158	46	15	23	31	53	109	86
New York, USA												
Av daily max (°C)	3	3	7	14	20	25	28	27	26	21	11	5
Rainfall (mm)	94	97	91	81	81	84	107	109	86	89	76	91
Rio de Janeiro, Brazil												
Av daily max (°C)	29	29	28	27	25	24	24	24	24	25	26	28
Rainfall (mm)	125	122	130	107	79	53	41	43	66	79	104	137
Rome, Italy												
Av daily max (°C)	11	13	15	19	23	28	30	30	26	22	16	13
Rainfall (mm)	71	62	57	51	46	37	15	21	63	99	129	93
San José, Costa Rica												
Av daily max (°C)	24	24	26	26	27	26	25	26	26	25	25	24
Rainfall (mm)	15	5	20	46	229	241	211	241	305	300	145	41
Santiago, Chile												
Av daily max (°C)	29	29	27	23	18	14	15	17	19	22	26	28
Rainfall (mm)	3	3	5	13	64	84	76	56	31	15	8	5
Suva, Fiji												
Av daily max (°C)	29	29	29	29	28	27	26	26	27	27	28	29
Rainfall(mm)	290	272	368	310	257	170	125	211	196	211	249	318
Sydney, Australia												
Av daily max (°C)	26	26	24	22	19	16	16	17	19	22	23	25
Rainfall (mm)	89	102	127	135	127	117	117	76	74	71	74	74
Tokyo, Japan												
Av daily max (°C)	2	2	6	13	18	21	24	26	22	17	11	5
Rainfall (mm)	25	43	61	84	102	160	188	155	160	147	56	38
Vancouver, Canada												
Av daily max (°C)	5	7	10	14	18	21	23	23	18	14	9	6
Rainfall (mm)	218	147	127	84	71	64	31	43	91	147	211	224

2

2

Dec–Feb: sweltering heat in the Outback. Dec–March: heavy rains in northern Australia can flood roads. Christmas summer holiday: resorts and transport busy.

● **Caribbean & Central America** June–Nov: hurricanes (can usually be avoided if you stay flexible and monitor the news).

● **Central Asia** Oct–June: the Karakoram Highway and the road between Srinigar and Leh (Kashmir to Ladakh) officially close. Nov–March: north central Asia can be wickedly cold. Mid-Dec to March: Himalayan trekking routes may get snowbound.

● **Europe and Russia** Aug: summer crowds along the coasts. Nov–Feb: northern and central Europe and Russia is cold and rainy and snow can disrupt travel, especially in the Alps.

● **Middle East** June–Aug: the heat can get downright uncivilized, especially if the Med isn't nearby for a cool swim. Keep an eye on the Jewish holiday calendar in Israel, as public transport and hotels can be swamped.

● **North America** May–Aug: central USA is prone to tornados (and high temps). June–Sept: hurricanes can hit the southeast coast, but are easily avoided. Dec–Feb: in mid- and northern USA, winter storms cause slow travel and severe cold can limit time possible outdoors.

● **South America** Jan–April: Inca trail can get awfully wet, and closes completely for clean-up in February. The Galápagos Islands are hot and rainy, although the waters are warmer and gentler for divers and the seas can be a bit rougher in late summer when many visit. Mid-Dec to Feb: Christmas holiday rush in Brazil, Venezuela, Argentina and Chile – coastal resorts and transport fills up.

● **South Pacific** Jan: rains can get heavy in the southern islands.

● **Southeast Asia** March–Oct: on the west coast, southwest monsoon rains disrupt diving visibility (and tanning opportunities). Nov–April: northwest monsoon drenches the eastern coast of Thailand and the islands, and the east coast of Malaysia.

How to plan around local holidays and events

Consider this scenario: your overnight train pulls into the station, you stagger over to the tourist information bureau, take a number and wait. When your number pops up, you head to the counter and say you're looking for some budget accommodation for a night or two. The person behind the counter is already shaking their head vehemently before you finish the sentence. There's a Rotary Club convention in town that has taken up all the rooms. The best the tourist office can do is find a room at the Ritz for $400/£252. Or, you can stay an hour's journey outside the city at a little hostel situated next to a maximum-security psychiatric ward.

Occasionally, scheduling conflicts occur. A rock concert, business convention or sporting event unexpectedly disrupts your travel plans. So what do you do? First, just try to avoid the situation by keeping an eye on your guidebook for national holidays or other events that might cause a hotel-booking frenzy. Then, if you expect the local accommodation to fill up, either email ahead for a reservation or stop at another town on the way and delay your arrival until a more auspicious day. It's an opportune time to head somewhere not mentioned in a guidebook. If you've already arrived, the easiest and most common solution is to simply move on to the next town. For this, the tourist office can be quite helpful. But before you do, ask for a list of accommodation the tourist bureau represents and try to get online. Crosscheck their list with the one in your guide and on the web. Often, there are several hotels, especially the cheaper digs, not on the tourist office's list. Give those places a call first; they're the most likely to have room. Or look for less conventional places to stay, such as camping grounds that rent out tents or university dormitories. Better yet, try ⓦwww.airbnb.com and other similar private rental solutions (ⓦwww .tripping.com aggregates many). Or stay for free with a local via a service like couchsurfing. If the weather is favorable, don't forget to ask about rooftop sleeping at hostels.

How much time should I spend in each place?

Traveling too fast and trying to see too much may be the number-one traveler mistake. Spend at least **two days longer** in each city than you think. Maybe even two weeks. The faster you go and the more ground you cover, tempting though it may be, the less you'll see. The same way that slowing down improves your peripheral vision when driving, reducing your speed allows you to take more in while you travel. If you're not pressed to press on, you may take an extra day to forge a friendship with another traveler you met over breakfast, or find out your favorite musician is giving a concert in an ancient amphitheatre nearby, or that the local cultural center is offering free palm-tree-climbing lessons. With enough time and curiosity, something interesting is bound to happen.

One of the most important things to plan: a break

Travel may sound romantic and adventurous, but finding your way around a city, coordinating train schedules, locating a place to stay, carting around three kilos of unexchangeable small coins, taking the stairs up every tall structure for a scenic overview, using perplexing toilets, sampling palate-numbing foods and happening on nose-tweaking smells – the things that give independent travel its bite – combine to form an exhausting experience, especially if you do them daily for months. Traveling is not the same thing as being on vacation, so give yourself a chance to relax.

2

30 festivals and events around the world

Festival planning usually takes some advance legwork, as cities and towns can get booked up over a year in advance. Last-minute accommodation, if indeed there is any, usually gets snatched up several days before the event. But the extra effort it takes to attend a festival is almost always worthwhile. There are thousands to choose from. In some you can participate, in some the spectators become part of the spectacle whether they want to or not, but the exuberance is nearly always palpable. See ⓦ www .festivalscom and ⓦ www.whatsonwhen.com

Africa

Great Migration Serengeti National Park, Tanzania. When a million wildebeest do anything together, it's pretty exciting to watch. Add 18,000 eland, about 200,000 zebras and up to half a million Thompson's gazelles. Now throw in a few crocodile-infested rivers that must be crossed and hundreds of hungry lions, and it gets really interesting. People pour in from around the globe to see this moving smorgasbord migrate, with hot-air balloons providing great lookouts for highly inflated prices. May to early June ⓦ www.wildwatch.com/great_migration/

Americas

Burning Man Project Black Rock Desert, Nevada, USA. This pop-pagan, post-apocalyptic gathering of 48,000-plus "burners" (gun-wielding prophets, nude chainsaw-jugglers and so on) has only one stated mission: to burn a giant wooden thing that, even in poor lighting, only barely looks like a man. Aug/Sept ⓦ www.burningman.com

Carnaval Rio de Janeiro and Salvador, Brazil. Carnaval is huge in all of South America, but these two are the biggest shows of all. You get a choice: you can watch the world's most colorful parade in Rio (two days, starting around 7pm and lasting until 5am), after which you'll never look at Liberace or Zsa Zsa Gabor the same way again. Or you can samba away three kilos a night dancing down the streets behind giant trucks loaded with speakers in Salvador. Feb/March (the week prior to Ash Wednesday) ⓦ ipanema.com/carnival

Day of the Dead Oaxaca, Mexico. There may not be life after death, but there's at least a party. The line between the breathing and the buried gets chucked aside for a day so the deceased can come out and play, complete with skeleton costumes and graveside bashes. Oct–Nov ⓦ www.mexonline.com/dayofthedead.htm

Greenwich Village Halloween Parade New York, USA. If you think New Yorkers are frightening in the daylight, check this out. The freak show gets even freakier during Halloween with over 50,000 kooks and spooks and two million spectators. Oct 31 ⓦ www.halloween-nyc.com

Junkanoo Nassau, Bahamas. Even Santa takes a back seat at this Christmas-time Caribbean-beat blowout. Bring a whistle, cowbell or anything else that makes noise. Dec 26 & Jan 1 ⓦ www.bahamas.co.uk/about-the-bahamas/junkanoo/what-is-junkanoo

Mardi Gras New Orleans, USA. Good times have been rolling here since 1699. Even the mayhem of Hurricane Katrina in 2005 couldn't stop this mother of all American streetfests, a bacchanalian party with parades that begin on January 6 (Epiphany) and build to a feverish pitch that culminates on Shrove Tuesday. Feb–March (the week prior to Ash Wednesday) ⓦ www.mardigrasneworleans.com

Monarch Butterfly Migration Angangueo, Mexico. With 100–250 million monarchs attending, it's likely the most spectacular convention of insects in the world. There's a butterfly carpet everywhere you look, and orange and black clouds in the middle of the day. The deep shade of the oyamel fir trees in the forests outside Mexico City lure these beasties from as far as 2000 miles away. Dec to mid-March ⓦ www.michoacanmonarchs.org

New Orleans Jazz and Heritage Festival New Orleans, USA. Ten days of mind-bending jazz, funk, gospel, blues, zydeco, folk and bluegrass – 4000 musicians-worth of it – plus great food. April–May Ⓦ www.nojazzfest.com

New Year's Eve Party Times Square, New York, USA. Wanna see a 500-pound ball slide down a pole? Sing *Auld Lang Syne* out of tune with half a million people? You may risk getting crushed to the size of this book but that's a small price to pay. More interesting than watching it on TV with 300 million others, anyway. Key West, Florida, offers an alternative crowd. Dec 31, arrive early Ⓦ www.timessquarenyc.org

Asia

Full Moon Party Ko Pha Ngan, Thailand. Possibly the best-known travelers' party on the planet – so infamous, in fact, its popularity has waned in recent years. With twelve raves per year, it's hard to miss. Howl at the moon, bark or just dance yourself into a trance. Thousands of lamps (and the odd fire-eater) illuminate the beach until sunrise. Monthly Ⓦ www.kohphangan.com/travel/fullmoon.html

Holi Festival Northern and eastern India. Welcome to the festival of flying colors. Powder dyes are dumped off balconies or playfully thrown at you from ground level (ears, nose, mouth… no orifice is safe from the technicolor assault). Feb–March during full moon Ⓦ www.holifestival.org

International Dragon Boat Championships Hong Kong. Paddle power propels the participants (fuelled with traditional pyramid-shaped *zongzi* dumplings) as they pull through the waters just off Hong Kong in 11.6m boats. The boats have been battling for over 2000 years to commemorate the suicide drowning of the poet-politician, Qu Yuan. The festival is tied to the lunar calendar, so check for dates. June Ⓦ www.dragonboat.org.hk

Naadam Festival Ulaanbaatar, Mongolia. Sometimes called the Mongolian Olympics, Naadam focuses on three main events: wrestling, archery and horse racing. Throw in some folk dancing and fermented mare's milk, and you've got yourself a festival. July Ⓦ www.csen.org/Mongol.Nadaam/Mongol.text.html

Pushkar Camel Fair Pushkar, India. If you ever need to get your hands on 30,000 camels, this is the place to go. In addition to the camel swap, there are races, camel polo matches and other events, but people-watching plays a big role as the town's population increases by 2000 percent during the week. Nov Ⓦ www.pushkar-camel-fair.com

Australia

Beer Can Regatta Darwin, Australia. Would-be yachtsmen can chug their way to the rank of captain in no time at this event: a coupling of aggressive drinking and aggressive sailing for the sake of charity. What more could you want from a pseudo-sporting event? Third Sunday of July. Ⓦ www.beercanregatta.org.au

Gay and Lesbian Mardi Gras Sydney, Australia. Gays, bis, straights and synthetic fibres are all warmly welcome as the gay and lesbian pride hits the streets, maximum exposure being the order of the day. Feb–March Ⓦ www.mardigras.org.au/

Europe

Ascot Races Berkshire, England. You can bet on the horses, but keep your eyes on the pomp on parade. Morning suits for men and formal dresses for women, not to mention hats of all sorts, from those with the shade coverage of a patio parasol to dainty little numbers not much bigger than a cinnamon roll. Third week in June, Tues–Sat Ⓦ www.ascot.co.uk

(continued....)

2

30 festivals and events around the world (....continued)

Carnevale Venice, Italy. A decadent renaissance festival, pyjama party and three-day rager against the backdrop of the world's most picturesque sinking city. The costumes are as elaborate as they are expensive. And guess what? They're for sale. Feb–March (the week prior to Ash Wednesday) Ⓦ www.carnevale.venezia.it

Cooper's Hill Cheese Roll Brockworth, England. People have been chasing a cheese down a sixty-degree slope here for over 200 years. Most tumble in a blur of legs, hands and dislocated shoulders all the way to the bottom. Don't worry, there are plenty of ambulances standing by. Last Mon in May Ⓦ www.cheese-rolling.co.uk

Glastonbury Music Festival Glastonbury, England. The biggest jam-fest in the UK. Performers on the three main stages have included Oasis, Paul McCartney, James Brown and a full cast of platinum-selling album holders. On the fringe of the concert you'll find market stalls (over 600 of them) offering everything from goat meat to henna tattoos. Not enough? Check out the freak show or help make a giant rhino out of mud. Late June Ⓦ www.glastonburyfestivals.co.uk

Kirkpinar Oil Wrestling Tournament Edirne, Turkey. Smear yourself with oil and wrestle for a camel and stack of cash? Believe it or not, it's been a winning formula for 600 years and it's still going. Over 1000 contestants sign up every year. July 5–11 Ⓦ www.kirkpinar.com

Oktoberfest Munich, Germany. Just grab a seat and a frothy "mas" and start slidin' back the brew. The atmosphere (fourteen tents with a combined capacity of almost 100,000 happy drinkers) makes the beer taste even better. But don't be fooled by the name; most of the event takes place in September. Sept–Oct Ⓦ www.oktoberfest.de

The Palio Siena, Italy. With bribes, religion and dirty tricks, this horse race is straight out of the Middle Ages. To be precise, 1147. Riders representing Siena's different neighborhoods battle and race around the town square for three laps. Medical personnel are on alert for both riders and horses. The party starts for days before each of the two big races. July 2 and Aug 16 Ⓦ www.ilpalio.org

Paris Air Show France. You don't need to be on the market for your own private F-15 to attend. The public, 300,000 of them, turn out to see new models unveiled and flown every other year on the spot Charles Lindbergh first landed. It's the biggest air show going. June (odd-numbered years only) Ⓦ www.paris-air-show.com

Running of the Bulls Pamplona, Spain. People have been testing out their insurance policies at this event for years. Eight days of drinking, reveling in the streets and, oh yes, attempting to avoid stampeding bulls on a narrow, winding, cobblestoned street armed with nothing more than a pair of tennis shoes and a hangover. (Two days before, animal activists stage a "Running of the Nudes" in protest.) July Ⓦ www .sanfermin.com

St Patrick's Day Dublin, Ireland. If you're not in green, you'd better have a good excuse. And a hangover that makes you feel green doesn't count. There's everything from Skyfest, an enormous fireworks display, to a treasure hunt that has families scurrying around the city. The full week of craic culminates with half a million lining the streets for Ireland's biggest parade. March 12–17 Ⓦ www.stpatricksday.ie

La Tomatina Buñol, Spain. Ingredients: one small town that produces cement, one town plaza, 30,000 lunatics (mostly drunk) and 40,000 kilos of tomatoes. Mix aggressively for one hour or until town is sufficiently red, then rinse at a local watering hole. Aug Ⓦ www.latomatina.org

Whirling Dervish Festival Konya, Turkey. The famed Whirling Dervishes spin their way closer to God only once a year, but the celebrations last a week. The dizzying ceremonial dance is accompanied with drums, flutes and camera shutters. Dec Ⓦ www.mevlana.net

To some extent, taking a break is going to happen on its own. You might stumble on a place you can't resist, get stuck waiting for a visa application to process or for a transport strike to end, find a fun person or group of travelers to hang out with or just hit the sensory overload wall.

The last one will occur if the first four don't. This exhaustion – think of it as cultural burnout – may creep up on you, or just descend on you at once. It typically occurs after two to four months of continuous, fairly fast-paced travel, but you'll need to find your own threshold. Here's the main symptom: you spend more and more time in cafés and hostel lounges and less out exploring towns and museums. There's a simple remedy for **recharging your wanderlust**: stay put.

Give yourself a chance to absorb and process what you've seen. Write some long letters, pen a song, start that novel. Get to know a few locals. Take the opportunity to earn some money. Who knows, stay in one place long enough and you might even fall in love.

On a long trip, allow yourself the flexibility to stop when you need it, or plan ahead so you end up at your dream white-sand hangout. If you hope to work or volunteer (see Chapter 6), or take a course or pay a relative an extended visit, you might try to plan some of that ahead of time as well. Whether or not you schedule a pit-stop in advance, you should factor in some "down time": approximately two weeks for every three months on the road.

The art of hanging out

It's been said that one of the most problematic aspects of doing nothing is that it's hard to know when you're finished. Hanging out, though, is hardly doing nothing. There's an art to this inertia.

Travelers who used to visit **hangouts** for weeks and end up staying for months or years are now more typically coming for days and leaving after weeks, or coming for days and leaving in days. They have tighter itineraries, more energy, and are about as politically active as Bart Simpson. You can still hear Pink Floyd tunes wafting through café terraces, but increasingly common is thumping electronic beats beckoning travelers to nightclubs or outdoor raves.

In **popular hangouts**, it's rarely just enough to find a beautiful beach with

Staying and leaving

A friend of mine would never leave a place until he'd had a good time there. Another friend would not leave a destination until he had learnt something encouraging about the people and their culture. Both are currently stuck in Brisbane.

I would never suggest that you set yourself such stringent criteria on what is in essence such an arbitrary decision. If you're having a good time – stay. If you've met someone you fancy and who fancies you – stay. If you're too buggered to move – stay. If the police are closing in on you – go.
Peter Moore
Author, *Vroom with a View* and *Swahili for the Broken-Hearted*

palms jutting out over cheap bungalows; they more often come equipped with traveler cafés and offer "adventure" activities, from diving to camel safaris.

Returning hippies may only recognize a few traits left on the Trail (namely, the funkadelic outfits derived from local handicraft), though the new batch of hangouts still serves as gathering points for gaggles of travelers in search of an escape from the very countries they came to see. The places may not be the bargains they once were, but they're still relatively cheap ($5–15/£3–9 for barebones accommodation). And the police seem to be employing the same law-enforcement techniques: a blind eye coupled with the occasional bust.

The classic refuges for relaxing and revelling are listed below.

Goa

Where is it? Southwest coast of India, about 17hr by bus south of Mumbai.

What's the attraction? Once known for its status as the crown jewel of do-nothingness on the Hippie Trail, it has turned into one of the world's largest rave scenes. Despite the place being almost completely taken over (and overrun) by Russians, thousands of techno-loving revellers (many over from Europe on a two-week holiday charter) continue to arrive and decorate the forests with fluorescent orange and lime paint. Groups of travelers rent dumpy cottages for weeks or months at a time, but short-term accommodation can be scarce. The beaches are spread out and each has its own scene with the exception of two common seaside roamers: hungry cows and hawkers.

Byron Bay (and Nimbin)

Where are they? Australia's east coast, 12hr north of Sydney by bus.

What's the attraction? Originally the surfing was the major pull in this otherwise sleepy town with 30km of unbroken sandy beaches. For some, it still is. The surfies were followed by the hippies, who brought with them enough crystals, herbs and tarot cards to transform it into Australia's New Age center. It was then discovered by the backpack set, who have been slowly pushing the once enchanting small community the way of Times Square, with mainstream developers licking their chops. If you don't mind the rather intestinal sound of Westerners trying to learn the didgeridoo, it can be extremely relaxing. The town of Nimbin, an hour inland, is known for its cookies and status as the unofficial marijuana capital of Australia.

Gili Islands

Where are they? In Indonesia, east of Bali, just northwest of Lombok.

What's the attraction? The major draws are beaches, beer and bongs.

There's also diving, snorkelling and nightly beach bashes. Most of this just occurs on the party island of the three, called Trawangan, with a ring of cottages and restaurants that stretches nearly all the way around the shore to house and feed all the merry-makers. Depending on the island you're headed to, it takes 20min to 1hr by *jukung*, a small outrigger that leaves from Lombok's Bangsal Harbour. It can be crowded at certain times of the year and may travelers find more tranquility in Lombok.

Ko Pha Ngan

Where is it? Thailand, 15hr by bus/ferry south from Bangkok.

What's the attraction? Drawn by the pill-popping, fire-eating, breast-exposing rave parties on the island's Haad Rin beach, about 5000 people show up every month to sacrifice their cerebellums under a full moon. Naturally, you need to get there a little earlier to secure accommodation, then stay a little longer to recover. The beaches and tranquil waters are likely to lure you into lingering.

Dahab

Where is it? On the Red Sea coast of Egypt's Sinai Peninsula, 8hr by bus from Cairo.

What's the attraction? Travelers coming from Israel are typically burnt-out kibbutz and moshav workers who have been picking fruit or milking cows for months. But wherever you've come from, the cushioned and carpeted Bedouin tents right on the shoreline with sweet-tobacco octopus-shaped water pipes offer a welcome break. Sadly, there's not much snorkelling any more. The coral reef, or what's left of it, has been trashed over the years and fished out by local restaurants. New "mini-Dahabs" are popping up all along the coast.

Pokhara

Where is it? Nepal, 6hr by bus west of Kathmandu.

What's the attraction? Trekkers these days gearing up for or returning from the Annapurna circuit can't seem to resist the charms of this serene lakeside town, which has one of the world's most spectacular mountain backdrops. You can rent a canoe, shop for excellent used climbing gear or just munch fresh brownies and play Battleship in a café.

Cape McClear

Where is it? Lake Malawi, Malawi, 5hr by bus from Blantyre, then a 20km lift in the back of a pick-up truck.

What's the attraction? It's a classic backpacker watering hole on the shores of the 570km-long freshwater Lake Malawi, serving up cold beer, thatched tents and a dreamy selection of hammocks. For the less lethargic, there's a full range of water activities, from kayaking to scuba diving.

2

The history of the hippie traveler hangout

The original **Hippie Trail** grew out of the 1960s the same way just about everything else did at the time: with a search for spiritual enlightenment. Or, at any rate, drug-induced enlightenment. Or, at any rate, drugs. Throw in sex, rock'n'roll, adventure and a VW bus and what self-respecting beatnik could possibly refuse? The word Kathmandu had a magical ring to it. And, more important, it had cheap ganja. The clothing was just an added psychedelic bonus: baggy leggings from India, embroidered Pakistani vests covered in little mirrors, Afghani sheepskins for evening wear and Nepali prayer beads for all occasions metaphysical. By the early 1970s, a multi-hued stream of near-penniless travelers had created a pulsating road to Kathmandu.

The most common **route** passed from northern and central Europe through the former Yugoslavia – Croatia and the Dalmatian Riviera, Sarajevo, Montenegro, Macedonia – into Bulgaria and on to Istanbul. Until the mid-60s, the trail just stopped in here: most hippies were content to drift to Marrakesh or Mediterranean havens (Tangier, Ibiza, Greece). But gradually Istanbul developed into a major launching pad to the East, with travelers passing through (or out) in droves. They stayed at "The Tent", a corrugated iron and canvas shelter on the roof of the *Gulhane Hotel* next to the Blue Mosque, while they gathered information at the Pudding Shop, the closest thing to a guidebook. Travelers swapped tips and directions to private homes with rooms for rent. From there, The Trail went across Turkey, northern Iran (with a stop in Tehran) and into Afghanistan. A major crossroads formed on Chicken Street in Kabul, which served as the halfway point (and halfway house) of the journey. With a fresh stash of hash, travelers traversed the breathtaking mountain passes and proceeded on to Pakistan, then over the border and into India. After paying homage in Manali, the supreme supply center of marijuana, and Dharamsala, the seat-in-exile of the Dalai Lama, it was over to Varanasi for a toxic splash in the Ganges river, and north to Kathmandu.

Meanwhile, back on the other side of the Atlantic, American hippies had worked their way down to a charming Guatemalan volcano-surrounded lake town called Panajachel. Before long, there was a virtual stockpile of stoned foreigners wearing mismatched Guatemalan outfits, and the town was dubbed Gringotenango.

The orally swapped travel information found its way into guidebooks, which helped pave the way for other travelers. More families turned their homes into guesthouses, and cafés started popping up to accommodate visitors reluctant to give up their Western eating habits. The quest for enlightenment, chemically induced or otherwise, has not diminished completely, but has been diluted by a newer breed in search of famous attractions, adventure excursions and passport stamps.

Dali

Where is it? Southwest China, 5hr by bus northwest of Kunming.

What's the attraction? It's said to be the best place in China to get away from China. Even among the Chinese in the region, it's known as a backpackers' paradise. Travelers are inclined to stay in the center of the ancient city on Yangren (Foreigners') Street, which isn't more than a short stumble away from the town's popular cafés. Pagodas, temples, lakes, mountains – it's a visual delight.

Vang Viang

Where is it? Northern Laos, 6hr by bus from Vientiane.

What's the attraction? In a word, drugs. This hangout, a modern-day Manali, is one of the budding centers of narco-tourism. Discount opium and weed beckon travelers (over 35 guesthouses full of them) to this otherwise easily missed hideaway. Muang Sing, another Laotian center for delirium, gets plenty of narco-traffic as well.

Lamu

Where is it? An island just off the northeast coast of Kenya, 7hr by bus north of Mombasa.

What's the attraction? Since the donkey sanctuary isn't a big draw, it must be the sloth-like pace of life (aside from the initial barrage of hustlers trying to help you find a place to stay) and dawdling dhows sailing travelers up and down the blinding beaches and off to distant islands. Zanzibar's sleepy northern cousin has Kenya's oldest functioning town (also called Lamu) and possesses much of the same medieval pulling power.

Researching your trip

Start online. Let's say you speak Spanish and you like scuba diving: got to your favorite web search engine. Type in "scuba" and "Spanish" and see what pops up, then narrow the search with words like "shark" or "tequila" or whatever diving aspects you deem essential. You can often find reviews and references online as well just by adding the words "reviews" or "references" to the search.

For specific activities, look in specialist **magazines or their online sites**. For a cooking course or fine dining, for example, you might look in *Gourmet Magazine*; for photography trips, *Outdoor Photographer*. If you're looking for general ideas, major-city or national **newspaper** travel section websites are invaluable.

For information directly from other travelers, you might try the straight-up reviews at Trip Advisor or look for more broad and specific tips at **discussion boards** such as ⓦwww.virtualtourist.com and ⓦwww .lonelyplanet.com's Thorn Tree, where you can post and read messages on thousands of specific travel topics. **Travel blogs** are another great source of first-hand – and often recent – information.

How to customize your itinerary

You've got a few places in mind, some weather you want to miss and a few dates you want to hit for festivals or seasonal activities. Before you start stringing it together with your chosen methods of transport (see p.140), there are a few more things to consider.

2

If it's your first big trip, **which countries you visit first is important**. If you're going to India, France and New Zealand, for example, India is the most challenging of the three and won't make the best starting point. Besides, after India, France and New Zealand won't seem quite as exciting. If you start in New Zealand, it will still be thrilling, but much easier. Once you get a feel of getting around on your own, move on to a country like France, where there's a solid infrastructure but, to some extent, a language barrier. After that, navigating the train stations and markets of India will be significantly easier to handle.

Take a moment and consider the **balance of your trip**. You want a good mix of attractions, adventure, a few courses, a little wandering, ample breaks, a measure of hiking, some kind of animal viewing, and maybe even a dose of meditation. And if you're traveling with a round-the-world ticket, add in an overland journey and maybe even some sea passage. Chances are your trip may be thin in a few of these areas. Just remember to space them out. You don't want to feel like you're trapped in a Jules Verne novel or a contestant on *The Amazing Race*.

To find out how to connect the dots using the transport best suited to the task, head on to Chapter 3. Just remember that by changing your departure date you may be able to neatly sidestep any meteorological conflicts, and that by stopping to work/volunteer/study/hang out, you can achieve the same effect.

Is it safe to go there? Where to check political stability

Try to get into the habit of picking up an international newspaper and scanning the headlines for any turmoil in the area. America's State Department website tends to play up the dangers. This may help prevent lawsuits, but it can also scare people away from a reasonably safe destination. Instead, or at least as a comparison, try the UK's Foreign Office (ⓦwww.fco.gov.uk), Australia's Smart Traveller (ⓦwww.smartraveller .gov.au)or Canada's traveladvice website (ⓦvoyage.gc.ca), which provide a more sensible synopses. Before heading anywhere you're not sure about, get a quick update from the web and learn how to be prepared (p.170) just in case things turn sour while you're there.

Remember: a **travel warning** does not necessarily mean you should not go – it just means you should investigate a step further (and check if your insurance provider will cover you once you get there). There's a big difference between the security for tourists in, for example, Iraq and in the far safer Israel or Philippines, yet both can be found on the same US State Department warning list. To figure out which countries really are dangerous and which just suffer from that misconception, but are actually safe (and often cheap and appealingly devoid of tourists), you'll need to do some basic research. Check with local tourist offices and

Ease of travel

Easy (traveler infrastructure, no language barrier): Australia, New Zealand, South Africa, Singapore, Israel, Canada, USA, UK, Ireland, Scandinavia
Moderate (traveler infrastructure, but language barriers for English speakers): France, Italy, Spain, Germany, Japan
Tougher (less infrastructure, language barrier): India, Bolivia, Syria, Uganda, China, Cambodia, El Salvador, Morocco

2

online travel chat rooms (see p.43) to get the traveler's perspective on how dangerous it really is. For volatile regions, it's important to keep checking the situation once you're on the road, too, so keep abreast of travel advice on the web during your trip, and talk to other travelers to check if it's wise to venture into potentially hazardous areas.

Likewise, most cities have more risky neighborhoods where you should think twice before venturing (especially at night). Check out a simple tip in the security section to figure out where not to go in the city (see p.172).

Register with the State Department/Foreign Office before you leave

The foreign offices have all gotten plugged in with some solid digital traveler assistance. Sign up for free to get the latest travel updates, and – more importantly – many offer travel alerts while you're on the move. If there's a natural disaster, terrorist act or coup d'état, those who are registered are more likely to get useful alerts about the help provided and direct assistance from the embassy. Depending on how you feel about it, it can be nice to have Big Brother know your whereabouts just in case. But remember to go online and update your travel plans if they change. (And this works well with short trips, too.)

Where to register
- **Australia** Ⓦ www.smartraveler.gov.au
- **Canada** Ⓦ www.voyage.gc.ca/register
- **New Zealand** Ⓦ www.safetravel.govt.nz
- **UK** Ⓦ www.fco.gov.uk/en/travel-and-living-abroad/staying-safe/locate
- **USA** Ⓦ https://step.state.gov/step

Why you need to book certain activities well in advance

Just because you find the ideal activity, that doesn't mean you have to book it. In fact, you can often save more than fifty percent of the cost by

2

Staying flexible

When I first traveled around Europe by train, I planned to go to London, Paris, Italy and Greece. Everything else, I figured out once I arrived. Today, I do a little more background reading, but the approach is the same. Months ahead of my trip, I read novels and classics set in the place I'm going to. I don't open my guidebook and start looking for places to stay until I'm on the plane heading there. If you make a detailed itinerary, you take away the excitement. And then it's easy to get disappointed because you often have to break with your plans. I think the joy and inspiration of travel comes from finding your own way.

Per Andersson
Editor, *Vagabond Magazine*

foregoing the middlemen and making arrangements once you arrive. However, there are some courses and tours that fill up well in advance. You can't always tell which these are, but it's possible to make a decent guess, or check on the web. If you reasoned, for example, that with constant treks heading out along the Inca Trail there would be no trouble to finding a group, you'd be wrong (there are only five hundred trail passes allotted per day and no more are sold even when there are cancellations, so most book about **three months in advance**). There may be some size limit to a pastry course at the Cordon Bleu, a Zambezi canoe safari or a trip to see the gorillas in Uganda — so these would be worth booking in advance; at the very least, send an email to find out about availability. Guidebooks often tell you which activities need to be booked in advance and which don't. When in doubt, check the web and follow up with a call or email. Keep in mind, though, that you'll hear about plenty of activities from travelers as you go, so don't knock yourself out researching. This is really only something you want to do for a "crown jewel" experience on your trip.

Hate to plan in advance? Consider this

Here's another way to go about it: get a passport, rustle up some cash and hop on the next bus that passes. Connect to an airport, train station or harbour, and head in whichever direction cries out. If you need a visa to get there, no worries, just pick somewhere else. Or fill out a visa application, find a cheap hotel and wait for the visa to be processed. While you're waiting, you might look into a few vaccinations, study the language and meet a few locals. Or don't. Go with the wind and your whims.

The drawback to planning your trip, free spirits claim, is that, to a large extent, you decide in advance what you're looking for. So, while you'll probably find "it", you'll likely miss many of the unpredictable things that are subtly trying to find you. On the other hand, you may miss some of your big ticket dream experiences… gorilla viewing, summitting a mountain, making a famous trek, catching a famous festival, If this doesn't bother you, then don't worry about the planning.

How to get around the world

3

You can hop on a freighter across the ocean, then buy a motorcycle, or maybe a horse, and trade it in for a plane ticket when you're ready to move on. You can work your way from continent to continent on a yacht, or circle most of the world on buses and trains. Price, length of journey, reliability and comfort vary drastically with each mode of transport, so you'll want to pick the ones that best fit your budget, itinerary (or lack thereof) and hardship threshold.

Making sense of the round-the-world flight tickets

The tickets come in two basic forms: a special RTW ticket provided by an airline alliance, and a series of cheap, often consolidated (airline talk for agents who purchase in bulk and pass on the savings) tickets sewn together by a booking agent. With an **alliance ticket**, the standard arrangement is this:

- The ticket is valid up to one year.
- You have to keep going in the same direction around the planet although some tickets do allow backtracking within a region.
- You pay based on the distance you cover (which increases the more you deviate from a direct route around the globe and decreases if you cover some of the ground in overland segments), or by the number of defined "zones" you stop in.
- You have to pick your stops and dates when you book the ticket.

3

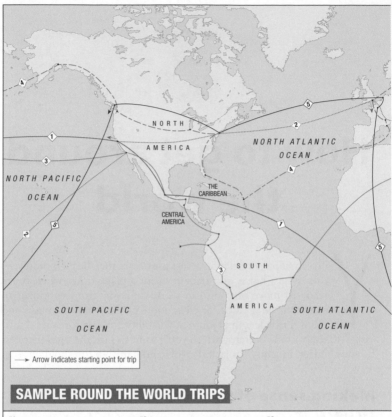

Arrow indicates starting point for trip

SAMPLE ROUND THE WORLD TRIPS

#1
Start in San Francisco; fly to Japan, work as an English teacher in karaoke bar; fly to Beijing; bus to Hong Kong, work as a private English tutor; fly to Hanoi; bus to Ho Chi Minh City; bus to Phnom Penh; fly to Bangkok, kickboxing school; bus to Kuala Lumpur; fly to Kathmandu; fly to Kenya, volunteer to build a school; overland truck to Cape Town; fly to Mexico City; bus to San Francisco.

#2
Start in Sydney; cheap one-way ticket to Christchurch, NZ; bus to Bay of Islands; catch lift on yacht to Fiji, work as a diving instructor in resort; one-way flight to Los Angeles; bus to San Francisco, work as a private gardener; car "drive-away" service to New York; one-way ticket to London, work in pub; Europe train pass, stop in Greece; one-way ticket to Mumbai; train to Kolkata; one-way ticket to Bangkok; bus to Malaysia, work as a diving instructor in a resort; bus to Singapore; bus/ferry to Bali; one-way ticket to Darwin; bus to Alice Springs; a lift to Sydney.

#3
Start in Israel; fly to Salvador for Carneval; bus to Bolivia, tour Salar de Uyuni salt flats; bus to La Paz, Passover; bus to Cuzco, walk the Inca Trail; bus to Colombia; fly to Guatemala, visit Tikal ruins; bus to Mexico City; bus to Los Angeles, work moving furniture; fly to Japan, sell fake designer bags on the street; fly to Bangkok; fly to Nepal for trekking; bus to India, New Year's rave party in Goa; fly to Israel.

Where to book tickets

So do you go with an alliance, a RTW spec list or just do it on your own with your favorite booking service? Our friends at Bootsnall.com just finished an eighteen-page analysis of the market called the "Around The World Airfare Report". Unfortunately, the exact prices of their findings will

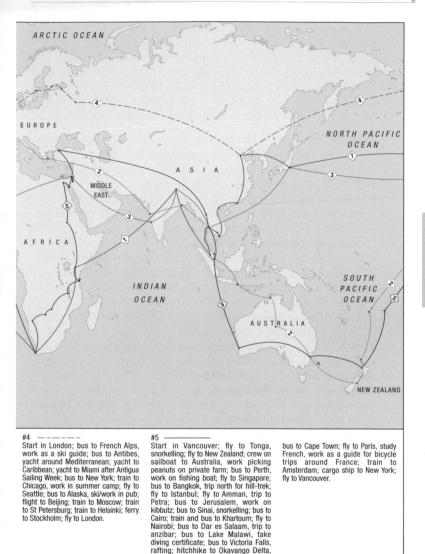

3

#4 ──────
Start in London; bus to French Alps, work as a ski guide; bus to Antibes, yacht around Mediterranean; yacht to Caribbean; yacht to Miami after Antigua Sailing Week; bus to New York; train to Chicago, work in summer camp; fly to Seattle; bus to Alaska, ski/work in pub; flight to Beijing; train to Moscow; train to St Petersburg; train to Helsinki; ferry to Stockholm; fly to London.

#5 ──────
Start in Vancouver; fly to Tonga, snorkelling; fly to New Zealand; crew on sailboat to Australia, work picking peanuts on private farm; bus to Perth, work on fishing boat; fly to Singapore; bus to Bangkok, trip north for hill-trek; fly to Istanbul; fly to Amman, trip to Petra; bus to Jerusalem, work on kibbutz; bus to Sinai, snorkelling; bus to Cairo; train and bus to Khartoum; fly to Nairobi; bus to Dar es Salaam, trip to anzibar; bus to Lake Malawi, take diving certificate; bus to Victoria Falls, rafting; hitchhike to Okavango Delta, safari; hitchhike to Windhoek;

bus to Cape Town; fly to Paris, study French, work as a guide for bicycle trips around France; train to Amsterdam; cargo ship to New York; fly to Vancouver.

likely be outdated a week or two after the report is published. But the essence of what they discovered, summed up here, should help you with your strategy no matter when or where you book. They compared a do-it-yourself option, booking a series of one-way tickets with Kayak (ⓦwww.kayak.com), with fares available from specialist travel agents

and alliance packages. For travel agents, they tried AirTreks (⊕www
.airtreks.com), Round About Travel (⊕www.roundabouttravel.com.au),
Round the World Flights (⊕www.roundtheworldflights.com) and STA
Travel (⊕www.statravel.co.uk). They also checked the alliance packages
from Star Alliance (⊕www.star-alliance.com) and OneWorld (⊕www
.oneworld.com). SkyTeam's packages (⊕www.skyteam.com) could not be
checked online and they were reportedly difficult to get quotes from.

- **Cheapest for basic RTW trips** Do-it-yourself booking came
  out ahead (eg New York–London–Delhi–Bangkok–New York
  was $1678/£1057 on Kayak.com and the most expensive was
  $4968/£3130 on Star Alliance). Again, the exact prices may vary
  from day to day, but this provides a sense of the basic range. They
  made several sample routes with major hubs using different starting
  base cities. STA Travel seemed to come in second.
- **Cheapest for complicated RTW trips** No clear winner. But the
  alliances seemed to be the clear losers with either highest prices
  or inability to even calculate the trip. The range for this sample
  trip: (New York–London–(overland)–Rome–Mumbai–(overland)–
  Varanasi–Bangkok–(overland)–Ho Chi Minh City–Perth–Sydney–
  Easter Island–Santiago–(overland)–Lima–Bogota–New York) was
  between $5200/£3276 and $9100/£5733. Most were in the
  $5500–7500/£3465–4725 range, which is about what you can
  expect to pay for complex RTW ticket.
- **Often cheapest for students and teachers** STA Travel.
- **Most likely to allow free changes** Alliance packages. They may be
  expensive, but free changes is one of the perks. The rest charge
  about $50–250/£32–158 depending on the change.
- **Best route flexibility** AirTreks and STA Travel.
- **Best customer service during booking** AirTreks and the USA
  branch of STA Travel.
- **Best website for trying out new itineraries and getting price quotes**
  AirTreks, followed by STA Travel. STA's takes a bit more savvy to
  get started, but offers better tools for free stopovers, which can be
  valuable.

Should you put an overland segment on your RTW ticket?

Numerous passes allow you to insert overland segments into your trip.
Some even come packaged that way. It can provide a great mission to
connect two points and you'll likely have a nice adventure along the way
and feel you're actually covering some of the globe by land. The problem
is, the longer and more interesting the overland route, the harder it will
be to guarantee you can (or will want to) make your next connecting

Typical RTW routes and sample fares

3-Stop RTW starting in London
London–Delhi–Bangkok–New York–London
DIY using Kayak: $1743/£1098
Round the World Flights: $1766/£1113
STA Travel: $2150/£1355
Air Treks: $2772/£1746
One World Alliance: $3612/£2276
Star Alliance: $4034/£2541
Sky Team Alliance: $4569/£2878

10-Stop RTW starting in London
London–Mumbai–(overland)–Varanasi–Bangkok–(overland)–Ho Chi Minh City–Perth–
Sydney–Easter Island–Santiago–(overland)–Lima–Bogota–London
Round the World Flights: $5049/£3181
Air Treks: $5746/£3620
DIY using Kayak: $5860/£3692
STA Travel: $6253/£3939
Star, OneWorld and Sky Team Alliances: too long to accommodate

16-stop RTW starting in Sydney
Sydney–Auckland–Fiji–Cook Islands–San Francisco–(overland)–Los Angeles–Mexico
City–(overland)–San Jose–Lima–(overland)–Buenos Aires–Cape Town–(overland)–
Johannesburg–Nairobi–Mumbai–(overland)–Delhi–Bangkok–(overland)–Singapore–
Sydney
STA Travel: $5167/£3633
DIY using Kayak: $5370/£3383
Air Treks: $5865/£3695
Round About Travel: $6600/£4158
Star, OneWorld and Sky Team Alliances: too long to accommodate

17-stop RTW starting in NYC
New York–Mexico City–(overland)–San Jose–Lima–(overland)–Buenos Aires–Cape
Town–(overland)–Johannesburg–Nairobi–Mumbai–(overland)–Delhi–Bangkok–
overland)–Singapore–Perth–Melbourne–(overland)–Sydney–Auckland–Fiji–Cook
Islands–New York
STA Travel: $5660/£3566
Air Treks: $5994/£3776
DIY using Kayak: $6600/£4158
Star, OneWorld and Sky Team Alliances: too long to accommodate

3

flight. Either your bus gets delayed at some washed-out bridge, or you find so many mind-boggling things to do that you feel like you've grossly underestimated your time allotment. Which gets back to the flexibility of your ticket. How are you possibly going to know when you book the ticket that seventeen days is exactly the right amount of time to spend in Thailand? The best approach is to take a look at your time management strategy (see p.24), coordinate with any special festivals or activities, and give it your best guess. Then pay a rebooking fee if you guess wrong.

A great RTW alternative: using a home hub

You can also book a series of round-trip tickets with lengthy stopovers and open-jaw tickets (which allow you to fly into one country, out of another and travel overland in between) and simply return home for a quick break between journeys as you head around the world. For example, starting in Vancouver, you might book a round-trip ticket to Santiago, Chile, make some kind of loop around southern South America and then fly back home. From there, after a short breather, you might fly to Delhi with Thai Airways, and take advantage of a free stopover in Bangkok (airlines often stop at their hub city and allow you to stay for days, weeks or months), then make your way overland from Delhi to Kathmandu, and fly back home again (with another stay in Bangkok if you like). You won't necessarily circumnavigate the planet this way, but that's just a technicality. It can be nice to sort out some of the mail that may have piled up in your absence (even if it's coming to your parents' house), spend some time going over your travel pictures, meet up with some friends, grab a change of clothes and work up some thirst for your next destination. If you don't feel like returning home, or just want to save some money, pick a city with great international fares like London, Bangkok or New York, and use it as a base.

Another great RTW alternative: wing it with locally purchased bargain flights

It's not only possible to book one-way flights as you go – **it's usually pretty easy and not necessarily that much more expensive**. Just pick up tickets from local travel agents and get any necessary visas and vaccinations at embassies and health clinics (respectively) along the way. If the country you're entering next requires an onward ticket, no problem: simply buy a fully refundable onward ticket and cancel it once you arrive. (Just remember to ask specifically where you can collect the refund, as some airlines will only perform the service where you bought the ticket or at the corporate headquarters.)

How do you find local deals?

Most of the smaller agencies have been steamrollered by the web in the West, but in many countries travel agencies still thrive. And many countries have well-established travel booking sites as well (locals should be able to tip you on the best ones to use).

Local agents make the deals and know the discounts. Depending on which points you're connecting, it's certainly possible to circle the globe this way (or zigzag around for a while) for the price of a mid-range RTW ticket. Some of these local travel agents are "**destination specialists**". In practice, the term usually refers to an agency run by first- or second-generation immigrants (ethnic neighborhoods are a good place to find them), which focuses on ultra-cheap tickets to "the homeland" by buying large quantities of seats on certain flights (sometimes charters) and operating with lower margins. Though all agencies like to claim that they are **specialists**, one giveaway is if they have a country-specific name (such as Athens Travel for Greek flights, Taj Mahal Tours for Indian flights and so forth).

Bear in mind too that international flights are almost always more expensive than domestic flights that cover the same distance. To get around costly international flights and taxes, it's often possible to string together domestic flights in neighboring countries with short overland connections on buses or trains across the border.

> ### Pay as you go
>
> Because I was traveling for more than a year, I bought my ticket in two halves: New York to New Delhi, then a year later (by phone), the next segment that took me back home. You don't have to return to your starting city within twelve months on all tickets.
>
> Jason Cochran
> Travel writer, *Frommer's Budget Travel Magazine*

3

Are courier flights a viable option?

The short answer is no. There are some ultra-low ticket prices available between major hubs (see Ⓦwww.courier.org) but piecing together any sort of round-the-world journey this way is not realistic.

How to travel the world by sea

Rather than zipping over dimpled oceans at 30,000 feet, you could head for the high seas, especially if you've got a strong stomach. As the saying goes, "If a man has anything in him, travel will bring it out – especially ocean travel." On the plus side though, no other form of transport quite conjures up that special feeling you get arriving by sea: a grand entrance in the style of the great explorers and nineteenth-century travelers. You can circle the world on one ship, skip from boat to boat, or simply make it a segment of your journey. Catching a lift on a **yacht** is the cheapest option. After that it's a toss-up between cruise ships and cargo vessels. To find out which will work out best for your journey, read on.

Yes, you can hitchhike on yachts (and even earn money doing it)

Private yachts of all types often need an extra pair of hands during a sea passage. Some are crewed by professional captains delivering a boat to a new owner and some by "old salt" couples who live aboard their vessels full time. They usually follow common routes across seas where anchorages are safe, the scenery is agreeable and (since many are retired) the prices are low – and simply want a little help or a little company on board. In other words, it doesn't necessarily mean seeing the world with a bunch of nouveau riche assholes.

It's possible to get a working passage or catch a free lift (though some may request $5–25/£3–16 per day to cover your food and drinks) while heading almost anywhere if you know the **sailing seasons, yachting centers and routes** (the big three regions are the Mediterranean, Caribbean and the South Pacific), and how to present yourself professionally. Most agreements to crew aboard a boat are made casually at the individual harbors, though you may have a written contract. Passages can be anything from a couple of days to a couple of months, depending on the destination.

You don't need to be a sailor to crew on a yacht, but if you're reasonably fit it certainly helps. Space is limited, so a compact kit will be appreciated. Show up pulling a Samsonite trolley and you've got a few strikes against you already. There's not much special gear involved, but in your collapsible bag you'll want some non-marking shoes, a good hat that won't land in the drink when the wind picks up, sun block, UV sunglasses with safety straps, motion sickness pills and some smart clothes that won't get you thrown out of the occasional yacht club.

You may be able to catch a ride right back to your departure point, but don't count on it. Even if you've prearranged a long round-trip berth, one thing or another may cause you to hop off earlier. Expect to cough up for a cheap one-way plane ticket, ferry ride or bus trip, depending on where you end up.

Useful yachting websites

Matching skippers and crew

Ⓦ www.crewseekers.co.uk
Ⓦ www.crewfile.com
Ⓦ www.globalcrewnetwork.com
Ⓦ www.partnersandcrews.com

Marina links

Ⓦ www.guam-online.com/myc /myclinks.htm
Ⓦ www.sailorschoice.com/YachtClubs.htm

Crewing agencies

These online crew agencies let you sign up free of charge, and then take a percentage fee from the hiring vessel:
Ⓦ www.crewfinders.com
Ⓦ www.crewunlimited.com

Where and when to find a yacht

The sailing season in the **Caribbean** begins in October, following the summer hurricanes, and lasts until May. If you want to head "down island" (south), show up in Miami or Fort Lauderdale between November and March. Antigua Sailing Week (end of April) is the big event, and the Antigua Yacht Club marina is an ideal place to pick up a berth to just about anywhere, especially South America, the USA or Europe.

The season in the **Mediterranean** kicks off in June when yachts need crew for their summer charters to cruise the Med. Nearly all major marinas are active, but especially Antibes, Las Palmas, Rhodes, Malta, Majorca, Alicante and Gibraltar. Then, from around November 20, there's a 2700-mile fun run (of sorts) from Las Palmas de Gran Canaria (Canary Islands) to Rodney Bay in St Lucia: the Atlantic Rally for Cruisers (ARC). Over two hundred boats participate in the rally, and even more make the crossing unofficially. If you show up in Las Palmas at the beginning of November or before, and chip in some food money for the crossing (about $250/£157), you've got a good chance of catching a lift. To get a step ahead of the competition, you could start your search a few weeks earlier in Mediterranean marinas around Spain or France to catch the yachts before they pass through the Strait of Gibraltar on their way to Las Palmas. But, unlike the typically smooth passage across the Atlantic, the leg from Gibraltar to Las Palmas can get rough.

The major springboard for the stunning islands of the **South Pacific** is a few marinas in northern New Zealand – Opua, Whangarei and Auckland (probably in that order). Most boats leave in the autumn (end February to end April). If you're looking for passage in the other direction (to New Zealand) or on to the USA, your best chances are between July and October. Some prefer to start in Australia – if so, try the marinas in the Whitsunday Islands, Airlie Beach and Townsville. May to July is a promising time to head north towards Indonesia.

Once there, how to look for passage

Head down to any major harbour and start by scanning the **noticeboards**. Then find the **harbourmaster** and ask if he knows any captains looking for crew. That way, you can slip in a personal reference ("The harbour master said I should speak to you about a crew position you're trying to fill"). If that doesn't yield any leads, ask if you can use his radio to announce on the local sailors' channel that you're looking for work. Before walking the docks in search of a captain, try a more informal place like the local sailing-supply shop or, better yet, the harbour bar. If you like to plan ahead, check the ads in yachting magazines and newsletters. There are also crewing placement agencies that specialize in this very service (see box opposite). Or, if you prefer to see the boat and meet the skipper first

3

3

Finding crew work

First, you don't need to know how to sail to do a crossing: you need to be neat, clean and trustworthy. If you're doing day work for a boat in the harbour – which is a good way to get your foot in the door – show up on time and take it seriously. My first boat was pretty shitty. And the captain was mostly incompetent. But I had been working day jobs on various boats in the harbour in Antibes for three weeks and was getting desperate. He did, however, give me a free lift across the Atlantic. And after that, finding boats was easy. I went after the nice boats first. They usually had the best, most talented captains – and the most money. I even got paid over $1000/£630 for the crossing back home after a few months in the Caribbean.

Jonas Persson

My friend and I flew right to Las Palmas, but there was so much competition, it took ten days of active looking before we got a free lift. We walked the docks, even borrowed a dinghy and rowed around to the boats that were anchored just offshore, but didn't get a lift until a captain saw me playing guitar at a party. He brought my friend and I along as onboard entertainment. It wasn't until we were well on our way across the Atlantic that I told him it was the only song I knew. Once we were in the Caribbean, it didn't take longer than five days to catch a lift. You just need to make sure that you don't get left someplace without a lot of yachts. Barbados, St Martin and Antigua are the places you want to be.

I saw a number of women hitching on boats alone, usually doing the cooking, but if it were me, I'd team up with another woman or man for safety.

Peter Laurin

(which is probably a good idea), you may be better off on your own.

If captains don't like how you look or conduct yourself, they may not reveal they have a position available. You need to **dress smartly** and demonstrate that you're easy-going and level-headed. Moreover, you'll need to learn some yachting manners – **always ask for "permission to board"** before letting your foot cross the rail, for example. If you're a good cook, mention it. If you've got technical experience, let the captain know. If you've got some solid job references, keep a few copies on hand. Tell the captain he's welcome to search your luggage (he may request this anyway) and that your travel documents are in order (make sure they are). The interview works both ways: you want to size up the captain and crew as well. Are these people you want to be stuck at sea with? Women travelers must especially be aware. Will you be the only woman on board? Can you speak to other women on board who have sailed with these men before? Find out. Once you set sail, it's too late.

Travel by cruise ship vs freighter

Here's the surprise: it's not much cheaper to take a freighter. There are some reasonably priced cruise ships – if your definition of reasonable is $150–300/£95–189 a day – that can take you across various stretches of ocean (a cruise-booking specialist can help find what's available). On a freighter, the average per day may be lower ($100–150/£63–95) as human freight, but it'll take a bit longer (nearly double the time on some routes), and you may end up staying in a hostel for a few weeks waiting for the ship to leave for its "scheduled" departure, so the total price can easily end up about the same.

There's more to do on a cruise ship, but, as far as hardcore budget travelers are concerned, the image can be an issue. That is, the leg of your journey you made by cruise ship isn't going to be a big hit at the next hostel story-swap.

Another little surprise: freighters tend to put you in fairly luxurious **officer staterooms** (bigger than what you get on cruise ship with a tight budget), many of which have been made available as the ships have replaced crew members with computers. Groups are usually small (about twelve – more than that and the ship is required to carry a doctor), but some freighters have become quasi-cruisers and take up to a hundred passengers.

Besides lengthy departure delays, one of the trickiest problems to overcome on many routes is the **one-way issue**. Ships give priority to round-trip travelers, so one-wayers generally end up on the waiting list. Also, single travelers may face a supplement of ten to twenty percent. If you're over 65, you'll want to bring a doctor's certificate of good health. And, finally, keep an eye out for pirates. The waters off the Horn of Africa (Somalia and the Gulf of Aden) have the highest risk of armed attacks; Nigeria comes in second and Indonesia third. Working aboard freighters for passage isn't likely to be a viable option, but they just might need some cleaning, an extra mechanic aboard or the services of a massage therapist. It never hurts to ask.

3

One more decision: container ship vs bulk freighter

The difference, as far as passengers are concerned, is the likelihood of delays and the number of days spent in each port. **Container ships** carry the giant metal-box eyesores that can be dropped onto the back of a truck, which expedites the loading and unloading process. This means you may only get six to twelve hours in port to look around, but it does help the ship keep on schedule. **Bulk freighters** may take two to three days in port, which gives you more time to explore, but increases the chances of falling behind schedule.

Sample freighter tours

Some of the more common (round-trip) routes include:

- **Australia/New Zealand–USA** 45–70 days
- **Mediterranean–USA** 60–70 days
- **South America–USA** 45–55 days
- **Around the world** 84–120 days

Check out:

Ⓦ www.freightercruises.com Ⓦ www.freighterworld.com
Ⓦ www.freighter-travel.com Ⓦ www.strandtravel.co.uk

What you need to know about traveling overland

Overlanding is usually the cheapest, and by no coincidence most exhausting, way to travel. Anything can happen... and usually does. Buses break down in scorching heat, leaving you trapped next to a tin speaker blasting out Hindi remixes of Britney Spears' songs at inhuman decibels; trains may stop for half a day for no discernible reason at all; and entire roads get washed away. There'll be times when you'll see a plane soar overhead and the thought of the cramped seats and rubber sandwiches of an economy-class cabin will send a wistful tear down your cheek. That said, kilometre for kilometre, overlanding is the **most interesting** way to get around, and no global trip would be complete without at least one land segment. Routes have sprung up over the years, some following ancient paths like China's Silk Road or Central America's Ruta Maya, or the 1960s contribution, The Hippie Trail (see p.42). Others have popped up to connect popular backpacker destinations, buttressed by glowing guidebook reviews. Some trails are better trod than others and sometimes the route branches then reconnects like a stream flowing around a rock, and you'll pass hundreds, if not thousands, of other backpackers along the way.

The best thing about public transport

This is perhaps the most culturally enriching way to get around. Passenger status places you on **equal footing** with those around you and allows a precious peek into the daily travel experience of locals. You might not enter their homes, but this is the next best way of experiencing how locals – especially low-income locals – live. It gives you a chance to strike up a conversation with them, or attempt one with a phrasebook and hand gestures.

Guidebooks contain the necessary travel details on major bus, train and ferry lines. With the exception of the Trans-Siberian railway, a few popular ferry connections and transport during local public holidays, tickets are rarely an issue and can be booked the same day (even a few minutes before departure).

Remember to buy your tickets at the **bus or train station**, not from an agent in the city (who may overcharge and take a commission, sometimes a large one). And with buses, always ask if they have a bathroom on board.

The overland tour – is it a good first step for you?

If you find the idea of overlanding exhilarating but intimidating, you're not alone. There's an entire industry comprising overland tour operators that load travelers into revamped army trucks (or some sort of steroid-enhanced

Border crossings

Having the right **visas**, **vaccination certificates** and **onward tickets** can be vital when you're passing through certain countries. Often you can obtain everything you need for onward travel at the various border crossings for free or for a small charge, at other times you need a stamp from an embassy, but count on the border guards turning you back if your papers aren't in order. Look ahead over your route and get updated visa information prior to departure, from either a guidebook or national websites.

transport), take care of all the paperwork and drive them across Africa, Asia or South America. You typically sleep in tents or cheap hostels, share the cooking and cleaning chores and take in the major attractions en route. It's not uncommon for travelers to use these tours as a sampler before heading off on their own or with a friend they've made in the group. However, there are some drawbacks: you're trapped with the same group of people for weeks or months and chances are reasonably high that at least one person is going to tweak your nerves; and you may feel ready to jump off and go it alone long before your financial commitment is up.

Overland tour companies are mostly UK-based and charge around $1000/£630 per week depending on location and length of journey. Try Dragoman (Ⓦwww.dragoman.com), Exodus (Ⓦwww.exodus.co.uk), IntrepidTravel (Ⓦintrepidtravel.com) or Overland Africa (Ⓦwww.overlandafrica.com).

The wonderful (or horrible) tour bus

This includes everything from four-star luxury tours to local packages that can be arranged in almost any mid-sized city. There are thousands of tour companies to choose from at any number of levels, and it certainly helps to get a personal recommendation or find some favorable reviews. In many areas, hostels team up with local tour operators (or allow tour operators to leave posters around, for which the hostel may get a commission); the operators typically offer off-road budget trips to scenic spots in the area that are hard to access by local transport. Often these tours are good fun, but it pays to try to get a sense of what the guide is like, and trust your instincts. For all the informative tips you get on the "real culture", you're unlikely to experience much of it with this sort of transport.

The essentials on buying a car or motorcycle in another country – or taking your own

It's possible to take a car or motorcycle across borders, and in Europe, North America, Australia and New Zealand, car travel can be a great way to save money and explore the backroads – though in Europe be prepared for motorway tolls and petrol priced like 12-year-old Scotch.

Guided excursions

Despite the general reluctance of independent travelers to sign up for just about anything, jumping on a tour for small portions of a longer trip can be an excellent way to get some **professional supervision** while you do something you haven't done before – and can work out cheaper and easier than arranging it on your own. There are glacier treks, journeys by dugout canoe into the Amazon, kayak trips around the Fijian islands, hippo-dodging African canoe safaris – the list goes on. You can usually get good, impartial information from your guidebook and other travelers while you're in the region.

A few good questions to ask when enquiring about an activity are:

• How easy is it to book on the spot without a reservation?
• Are there any possible (likely) weather-related conflicts with the intended activities or refunds if they're not available when you arrive?
• Does the price include taxes and tips? If not, what's the total cost?
• What are the living conditions like? Private room? Bathroom in room? Washing facilities?
• What meals are included?
• For walking and cycling tours, are baggage transfers or porters included?
• What is the cancellation policy, and what kind of insurance is included?

In Asia, Africa and Latin America, prepare yourself well in advance for the mountain of paperwork and fees ahead. After you've specially prepped your vehicle for the trip, you'll need to get it a "Carnet de Passage" (see box opposite). For more details on documentation, preparation and international hassles you may encounter, take a look at *The Adventure Motorcycling Handbook* (Trailblazer). And you'll see a few more suggestions in the "Regional profiles" section at the end of this book.

Third-world driving tips

• Have multiple copies of everything. Even get some color copies of your driving licence laminated so you can leave them with border guards who threaten to hold them for a bribe.

• Take a course in vehicle maintenance so you can fix minor problems yourself. If you can't find one, go to a garage and ask to pay by the hour for a half-day or day's worth of lessons. It's likely to be more expensive, but you'll get to practice on your own car and can buy any spare parts you need at the same time.

• Cross-check maps in remote areas with local drivers. Some of the roads marked on your map may only be in the planning stage, while others may simply not exist.

• Crossing borders is more time-consuming for vehicle owners, so get there early or just after lunch to avoid the crowds, and try to steer clear of crossings during weekends or local holidays.

• Keep things friendly at the border. Patience is paramount. If the border officers or police ask for money (a bribe), cheerfully asking for a receipt and their names so you can send a note to the tourist board might discourage them a little. Or have some small bribes ready: little souvenirs, cigarettes, candy and the like can help circumvent more costly cash bribes.

Bringing your own vehicle

If you want to take your car or motorcycle around the world, you're going to need a **Carnet de Pasage en Douane (CPD)**. It's not necessary if you're bringing a car to Europe or North America, but for crossing continents the document works like a passport for your vehicle, allowing it to pass through customs with a set of stamps. The actual purpose of it, however, is to keep you from selling your vehicle in countries you're traveling in (thus circumventing local import taxes). So, while the carnet itself only costs $293–310/£185–195 (depending on how many blank pages you want in it for stamps and on whether you're a member of the automobile association that issues it), to get it guaranteed you need to put down a **refundable deposit** of as much as six times the value of the vehicle. That means that if you're taking a Land Rover worth $30,000/£18,900, you may have to leave as much as $180,000/£113,400 (and probably not less than $90,000/£56,700) to get a carnet – though you can also pay an insurance company a fraction of that amount to guarantee the carnet gets paid in the event you and your vehicle become separated. If you leave the country without the vehicle you came in with or overstay your visiting time allotment, they'll presume you sold it (even if it died and you left it in a scrapyard), and the country is legally entitled to collect from the carnet issuer an amount equalling whatever the import duties would have been, which can – you guessed it – be up to 600 percent of the vehicle's value in some countries.

However, if you're just shipping a vehicle to one country, such as Australia, you should look into the local import duties. It may well be easier and cheaper to pay those than to get a carnet.

In the UK, pick up a carnet from the AA (🌐 www.theaa.com) or RAC (🌐 www.rac.co.uk). In the USA and Canada, this is handled by the CAA (🌐 www.caa.ca). The AA also issues carnets in South Africa (🌐 www.aasa.co.za), Australia (🌐 www.aaa.asn.au) and New Zealand (🌐 www.aa.co.nz). Outside these areas, try the Swiss-based Alliance Internationale de Tourisme (🌐 www.aitgva.ch), which administers the carnet system; the public part of its website has a listing of affiliated members.

Countries that require carnets (or where it facilitates importation)

Africa
Benin, Botswana, Burkina Faso, Burundi, Cameroon, Central African Republic, Chad, Comoros, Congo, Egypt, Gabon, Ghana, Guinea-Bissau, Ivory Coast, Kenya, Lesotho, Libya, Malawi, Mauritania, Namibia, Niger, Senegal, Somalia, South Africa, Sudan, Swaziland, Tanzania, Togo, Uganda, Zimbabwe

Asia
Bangladesh, India, Indonesia, Japan, Malaysia, Burma (Myanmar), Pakistan, Singapore, Sri Lanka

Australia, New Zealand and the South Pacific
Australia, New Zealand, Vanatu

Latin America and the Caribbean
Argentina, Brazil (only required for vehicles arriving by boat), Chile, Colombia, Costa Rica, Dutch Antilles, Ecuador, Jamaica, Paraguay, Peru, Suriname, Trinidad and Tobago, Uruguay, Venezuela

Middle East
Bahrain, Iran, Iraq, Japan, Jordan, Kuwait, Lebanon, Oman, Qatar, Syria, United Arab Emirates, Yemen

3

The Trans-Siberian Express

Matronly Russian train attendants with enough facial hair to knit a pair of leg-warmers, food that most travelers would only eat on a dare, and smoke in some cabins so thick you could conceivably cut off a piece of the seat and use it for a nicotine patch if you ran out of cigarettes… you might wonder how the **Trans-Siberian Express** has managed to maintain its exotic appeal. Still, it feels like the right way a traveler should head across Asia, whether on the way out or on the way home – going both ways may be overkill. The actual Trans-Siberian line runs from Vladivostok (a Russian port city just north of China) to Moscow. Instead, most travelers take one of two lines from Beijing to Moscow, neither of which (confusingly) is called the Trans-Siberian, though people refer to them as such. There's the **Trans-Mongolian**, which takes six nights to cover 7865km and passes through Mongolia (Russian and Mongolian visas required), and the seven-night **Trans-Manchurian** (9001km), which passes just north of Mongolia (Russian visa only). Though you can hop on and off along the way, the ten-day Russian transit visa won't give you much time to explore.

Budget travelers usually opt for a four-bunk cabin, which has relatively comfortable bunk beds and luggage space. You can also ride in a more expensive first-class compartment with two beds, slightly softer seats and, on the Chinese trains, a shower. In both classes, attendants keep things clean and make your bed with rented sheets ($3/£2). The dining facilities on both trains may receive less than stellar reviews, but more interesting fare can be found off the train during the brief stops in Russia: here, fresh smoked fish from Lake Baikal and other goodies are available for pocket change. There are also samovars at the end of each car filled with hot water you can use to make your own soups and teas. Many travelers cross Asia on Cup-a-Soup and Earl Grey.

If you're not crossing in summer, bring warm clothes to stretch your legs comfortably at the border checkpoint or when the trains get a wheel change. (Russian and Chinese rails have different gauges, so they actually switch the train cars onto different wheel bases; this takes several hours, so a good novel will come in handy as well.)

Bring something to clean the outside windows. A cheap squeegee fastened to a long stick will make you tremendously popular, as many windows are coated in thick dust. Who knows, you might even be able to trade your window-washing services for a few drinks. In second class, ask for a top bunk so you can sleep when you want, not when your cabin-mates decide to relinquish your seat-bed. And pick up a copy of Bryn Thomas's *Trans-Siberian Handbook* (Trailblazer).

Both the Trans-Mongolian and Trans-Manchurian depart once per week. See Ⓦ www .seat61.com for good, in-depth information. You can book tickets on Ⓦ www.realrussia .co.uk. They have a booking widget that uses data directly from the RZD (Russian Railways) database. You'll want to do this in advance, before you land in Russia.

Buying a Trans-Siberian ticket in China

They don't let you walk into the train station and buy a ticket at the counter. If you want to take the easy, more expensive, route you can find a local **travel agent** in China to sell you a ticket. If you want to save a bit (the exact amount is hard to say – it depends

---

- On a map, a town does not always equal a filling station, so tank up whenever you get the chance.

The pros and cons of taking a bicycle

A bicycle involves much less paperwork than a car or motorbike, but few countries are set up for cyclists (not to mention people wearing

on the travel agency) you can pick up a Russian visa and head to the **Chinese Tourist Board's** official agency, CITS. Chinese readers might check out the website. But if your visa and forms are in order (the forms are in English) it should be fine. CITS has an office in the Beijing International Hotel (Mon–Fri 9am–12pm and 1.30–5pm; Sat, Sun & holidays 9am–12noon) where you can even find English-speaking staff. They don't sell trans-Mongolian tickets though. Those you need to get via a travel agent and require a Mongolian visa.

Stopovers are a bit tricky to arrange on your own since CITS insists that you buy separate tickets for each leg of your trip (eg one to Ulaanbaatar and one from Ulaanbaatar to Moscow), but will only sell you the leg from Beijing to Ulaanbaatar. The Ulaanbaatar to Moscow leg must be bought in Ulaanbaatar. That brings most people back to a booking agency.

A **Russian visa** can be picked up at the Russian embassy in Beijing. You have the option of having it processed within 6–10 working days, 3–5, the next day or the same day, with prices varying accordingly from $131/£83 to $300/£189 for US citizens, and $30–50/£19–32 for EU citizens. You can pick up the Mongolian visa at the Mongolian embassy ($30/£19 for two working days or $100/£63 for eight-hour service), which gets you 30 days in the country. Note that citizens of Canada and the UK pay $55/£35 instead of $30/£19, and that US citizens don't need a Mongolian visa for visits of up to 90 days. Remember to buy your train ticket before pursuing the visas.

Buying a Trans-Siberian ticket in Russia or Finland

To do it yourself, head to **Central Railway Agency** in Moscow. The Trans-Mongolian should cost around $300/£189 and requires Chinese and Mongolian visas. The Trans-Manchurian costs around $310/£195 (Chinese visa only). For first-class fares, for which you get a two-bed compartment, add about $200/£126. Booking with a local travel agent will add about $50/£32 to the fare, but will allow you to make arrangements in advance and give you assistance with stopovers. In Moscow, try **G&R International** (Ⓦ www.hostels.ru). In St Petersburg, the **International Hostel** (Ⓦ www.ryh.ru) can book tickets through its travel-agency arm. In Finland, tickets are available at the train station in Helsinki, though it will cost more than in Russia. If money is less of a concern, and you want a choice of diverse excursions during stopovers, try the Russian Experience (Ⓦ www.trans-siberian.co.uk), where a trip might cost around $2800/£1770.

A **Mongolian visa** can be picked up at the consular office in Moscow once you already have your Chinese visa. Americans don't need a visa. For anything more than a transit stay in Mongolia, you'll need an invitation. Moscow isn't the best place to pick up a Chinese visa, but it can be done, again in about three working days – you'll need to show your train ticket and onward ticket from China. If you're leaving by an overland route you're making up as you go, try getting a letter of introduction from your country's embassy. If you're planning stops along the way, there are several alternative trains you'll be able to catch throughout the week that don't go all the way to China.

3

spandex shorts with built-in crotch padding), which can work both for and against you. In small towns off the main routes where few people with motors care to stop, you're an instant celebrity (or freak). But getting between those towns can be a dusty, muddy, traffic-dodging experience. Some countries, however, such as the Netherlands or Denmark, are especially well suited for cycling (Norway too, if you don't mind hills). Find out what you're in for before packing the bike. On the downside, you may not always feel like biking, especially when the weather conspires against you. And if you start trying to put it on a bus or train, you're likely to face extra costs. With all the locking and carrying, it can feel at times as much of a burden as it does a liberty.

If spare parts are a major concern or you want to get a first-hand look at local cycling conditions, wait until you arrive and then buy a sturdy local model. And just because your bike holds four **saddlebags**, that doesn't mean you should bring all four. You will probably need four if you're camping, but if you're planning to stay at hostels or pensions, two saddlebags should be sufficient, and the reduced weight

3

Classic overland routes

New York to Los Angeles
Distance: 4050km
New York–Philadelphia–Cleveland–Chicago–Denver–Grand Canyon–Las Vegas–Los Angeles

London to Sydney
Distance: 19,900km
England–Belgium–Netherlands–Germany–Czech Republic–Slovakia–Hungary–Romania–Bulgaria–Turkey–Iran–Pakistan–India–Nepal–Tibet–China–Laos–Thailand–Singapore–Indonesia–Australia

Istanbul to Kathmandu
Distance: 16,997km
Turkey–Iran–Pakistan–India–Nepal

Beijing to Berlin
Distance: 7379km
China–Mongolia–Russia–Finland–Sweden–Denmark–Germany

Cairo to Cape Town
Distance: 8000km
Egypt–Sudan–Eritrea–Ethiopia–Kenya–Tanzania–Malawi–Zambia–Zimbabwe–Botswana–Namibia–South Africa (Sudan/Eritrea/Ethiopia borders can be problematic)

Anchorage to Tierra del Fuego
Distance: 14,500km
Alaska–Canada–USA–Mexico–Guatemala–Honduras–Nicaragua–Costa Rica–Panama–Colombia–Ecuador–Peru–Chile–Argentina (Darién Gap, between Panama and Colombia, can be problematic)

Amman to Cairo
Distance: 1000km
Jordan–Israel–Egypt

Note: Remember that political turmoil, natural disasters and the like can rapidly change the security situation in most countries. See Chapter 15 for more on staying safe on the road.

is a godsend going up hills. More important, it makes daily security less of an issue. If you want to head into a market or restaurant or up a flight of stairs to check the availability of a hostel (something you'll be doing daily), it's easy to lock up the bike and carry two bags along. With four bags (or five including a front bag), that's not much of an option, so someone will get stuck guarding the gear – or you'll need one impressive security system.

3

How to choose: traveling alone or with friends

One of the biggest decisions facing any traveler is whether or not to go it alone. There are several factors to consider before making this choice and sizeable pros and cons for each, but, all things being equal, you'll probably want to travel solo, at least for some portion of your trip. Even if all things aren't equal and there's someone you'd really like to travel with, read through this section to find out the risks and learn how to minimize them.

Why you should at least consider traveling alone

Obviously, this is the more intimidating path. But it's also the most potentially rewarding. And it's not nearly as frightening as it may sound.

1. Traveling solo does not necessarily mean you'll be traveling alone for the bulk of your trip. Quite the opposite, in fact. Most solo travelers just end up traveling with different people for different legs of their journey. Everywhere you go, from museums to hostels to cafés, you'll run into other solo travelers who'll be delighted to travel with someone and, because there are often significant price breaks on rooms for pairs, there's a good chance you'll be sharing accommodation. Even the shyest travelers find the dialogue easy to start: you already have your travel destination and independent spirit in common, not to mention doubtless shared frustrating experiences. At times, it can almost be more difficult to find periods to be on your own. For those who are still uncertain about their ability to meet travel partners on the trail, you can, virtually everywhere, sign up for a group tour along the way and surround yourself with an entire platoon of companions.

2. You learn about yourself. You'll find out what your likes and dislikes are, and be able to act on them. Often travelers spur each other on to check off a "to do" list (with no one looking, maybe you'll give that famous museum a miss and rent a bike and head for the countryside instead). You'll spend more time writing your journal, taking photos, reading, studying the culture – absorbing more of the country you're traveling in.

3. You'll be less distracted by a friend and more likely to notice the small things happening around you. As a single traveler it can be easier to blend in, and you're less likely to be attracting attention by speaking English with your partner. Single travelers attract single travelers.

4. You'll be approached by more locals. They're often anxious to meet foreigners but can be intimidated by couples, feeling reluctant to interrupt a conversation or intrude. Which means solo travelers are much more likely to return home with an address book filled with great contacts from around the world.

4

Is it safe for women to go alone?

Women can and do travel solo throughout the world. Some countries and regions make this quite easy, and thus provide a better starting point: northern Europe, Australia, New Zealand, the USA and Canada. In southern Europe and parts of Latin America, catcalls are common, but you'll rarely feel threatened. Dressing and safety tips can be found in the security chapter (p.169). In much of the world, however, you'll be seen as an oddity. All backpackers are a bit of an oddity (forsaking our creature comforts and spending more money than many locals will ever possess to wander about the globe with our worldly possessions in a nylon sack), but people may assume you have left your husband and children behind to undertake this journey. So long as your wardrobe is conservative, you'll often be afforded the same status as male travelers in most developing countries you visit, but expect numerous enquiries. It's helpful to have a story for the men (such as you're meeting your husband in the next town), but many questions will come from women, which is a great conversation-starter and can offer interesting insights.

The possibility of rape and robbery should be taken seriously, but these are risks that can be minimized (see Chapter 15). Most likely the harassment you get will be a mild irritant: an admirer on a long train ride who thinks he can charm you with a six-hour story. The trick is being able

4

Covering up in India

When I started traveling on my own I was making all the typical mistakes. Perhaps the one I paid the highest price for was wearing tight-fitting clothes in India. I was often harassed on public transport and in crowded streets. It was at times so frustrating, some evenings I'd just go back to my room and cry.

After two years, I've learned to deal with it. I wear much baggier clothing now and keep my legs and shoulders well covered. I stopped initiating conversations with men and have become more abrupt with the ones who've approached me, as that too often seemed to signal some sort of green light. And I pay a little extra for the perks of air-conditioned second-class trains: doors that remain shut and passengers who are less likely to harass.

One of my favorite tricks is carrying my small daypack on my front in crowded areas. At least that protects my front from the anonymous hands searching for a quick feel. I'm also no longer afraid to lash out when I do get grabbed – and a little yelling helps get it out of my system.

If foreign women would cover up and respect local customs – as I wish I'd done from the start – it would make life easier for the rest of us.

Beth Wooldridge
Author, *Rough Guide to India*

to distinguish between a tactless man and a dangerous one. Always **trust your instincts**. If any man makes you feel at risk, simply move to a train compartment where there are more safe-looking people (preferably women or other travelers), head to a more crowded street, pop into a busy store or stop a police officer.

If you're heading overland into a country or region that you're a little unsure of, you can almost always find a trustworthy travel companion (even a male companion, if limiting the sexual harassment is important) to accompany you for at least a few days, if not longer, provided you're going in the same direction. It may take a day or three to find the right person, but in places where the hassle factor is high, such as arriving in Morocco from Spain, a male companion can make things much easier, especially if you tell people that he's your husband.

The benefits of bringing a companion

Traveling with a friend isn't all bad. In fact, there are some nice benefits: minimized culture shock; medical security (they can help get you to a doctor if you get sick or carry you back to the hostel after you've passed out in a bar); money saved when staying in double rooms and taking taxis. For many, though, a travel partner's most important role is offering **moral support** for the never-ending onslaught of new situations to face. And helping avoid the fairly frequent party-of-one meals or having your ear bent by some garrulous locals.

How it can risk your friendship

Twenty-four hours a day of reassurance and sharing for months on end can put a serious strain on any relationship. Having to make decisions constantly, often in uncomfortable conditions, can strain the tightest bonds. Remember: compromise means that on this "trip of a lifetime" you probably won't get to see everything you want, and certainly not at your own pace. Just because you're the best of friends, or even partners, there is no guarantee you'll travel well together. Something else for friends traveling together to keep in mind: if you think it would be nice to stumble on some romance on the road, you better pray you meet twins going in the same direction, because your friend isn't going to want to hang around while you fall in love.

How to keep the travel friendship from unraveling

If you do decide to go with another person, give yourselves the option of **separating** for a while. Even just a morning or afternoon apart every few days can be enough breathing room to sustain a travel relationship. A better bet, however, is to build some solo time into the trip. Perhaps a week or two apart every other month: sign up for different courses or adventure activities in the same region or tackle a city separately. Pick a meeting time and figure out a few fallback ways to get in touch in case one person can't make it, such as email or a note at a certain hostel.

What to look for in a travel partner

First, you want someone with the **same budget**. If you don't see eye to eye (or wallet to wallet), it's going to be a straining trip. If one person is going down the comfort route while the other is on a tight budget, you won't be staying at the same places, eating at the same restaurants or doing as many activities together. Or, more likely, you will, but neither of you will be having a good time doing it. The one on a tight budget will feel like a scrooge, always getting their budget pushed too far, having to eat plain rice at a nice restaurant or sit outside while the other goes to a string of expensive museums. The one on the bigger budget will be roughing it more than they'd like, yet feel they're shamelessly indulging in front of their companion the entire time.

Having checked if your budgets are in alignment, then see if your itineraries are. Talk about what you hope to do

Traveling solo

My first trip alone was to Europe. I was 22. It was probably the three most eye-opening weeks of my life. I realized, for starters, that I could go to another continent and be entirely self-sufficient. I could travel from country to country, from one foreign language to another, order a meal, get a night in a room and make friends with people all over the world. Learning I could do all that on my own was a revelation. If I had gone with a friend, I wouldn't have returned home with the same sense of accomplishment and satisfaction.

Jim Benning
Editor, ⓦworldhum.com

I did not travel alone for my entire journey – I traveled with another traveler for part of it (a friend flew out to join me for two weeks) and I joined a few organized tours. The best fun and most rewarding, though, was traveling solo.

Becky Robinson

4

during **a typical day**. Will you get up early and aggressively pound the pavement of a city, or sleep until noon, then linger in a café and read a book? Will you be pursuing cultural activities or flopping on beaches? Are you keeping things flexible or planning all the details? These are not the sort of things you want to discover after you've started traveling.

Does it make sense to find a travel partner before leaving?

Not really. Many people find the prospect of traveling alone so daunting they try to line up a travel partner before leaving. They place personal ads in travel magazines, newspapers and on websites. These correspondence-arranged partnerships may work out, but all too often they don't: heading out on the road together is like getting married after one blind date. There's no need to do this, especially without taking at least one short local trip together first. You'll meet so many travelers during your trip, it's much more natural and sensible to make friends first, travel for a while without commitment and only continue together as long as it's working out. This is extremely common and no one gets insulted if and when you part ways.

4   Traveling with a crowd

With more than two people you're going to find yourself taking votes, which is a fine way to run a democracy but a maddening way to set an itinerary. Whether you leave with a group or simply snowball into an international party on the move, beware: you're going to be about as subtle as a G-20 protest rally. Another potential problem is getting anything done. Before you can all head out to explore a famous museum together, a few people will have to use the bathroom, someone will have to fix a button that's about to fall off, someone else will need to mail a postcard, two others will have to stop at a bank and one will have to bargain for a souvenir on the way. What's more, you're going to have a difficult time finding hostels, buses and restaurants that can accommodate all of you. It's nice to find a social group. But instead of corralling yourself into a tour group, a better idea is to pick a bar or restaurant in the next town and a time and say you'll meet there. Then everyone breaks up and goes their own way.

Friendships on a long organized tour

This locks you in with a group for the duration of the tour, for good and bad. Such trips tend to bring out the best in some and the worst in others. Life-long friendships are common, but so are group conflicts, and you won't be likely to see much about the latter in the brochure. So make sure you ask about how much time is available away from the group, then take advantage of it when you get the chance.

Costs and savings

What does it cost to travel around the world? Reasonable question. Unfortunately, a personalized, independent journey doesn't come with a standard price tag, so you're going to have to take a different approach. You can **calculate your budget** – and this chapter will show you how – but before that's possible you'll need to figure out your level of comfort, where you want to go, and which activities you want to do. Without narrowing down these factors, you'll have a hard time getting within $10,000/£6300 of an accurate figure on a year-long trip. Why? Take a typical budget of $50/£32 per day, plus $5000/£3150 for a RTW ticket, insurance, vaccinations and gear, and you get a yearly total of $22,200/£13,986. If you stop and work for three months of that, you're down to $18,000/£11,340 plus whatever you earn, which might bring the total down to $15,500/£9450. If you stay with relatives for a few weeks and spend a month in a cheap hangout, you're down to $14,500/£9135. If you confine your travels exclusively to developing countries, that may drop the figure to $11,500/£7245. If you Couchsurf (see box, p.79) half the time, that drops it to about $7500/£4725. Cut the trip back to nine months, and you're down to about $5500/£3465.

Starting costs

Backpack: $150–250/£95–158
Travel gear, toiletries, medical kit, emergency kit (depending on what you have already): $150–500/£95–315
Insurance for 12 months: $400–1000/£252–630
Vaccinations: $100–350/£63–220
RTW ticket or other long-range transport: $2000–5000/£1260–3150
Approximate total: $6000/£3780

5

Daily costs

You could spend anywhere between $10,000/£6300 and $100,000/ £63,000 on a yearly trip around the world, and with the myriad spending choices you make every day, it's impossible to knock out an itemized cost sheet before leaving. And it's also impossible to know what the exact right amount is you'll need. If you allow some flexibility with your return ticket, just save the best you can as you go and return home (or find a local job) when you run out of cash.

How long will your money last? Depends where you go… Picking even a slightly cheaper country can save you a fortune on a long trip. Traveling on a mid-level budget, the chart below gives you a rough idea how long you can go with $1000/£630.

Spendometer

Days of travel with $1000/£630

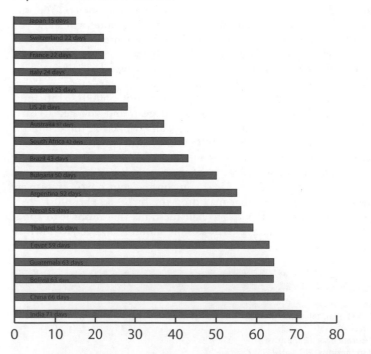

Note: Prices represent a barebones budget (hostel dormitories, street food) with about sixty percent of the time spent outside the more expensive major cities in each country.

Calculating your budget

5

Within the range of **budget travel**, the daily costs can vary enormously over the course of a year. Just between the middle and upper levels, there's roughly $18,000/£11,340 of savings to be had. By traveling in developing (read: cheaper) countries you can obviously save a fortune: $5000–20,000/£3150–12,600 over a year, depending on your comfort level. Put these together and the difference between traveling for a year on a more comfortable daily budget in Europe ($40,000/£25,200) and a tight daily budget in Southeast Asia ($6500/£4095) is pretty significant.

Select your **level of comfort**, then figure out how many weeks or months you plan to stay in developed or developing countries and add up the costs. For example, if you plan to spend three months in Europe, four in Southeast Asia and two in Central America, all on the lowest budget, that's six months at $600/£378 plus three months at $1500/£945 plus about $4000/£2520 for start-up costs (see box, p.71). Which makes a total of $12,100/£7623 for the nine-month trip. A mid-level budget on the same trip will cost roughly $19,750/£12,443. A bit of financial discipline and lifestyle readjustment will net you a cool $7000/£4410 on such a trip.

Note that all of these costs assume that you're not Couchsurfing (see box, p.79). If you were to do this exclusively, you could virtually cut your costs in half.

Low-budget backpacker (extreme scrimping)

Expenses in developing countries: daily: $20/£13; monthly: $600/£378; yearly: $7200/£4336
Expenses in developed countries: daily: $50/£32; monthly: $1500/£945; yearly: $18,000/£11,340
Lifestyle: Sleeping in hostel dormitory rooms; sharing rooms in the very cheapest hotels (no matter how bad the guidebook description); camping or renting a tent at camping grounds; sleeping on trains and buses. Eating cheap food purchased at supermarkets and the lowest-priced side dishes at budget restaurants or at street stalls. No clubbing and nothing more than the occasional beer. Limited museum visits and no lingering drinks at nice cafés.

Middle-end backpacker (budget-minded)

Expenses in developing countries: daily: $50£32; monthly: $1500/£945; yearly: $18,000/£11,340
Expenses in developed countries: daily: $85/£53; monthly: $2250/£1418; yearly: $31,0250/£19,545
Lifestyle: Same basic accommodation as "lowest" category but in smaller dorms, or occasionally sharing a two-person room with another traveler, plus a few coffees at nice cafés per week. Museums are not limited but adventure activities are. The occasional night on the town, but not more than one reasonably priced drink (beer, wine, cappuccino etc) per day.

Upper-end backpacker (comfort)

Expenses in developing countries: daily: $100/£63; monthly: $3000/£1890; yearly: $36,500/£22,995
Expenses in developed countries: daily: $150/£95; monthly: $4500/£2835; yearly: $54,000/£34,020
Lifestyle: Decent budget hotels or private rooms in hostels/guesthouses. Unlimited coffee, liberal drinking, several nights out per week and a nice restaurant and good breakfast per day.

5

How do you travel cheaper?

Without a number of budget tricks, you may end up traveling on a high-end budget while only getting mid-range value. The key to saving money on the road is not to concentrate exclusively on the big expenditures, but to find **small savings** along every step of the way. Beyond picking countries where your funds will last longer, savvy saving is about a deliberate lifestyle adjustment that rations out the creature comforts, or drops them altogether. People love to spend countless hours surfing the web and calling around to find the cheapest plane ticket. Of course, you don't want to end up paying more than the guy sitting next to you on the airfare, but, aside from a big RTW ticket (where prices can vary by over $1000/£630), don't knock yourself out searching for a flight or two in a massive effort that probably won't save you more than $50–200/£32–126. Why? Because that's not where the real savings are found. With some self-discipline – while hopefully avoiding full-blown "budgetitis" (see box opposite) – you can reduce your **daily budget** by as much as $20/£13 or by $35/£22 if you're Couchsurfing. Over a three-month-long trip, that's a saving of over $3000/£1890. Even on a one-month trip, that's over $1000/£630 you can leave in the bank.

Discount cards

There's no magic wand to wave to guarantee savings everywhere you go, but for $22/£14 an **International Student Identity Card** (ISIC; ⓦwww .isiccard.com) comes close. ISIC also issues youth cards (for under-26s who aren't students) and cards for teachers, all of which offer similar discounts on museums, city transport tickets, plane tickets and more; in fact you may even make up the cost of the card on the flight over. The trick is remembering to ask for the discount. It won't help you much in restaurants, but nearly anywhere a ticket is required, be sure to ask. Also, you can use it as a back-up ID card to leave behind when renting bikes and so on.

Another popular discount card is the **Hostelling International Card** ($28/£15, or $18/£11 if you're 55 or older; ⓦwww.hiayh.org), which, on top of many of the transport discounts available with the ISIC or youth cards, gets you reductions on about two thousand affiliated hostels around Europe. The card will pay for itself within four nights. The downside (or perhaps upside) is that these official hostels invariably don't pack the party atmosphere of private hostels and are often not centrally located. You'll need to buy this card before leaving as it's only available in your home country. Before you splash out on that, you may check out the section on accommodation to find out if you like the sound of hostelling (p.150).

5

Budgetitis syndrome

When you first start traveling, **spending comes naturally**. Almost too naturally. A beer here, a T-shirt there, a few museum passes, a nice meal. Maybe you're too caught up in the excitement of arriving or spending to cushion your landing into a new culture. Whatever the case, after a few days or weeks, you'll probably realize that you're over budget; you'll begin to feel the stress of your money belt getting thinner. The natural response to this relentless stream of expenditure is an attempt to stem the outflow. And when you meet other travelers to compare notes, boasting rights go to the one surviving on the lowest funds. When it gets competitive, that's when **budgetitis** really sets in.

Symptoms include: walking an extra twenty minutes to find a bread shop whose loaves are three cents cheaper; full-blown arguments with taxi drivers over the equivalent of 25 cents; and skipping a meal because the local supermarket prices seem a little high. In extreme cases, you might party all night (without drinking… well, not much), then sleep in a park during the day. You'll only travel by hitchhiking and show up at soup kitchens for food, paying with the minimum donation. This is one of the most common budget travel afflictions (followed closely by exaggerated storytelling) and at some point during a long trip you'll likely suffer from it.

If you can sense this happening, you have to take a step back and remember why you're traveling. It's fine to save money while you're on the road, but you need to balance this with the fact that you're not traveling in order to save money. Better to come home a week or two early and suffer a little less.

If you find you're staying at a number of Australian-managed VIP-affiliated private hostels (Ⓦwww.vipbackpackers.com), of which there are roughly 1200 in 83 countries worldwide, you might as well pick up a **VIP Backpackers membership card** (Aus$43/£29 online with shipping) while you're on the road. The discount is only one percent off at 1200 backpackers but has substantial savings on transport and activities and comes with a free SIM card for local and international calls. You can also download their app and it will tell you all the specific places it can be used around your current location.

Fake versions of some of these cards (including journalist's press passes) can be picked up in Cairo and Bangkok for about $5/£3 each.

Buying cheap international flight tickets

There is some truth to the airline axiom that savings come with restrictions, discomfort and stopovers. But only some truth – it is possible to get reduced prices on direct flights with reputable airlines as well.

A good basic guideline to follow before booking any flights is to do a little checking on your own so you'll know a good price when you see one. Many **flight search engines** will now show you the cheapest available ticket during the period you're searching so you'll know your target price. Start looking on your favorite sites, then try a few others just to compare. The major online players include: Ⓦwww.expedia.com,

5

ⓦwww.priceline.com, ⓦwww.travelocity.com, ⓦwww.kayak.com, ⓦwww
.hipmunk.com and ⓦwww.skyscanner.net.

All things being relatively equal, it can help to book with a well-informed **travel agent** just so you have someone to call in a crisis. Imagine, for example, that you're stuck in an airport during Iceland's volcanic ash cloud. You may not have many online tools at your disposal and the queues are likely long. Wouldn't it be great if you could make a call and get rerouted while the others are waiting around? In that sense, it's like insurance. Plus a good travel agent can point out things you can easily forget while booking on your own (such as a flight that leaves at 6am from a certain airport will cost you more because there's no cheap transport running to the airport at that time).

Bear in mind that:

- Whether you're with an agent or surfing the web, play around with dates. Often just a day or two can make a surprising price difference.
- If you know where you want to go and when, sign up for online alerts so you can grab deals as soon as they become available.
- Once you find a good deal, check that airline's site directly to see if they're offering any other special promotions to places nearby that are even cheaper.
- Keep in mind that the cheapest fares are often less direct, less conveniently scheduled, and may involve an airline you've never even heard of. If you have more time than money, this is a fine way to grab a deal.
- There's no need to let your frequent-flyer plan get in the way of finding the best ticket. First, look for the best deal, then if two or three similar fares come up, pick the one that fits with your mileage plan.

Buying a train pass before you leave home

If you're doing anything more than zipping across a country by rail (and even if that's all you're doing), your best bet will most likely be to buy a rail pass, whether you're in Europe, Japan or North America.

Most rail passes can only be purchased in your **home country**, but with the internet, this isn't such a problem. If you're already there, or on your way, you can order it online, have it sent to your parents or friends and then get them to forward it to you. The more difficult task is selecting the right type of pass.

In Europe, for example, it is well worth considering a flexi-pass (valid for a certain number of travel days within a fixed time period) instead of an unlimited travel pass. You won't want to spend every day on the train anyway. Then, supplement your flexi-pass with cheap, shorter trips; this is a good option typically if the journey lasts less than an hour and you're not on a high-speed train. The value of a flexi-pass works out to around $40/£25 per day. If you're traveling, say, the 97km from Florence to Siena in Italy, a second-class one-way ticket costs around $10/£6, so it's going to be cheaper to buy a ticket at the window and save travel days on your pass. Check too for weekend deals before using your flexi-pass.

Don't be afraid to use flights just because you have a rail ticket. You need to balance this, of course, with your environmental philosophy. But you'd spend a few days of your trip on the train (and use up a few days of your rail pass, plus some not-so-ecological packaged food and drinks) to get, for example, from London to Portugal or Greece. With cut-throat budget airlines practically giving tickets away, chances are you can find a one-way flight for less than $100/£63, possibly even less than $30/£19. That will save you time and roughly $100/£63 worth of travel on your flexi rail pass; not needing to pay overnight and reserved-seating supplements will push the total saving to over $150/£95.

As a rule of thumb, the less flexible the rail pass, the cheaper it is. In other words, if you know more or less where you plan to go (and you don't feel obliged to hit every single region or country), you can get a much better deal.

If you only want to travel in one country and can't decide which, bear in mind that some **single-country passes** cost more than others. In Portugal, you get four days of travel, valid over one month, for €98 (second class); in Norway, four days within one month is €210 (second class).

Finally, if you plan to stay in one spot for a while, try to time it at the beginning or end of your journey so your active pass isn't sitting idle more than it need be.

To purchase passes directly from the sellers, visit ⓦwww.eurail.com or ⓦwww.raileurope.com.

The extended bus tour

You don't need to buy bus passes (popular in Europe, Australia and New Zealand) before arriving. The hop-on-hop-off buses are easy to use and make it even easier to meet fellow travelers, but they do remove much of the navigating as well as contact with locals. There are sometimes kick-backs involved as buses may stop at some "preferred" restaurants along the way. That doesn't make them bad, just something to keep in mind.

Bus tour companies

AUS ⓦwww.ozexperience.com
Europe ⓦwww.busabout.com, ⓦwww.contiki.com
NZ ⓦwww.kiwiexperience.com
South Africa ⓦwww.bazbus.com

5

The trick to buying individual bus tickets

Buses, unlike trains, tend to be run by private companies and are not subject to the sort of regulation that trains are. Which means that on most popular routes in developing countries, you can and should **haggle** for your ticket. This can be some of the most intimidating bargaining you'll ever do, as bus touts often move about the station in packs, then swarm you with offers, all speaking at once. If you trade stocks on Wall Street, you'll probably feel right at home. If not, it takes some getting used to. The coaches vary dramatically in quality from third-class "chicken buses" to fully reclining sleepers. So, just because you hear someone shout a nice price doesn't mean it applies to the bus you want. Ask questions to find out how many stops it makes (some make local stops while others offer express service), if the seats go all the way back and if there's air conditioning. If you're planning a long-haul trip, ask if the bus has a working toilet.

The best approach is to politely but firmly get past the touts, insisting you know where you're going, and make for the ticket windows of the various companies, where you'll hopefully be able to play them off against one another. A few will be selling tickets to the same location. Get the timetable, information on the bus and the best price from the person at the window. Thank them, then walk off and gather information on the others. Once you have them all (this shouldn't take more than ten minutes), decide on the bus you want and approach the window. Say that it was cheaper with another company, but that their buses didn't look as nice and you heard a tout mentioning a special price with this company (pick a price a little under the one they originally offered) and if that's the case you'd like to buy a ticket. And let the bargaining begin. If they can drop their price they probably will. If they don't, chances are you should try the next company. If you want to skip the hassle and buy a ticket from a local **travel agent**, keep in mind that this service is likely to cost you between 10 and 40 percent extra.

In the UK, **Megabus** (ⓦwww.megabus.com) offers discount deals around the country for as little as $2, and has started taking passengers to Paris and Amsterdam as well. Otherwise, Eurolines (ⓦwww.eurolines .com) provides the main long-distance bus service in Europe, Greyhound in North America (ⓦwww.greyhound.com) and Down Under, Greyhound Australia (ⓦwww.greyhound.com.au).

Saving on accommodation

One of the best things you can do to save money on the road is get accustomed to sleeping in no-star accommodation. That means sleeping in **dorm rooms** when available, trying to **share a room** with another

5

How to find free – yes FREE! – accommodation

In 2001, a 24-year-old Dutch traveler named Ramon Stoppelenburg hitchhiked his way around the world for two years "without any money" by setting up a website called Letmestayforaday.com, through which he found sponsors and took up the 3577 invitations to stay which came in from 77 countries. Seems like a cool idea? Well, these days, it's available for everyone. You may have heard of it; it's called **Couchsurfing** (also see Ⓦ www.tripping.com and Ⓦ www.triptrotting.com…) and as well as being a great way to meet locals, it's probably the single most effective thing you can do to save money during your trip.

After all the bogus offers from Nigerian billionaires and Viagra pill salesmen, you'll be happy to know that this social hosting is proof positive you can get something for nothing on the internet. At Ⓦ www.couchsurfing.com or the other sites listed above, you'll find a network of people willing to host travelers for free, and a network of travelers happy to get a free place to crash – it's a 2.0 spin on the concept that Servas (Ⓦ www.servas.org) has been conducting for years (though they charge a $30/£19 membership/host list fee and have a face-to-face interview system for qualification). The Couchsurfing version has proven overwhelmingly popular with younger travelers, and now has over three million members around the world. It works like this: you register your "couch" (or guest room, or your parents' guest room) for free and agree to let travelers stay for free when it's convenient for you; in return, you get access to everyone else's sofas or guest rooms. **You're not required to allow anyone stay when you get a request** – you can say you're away or the couch is occupied. You can also view the profile of anyone who requests a stay online – people get recommended both as hosts and guests – and see if they seem like the sort of guest you'd like to invite into your home. The site accepts donations, and will use your donation (combined with verification of your mailing address) to give you another level of security recommendation. Otherwise, **the main security comes from the reviews you get, both when you visit someone and host**. If you see someone who has hosted several travelers and received great reviews, chances are they're a lovely and safe host. Likewise, any traveler who has received great reviews is likely a safe and good guest.

It takes a bit of advance planning to make arrangements, but the advantages of Couchsurfing are enormous. Travelers on a budget can save $20/£13 to $100/£63 (whatever you normally spend) a day on hotel expenses, which adds up quickly to several thousand on an extended trip. In fact, **there's virtually nothing you can do that will save you more money**, and into the bargain you'll meet locals, get a look into their home and often try home-made cuisine. (It's even safe for females travelers going it alone, but you should be more picky about your hosts, or take a friend with you the first time for a little extra security.) For hosts, it's a great way of traveling without leaving home.

If you don't mind staying in one place a bit longer, you might consider a house-sit via Ⓦ www.caretaker.org. For an annual membership of $30/£19 you get access to a list of homeowners looking for someone to water their plants, turn the lights on and off, feed the family pet or help keep an eye on grandma. Some will even pay you for your house-sitting skills.

traveler if there are doubles with lower rates, and not letting yourself be put off by places described in your guidebook as basic, or even grungy. If you're armed with earplugs and a good sleep sheet, you'll be fine. These are some other money-saving facts about and suggestions for bottom-end digs.

5

- Hostels and pensions in large cities pay the most rent, and pass the costs on to travelers. It's almost always cheaper to stay in small towns and rural areas.
- Ask about sleeping on the roof. In fair-weather climates this is often possible for roughly half the price of a room. Many places provide mattresses.
- Make a point of getting addresses of travelers you meet, and stay with them if you're heading to their home town. Try to give a few days' or weeks' notice with an email.
- Head to campsites just out of town and rent their walk-in tents (with real beds).
- Check out accommodation at universities over the summer. Empty dorm rooms are often rented out at cut-rate prices.
- In Eastern European countries, you can find deals at train stations; often, old ladies wait around to try to rent out their spare rooms (typically those no longer occupied by their adult children) to travelers.
- A hotel that notices that it is listed in a guidebook is likely to raise its prices, so don't be surprised if your book is off the mark.

Flat rentals

Another route is to rent someone's flat or even just a room in it. The website www.Airbnb.com has jumpstarted an entire industry and turned almost everyone into a potential bed & breakfast owner. It's a great way for hosts to augment their income and visitors to find a reasonably priced authentic local place to crash.

In addition to ⓦwww.airbnb.com, you might take a look at a few of these: ⓦwww.roomorama.com, ⓦwww.istopover.com, ⓦwww.flipkey .com and ⓦwww.homeaway.com (or try an aggregated search on ⓦwww .tripping.com).

Backyard rentals

Yes, you read that correctly. Thanks to the new website ⓦwww.campin mygarden.com, people are now renting space in their backyards for travelers who bring their own tents and just need a place to use the toilet and perhaps get access to wi-fi (all depends on what the owners specify they are willing to provide). Costs range from about $12/£8 to over $40/£25 (when there's a big concert/event nearby).

Finding reasonably priced good food

Cosy restaurants and old-world cafés are tempting places to relax, socialize with other travelers and people-watch. They're also nice places to run down your budget: those double café lattes add up in a hurry.

5

Minimizing these **little luxuries** is going to be the first unpleasant step. Here are a few others:

- Stick to restaurants that don't take credit cards or have English menus. Places smart enough to do this are usually smart enough to jack up their prices as well. Another approach is to choose places where you don't see other foreigners.

- Look for restaurants near universities. Students worldwide have little money for eating, and there's almost always a cottage industry set up to serve them.

- Sample the street food, find a few favorites and make meals out of them. Two full days of street-vendor-bought meals costs the equivalent of one decent restaurant meal.

- Cook in hostels (or the flat you rented). Check your guidebook for hostels with kitchen access. It's always cheaper to cook as a group, so don't be afraid to stick your head into the lounge and ask if anyone wants to pitch in and make a communal dinner.

- Supermarket-dining works. You'll soon learn how to survive on fruit, yoghurt, sandwiches and crisps.

- Try the samples at supermarkets. During weekends and busy shopping times in large supermarkets in developed countries, you can often find a tremendous range of free samples available. With a little luck, you can get an entire meal, as long as you don't mind getting it in fifteen small servings.

Is there a standard rule to tipping in restaurants?

In the USA, it's 15 percent for respectable service, 20 percent and up for exceptional service and 0–10 percent for buffets, or if you want to make a statement to a particularly bad waiter. In Iceland there's no tipping at all. Beyond that, not even Stephen Hawking has successfully unraveled the **complexities** of global tipping. You can take some comfort knowing that it baffles nearly everyone, often including the people who live in the country you're visiting.

Many restaurants utilize a **service compris** method, meaning a 0–15 percent service charge will be summarily tacked onto your bill no matter what you think of the service. You can usually find this information on the menu or bill, but you may have to ask. The thorny part is that, if the service is anywhere from decent to superior, you're often expected to give a little extra, from a few small coins for lunch in a café to 10 percent for immaculate service at an upscale restaurant.

One approach is to simply wait for the bill total, then round up. If your lunch tab comes to, say, $5.60, you might leave an even $6. With a tab of $9.80, round up to $10 for service you could have just as easily done without and $11 for excellent service.

In a crunch, you can always ask a fellow diner or your hotel concierge for some guidance, or play it safe and give ten percent when service isn't included. But the final decision is up to you. Give what you feel is appropriate and leave the restaurant with confidence.

5

- Walk for ten minutes away from major tourist areas and watch the prices drop by the block.
- To increase your options in markets, keep a kit of salt, pepper, olive oil, knife and spoon in a small container, and use it to prepare salads and the like.
- Bring food onto trains. Throughout the world, trains are united by one common theme: bad food at ridiculous prices. Bring more than you think you'll need, plus water. And if you walk a block or two from the train station, chances are you'll find a better-priced and better stocked supermarket.
- Buffets and salad bars: look for a cheap salad bar or buffet and then stack your plate about a metre high. This may require some advanced engineering skills.
- Pizza gathering is not officially recommended, but it works. Travelers have been known to hang out in franchise pizza joints, order a small salad, then grab the untouched slices from other tables when groups get up to leave.
- Waiters may play more tricks than just serving warm drinks and seeming to squeeze in a round of golf before getting the food to your table. They may also incorrectly add up the bill, conveniently in their favor. Always double-check it. If the menu says that tax is included in the prices, make sure that an extra tax charge isn't being added on top.
- Likewise, avoid places with a cover charge (or "service fee"), a charge for just sitting down at the table. If you've asked, and there isn't one, make sure it doesn't magically appear on the bill.
- Order economically. A restaurant is a great place to rest your feet and socialize, but to keep the bill down consider ordering one appetizer and a few filling side dishes instead of a main meal.

Museums and attractions – worth the cost or the wait?

It can be painful to cough up $20/£13 for a museum – and many travelers in the budget mode opt not to go. But also remember to put this in an equation that factors in how much it cost to get there and when you might be returning. Pity to pay $1000/£630 to get there, then skimp on the last $20/£13. Though, to be fair to those who've balked at the fees, many of these cultural wonders do seem to be pushing the limits of what they can get away with. The most strapped travelers have been known to try to hop onto a tour group entering a museum and try to pass themselves off as a member of the paid group.

5

Passes covering a number of attractions in the same city or country are often worth looking at, especially if extremely popular places are involved. The Paris Museum Pass, for example, pays for itself in just a few visits and lets you stroll by the snaking queues. Even a single pass to the Louvre is worth picking up in advance. Several museums in London request a donation, but are completely free.

Changing money – the cheaper way

Changing money, even when there is no black market, isn't as straight-forward as moneychangers would like you to believe. It's not exactly a science, but there are a few tips that will help you save a bit of money:

- Minimize transactions. Take a moment to calculate what you'll need because every time you change cash, travelers' checks or withdraw money from a bank machine, you're paying for the transaction. Cash machines typically tack on $5/£3 fees.
- Use a cash card. In addition to the ATM fees, credit cards hit you with ungodly interest on cash advances. If you're going to use a credit card, try to do so nearer to your monthly payment date so the interest is minimized.
- Avoid changing money at hotels and *bureaux de change*. They're well situated, have great opening hours and typically charge you for all that convenience. Don't be fooled by nice rates. They specialize in sneaky transaction fees.
- Always compare before changing money. The rates can differ even on the same street. Check banks or the post office.
- Some countries require official exchange receipts if you want to change your leftover currency back on the way out. That doesn't mean you need to keep every receipt. Just enough to cover your leftovers: one or two is plenty.
- Make deals with other travelers who are leaving the country and have some extra money. By eliminating the third party you can both get an excellent deal. Just check at one of the changing offices and use the rate halfway between the buy and sell price for that currency. Or check online.
- You can't easily exchange coins, so if you don't spend them or get them

Finding the black market

In most places where there's an active black market, this is something you won't have to worry about. Just walk down the street in all your Western-ness and it will find you. In fact, in places like Kathmandu, you'll be convinced that your name has been changed to "Change Money".

Peter Moore
Author, *Wrong Way Home* and *No Shitting in the Toilet*

5

Learn the exchange-rate tricks

Let's say you want to change $100 to Thai baht. Bank 1 is offering 44 baht to the dollar with a two percent **commission** and a 41 baht minimum fee. Bank 2 is offering 43 baht to the dollar with a 1.5 percent commission and a 120 baht minimum fee. And bank 3 is offering 45 baht to the dollar with a six percent commission and no minimum fee. At bank 1, you'll get 4271 baht. At bank 2, you'll get 4116 baht. And at bank 3 (the one with apparently the best exchange rate) you'll get 4230 baht. Earning about $4 for a minute of elementary-level arithmetic may sound OK on paper, but it seems like cruel and unusual punishment when you're there.

Of course, you can bypass all of this by using an ATM.

converted to paper money, they turn into souvenirs when you leave the country.
- Be wary of black-market changers (they're the people who approach you about thirty times a day as you walk down the street to see if you want to change money). They can be the best deal in town if you bargain and make sure you don't get ripped off – but always count your money (see p.177).
- Change money in larger cities. Rural areas are less likely to give you a competitive price.

The art of bargaining

Shopping isn't always as simple as bringing an item up to the cash register for purchase. Sometimes you've got to haggle for it. The golden rule of bartering is to keep a smile on your face. It's okay to be firm with your offer, even walk away at an impasse, but if you think of it as a game and keep the atmosphere **light and friendly**, it's hard to go wrong.

Getting an excellent price on an item, however, is another story. The first thing to do is find out from a local or fellow traveler who's familiar with the market what the real **going rate** is. Now you've got a goal. You may not get the local price, but if you come close, you've done well. More importantly, this little bit of research will help you recognize any serious swindling. That is, sometimes vendors, just for sport, like to see how much they can get for an item and may throw out a completely outlandish price and see if you'll take the bait.

Take a look at what you're wearing. It's hard to haggle a price down with a ring on every other finger or a watch on your wrist that will tell you the time 300 metres under water. Leave the expensive camera, jewelery and sharp clothes in the hotel room if you know you're heading to a market to do some bargaining. Then **go early**. Many vendors share the belief that a sale early in the day will bring them good fortune, so they may be more likely to lower their prices than they would otherwise.

This also increases your chances that you'll be alone with the vendor, which works to your advantage. With other potential customers browsing within earshot, the vendor may feel pressure to keep prices high.

The next step may be the most difficult: **hide the true extent of your interest**. That is, you don't want to hold something up to show your travel partner and say: "Look at this. It's perfect!" The vendors may not be fluent in English, but this exchange won't escape them. If you have a salesperson hovering around you, look at the item closely and wait for them to pick it up. Once they do, start to back off. "Why would I want that? I don't even know what it is." Let them try to sell it to you. "It's an X. It does this and that. And I'll give you a good price." If you do decide to pick it up, don't hold onto the item very long, or give any other clues that you're becoming attached to it. Instead, you might start out by lifting it for a moment and casually asking how much it costs. (If you don't know the local word for the item, you might take the opposite approach and use the word "thing", as if you're not sure what, exactly, it is, and therefore have relatively little use for it.)

They'll either respond with an inflated price, a decent price or this question: "How much will you give me for it?" If you've done your research, you're in good shape for any of these. If you get an inflated price, offer a price that's equally below your target price. The vendor will immediately dismiss it as unfair, and you – and here's where that smile really comes in handy – can say: "I was just having fun. Maybe we could start the bargaining over again, but this time at a more reasonable level." Your next offer should be just under your target price. On the other hand, if the vendor starts the bargaining at a very reasonable level, don't expect it to go down much. Pick a price just under your target and be prepared to come up in price fairly quickly. They may simply not be in a mood for bargaining much. And finally, if you're asked to start the bidding, you might say: "Actually, I spoke to a few locals who bought these as gifts, and they told me I shouldn't pay more than [insert the local price here]." The vendor will immediately know that you've been doing your homework, but may not be ready to give it up to you at that price. If that's the sense you get, you can say: "Perhaps that's the local price I heard about. As a visitor to your country, I'd be willing to give you a little more." Then offer a price that's one or two percent higher.

Often, sellers like to point out the unique craftsmanship in defence of their inflated prices. To counter, you might say: "I'm sorry, I'm not a professional craftsman, so some of the details are difficult for me to fully appreciate." There's no need to insult the **quality** of their merchandise during the bargaining. A more subtle way to express your sentiments is to pick the item up and inspect it closely, letting your face show your indifference, then say: "Well, I'd be willing to give you $X for it."

5

If you'd rather take a more complimentary approach, you might say something like this: "It's certainly a very nice [whatever it is], and I appreciate the time you've taken to point out its features and fine craftsmanship. And I certainly believe you when you say it's worth [his last offer]. In fact, it may even be worth more. Unfortunately, I'm not able to pay that price. I'm embarrassed to say that it's not within my budget. If you'd be willing to grant me a very special price, I would very much like to bring this home as a memory of my journey and our meeting. And I'd be most grateful. If not, I completely understand." Of course, you should be prepared to walk off if you get a no. But if you leave on such a friendly note, there's a good chance the vendor may beckon you back after you've made it halfway down the street. If they don't, and you still want it, you can either return with your tail between your legs or simply buy it somewhere else.

Another more businesslike approach is to introduce yourself to the vendor and tell them that you're considering doing all of your shopping in their boutique. Say that you're familiar with the typical market prices for each of the items and if the vendor is willing to give you a good price on them this could work out well for both of you. You'll be asked to pick out the items you're interested in and then take a seat. After some small talk (and complimentary tea and snacks in Arab countries), the vendor will probably let you steer the conversation to prices. If you're still not close by the second round, let them know that you're sorry it doesn't sound like it's working out and thank them for the tea. They've already paid for some tea and won't want to lose a fairly substantial customer so probably won't let you go that easily.

In the end, it should be a win-win experience. And if you keep the negotiation friendly, **keep your cool** and only buy at a price you feel good about, it will be. Despite any dramatic claims of losing money, a vendor will never sell you merchandise at a loss, so you shouldn't leave feeling guilty that you obtained an unjustly low price.

Working, volunteering and studying

No matter how many museums and handicraft markets you hit, no matter how long you bounce around from bus to train to tuk-tuk, no matter how little you pay for your night's accommodation, you're not likely to get under the skin of a place until you stop and engage yourself. It doesn't matter if you're working, volunteering or studying, all it takes is some ongoing interaction with locals to develop a connection and make some friends. If you've studied, consider the relationship you've had with your closer classmates compared to the one you've had with people you've shared a bus ride with. It's a different level entirely. Some jobs, volunteer projects and courses immerse you in the culture more than others, and it's not always easy to tell in advance which will and which won't, but at least you'll still be earning money, helping others or learning a skill – not a bad way to see the world.

Most wages for travel jobs are firmly set by employers. Therefore, to increase the chances that you'll make some cash to keep you on the road, you'll do well to follow this basic concept: work where the currency is strong and spend it where it's weak. An hourly wage in Japan will get you three nights in a cheap Indian hotel, whereas an hourly wage in India wouldn't cover a tip in a cheap Japanese hotel.

If you plan to work, learn how to recognize a good travel job

Worried you might run out of funds before you run out of wanderlust? Not a problem. Travelers have gone for years with just a few months' worth of cash in their pockets. Depending on your age, nationality and professional skills, you can get legal permission to work nearly anywhere. If you don't qualify under the country's regulations, or can't be bothered with the paperwork, that doesn't mean you can't work. It just means you can't work legally. Thousands of work-visa-deprived travelers manage to earn money overseas every year, especially in **short-term seasonal positions**, many of which require language skills that the locals don't possess. Of course, working illegally carries a serious risk that should be weighed carefully.

Many travelers who work abroad needlessly end up in the worst travel jobs. The reason? They take the first one that comes along and never bother to see if it fits with the travel experience they're after. (Plus, many take jobs without securing proper work permits, so they figure they need to take whatever they can get.) Let's say you want to work in a ski resort. You go to the Alps, search frantically for a job and land one washing dishes. You're thrilled to have work, but the minimum wage doesn't get you very far in a pricey resort. You get by working eight-hour days six days a week (fairly standard). After a few weeks you realize you've only put your skis on once and, as the lone washer, you've been kept too busy to meet anyone at the restaurant. It's not uncommon. In fact, very few jobs in ski resorts pay well (considering the high cost of living) and many don't allow you much time to ski. Eventually, you'll wonder what the point is. If you can't answer "yes" to at least one of these questions, you'd do well to look for a different job:

- Factoring in living costs, does the job bring in enough money to cover future travel?
- Does it make for an interesting experience or provide you with a valued skill?
- Is it a relatively easy workload and/or does it offer a lenient schedule that allows you to partake in activities you enjoy?

How to find work abroad

Wake up early, check the classified ads in the paper, check notice boards, put up your own messages, dress smartly, don't wear sunglasses, take off that hat, lose the body piercings, cover any tattoos that may frighten small children, dye your hair back to a color that could at least pass for real hair, double-check your letters for typos, return calls promptly. In short, don't give them a reason to pass you over.

If you are rejected, take it with a smile, thank the company for their consideration, and always take the opportunity to ask them where you might find work. If you've made a good impression, most people won't mind providing a few leads.

Furthermore, don't cross off a potential employer just because they said no a few days or a week earlier. Things change. One of their employees may have quit or been sacked. Or perhaps someone they were expecting never showed up. They might even realize that they needed more help than they thought. And as long as your approach is polite, your perseverance will be respected.

To make a start with your job hunt, try ⓦwww.kareeve.com, ⓦwww.transitions abroad.com, ⓦwww.jobmonkey.com, ⓦwww .payaway.co.uk or ⓦwww.jobs4travellers .com.au.

Not all illegal jobs will land you in jail

If you do illegal work (not drug trafficking… more like babysitting, tutoring, web design, garden help, etc), you could very well – depending on the laws of that country, which are certainly worth looking into – find yourself slapped with a fine, thrown out of the country (guess who gets to pay for the ticket home?) or landed behind bars learning language skills from your cellmates. With that little disclaimer out of the way, there are scores of employers who don't mind hiring unregistered foreign help and, from experience, know that the authorities will turn a blind eye. In fact, you may go to great lengths to secure a work permit only to be paid under the table. They often just like to know that you have a permit in case the police show up requesting documents.

Seasonal work

One of your best chances of turning up and landing a decent-paying job with no previous skills (or a work permit) is going to be taking advantage of the seasonal openings that, at any given moment, are

Funding a trip

To finance my year-long trip, I spent six months living with my parents while waitressing in a restaurant renowned for its hefty tippers. I managed to save about £5000, even after buying my flight. I chose cheaper countries and budgeted for just under £15 a day. This worked out fine for accommodation, food and local buses, but to help cover the occasional beers, decent meals and a few once-in-a-lifetime activities (whitewater rafting, hiking to Machu Picchu, etc), I took the odd job I found along the way. I worked in bars in Chile and Peru and taught English in Quito. The wages were in line with the meagre local rates, but they were enough to stop me from dipping into my savings. I ended up renting shared flats in these places, which allowed me to make local friends, improve my Spanish and get an insider perspective on day-to-day living so different from home in the UK.

Claire Southern

6

6

The classroom vs tutoring

I went over to Korea on a teaching contract for eight months. I had a university degree but no ESL. They took care of my work visa, which was a relief. The experience on the whole was so-so. There was more work than I expected. It's not uncommon to teach a class before businessmen go to work, which is at 6.30am, and your last class for college students and businessmen may be at 10.30pm. You work six days a week and get Korean holidays, plus one day for Christmas and one day for Thanksgiving. The academy did provide supplies and help structure the classes. On the other hand, I was at their mercy – you can't legally leave that school and stay in the country. Stories of academies withholding final pay checks, skipping a month's salary or adding up hours incorrectly were not uncommon.

When I decided to go back a few months later, I opted not to go back to the school. I started teaching on my own.

It took a couple of weeks to build up my client list. Some people just ask you in an elevator in a nice apartment complex while you're leaving another student's house. Plus the usual networking. I ended up making more than twice as much per hour as with the program, saving (with my wife) over $10,000 in six months. And I could take vacations when I wanted – actually I had to leave the country every three months because of a tourist visa. The trick was changing money because they limited the withdrawal for foreigners. There were many foreigners teaching this way so they must have found a loophole. Mine was to have the family I was staying with convert my earnings to dollars. Then I took the dollars and transfered them to travelers' checks and took them out of the country that way. The other trick was not getting caught – teaching or changing money. You can get fined and kicked out of the country for both, though they're more likely to catch you changing money.

Ken Johnson

available somewhere in the world. It's a matter of being in the right place at the right time; if you know what you're looking for, it's easy to coordinate.

Summer-resort work

For summer resorts (June–Sept in the northern hemisphere, Nov–Feb in the southern hemisphere), you may want to turn up a month or two before the season begins to **beat the rush** for jobs, then, once you've secured a job, go traveling and return when the job starts. Women tend to have a much easier time finding work on the hotel/bar/restaurant end than men. Possible jobs include: camp counsellor for kids, bartender, waiter, hotel receptionist, hotel housekeeper, cook, baker, sales clerk, supply driver, DJ, rental shop clerk, cleaner, bouncer, guide, sports instructor, lifeguard, scuba instructor and campsite maintainer.

Winter-resort work

For ski-resort work, either apply in writing for work with a tour company in your home country six to eight months in advance, or arrive at your desired resort around a month before the season begins (Dec–April in the northern hemisphere, June–Oct in the southern hemisphere). Be especially careful about hiring yourself out as a freelance ski instructor – most resorts keep a keen eye out for unofficial lessons on the slopes and prosecute. Possible jobs include: ski tuner, lift operator, snowmobile guide, ski guide, ski rental shop clerk, chalet cleaner, bartender, waiter, hotel receptionist, hotel house-keeper, cook, sales clerk, supply driver, cleaner, bouncer and DJ. Countries with ski resorts include: Switzerland, France, Italy, Germany, Norway, Sweden, Spain, Scotland, Austria, Slovenia, Argentina, Chile, USA, Canada, Japan, Iran, Lebanon, Israel, New Zealand, Australia, South Africa and, strangely, Dubai.

Harvest-season work

6

If you can eat it, you can probably find work picking it if you turn up at the right place in the right season. The best place for pre-trip research is the internet:

- **Fruitful Jobs** (🌐www.fruitfuljobs.com). Farming jobs in the UK for foreigners
- **Grape Picking** (🌐www.grapepicking.co.uk). Grape picking/wine harvest jobs for English speakers in France
- **Jobs 4 Travellers** (🌐www.jobs4travellers.com.au). Good info on harvest jobs in Australia.

Pay is often based on the amount you pick, and it may take a few days to get up to speed. Remember to ask for adequate protection when pesticides and other noxious chemicals are sprayed. Europe, Australia, New Zealand and North America are likely to offer the best rates.

Manual labor

Construction jobs tend to be underpaid and backbreaking. There's often a spot or two in cities where laborers show up each morning and get selected by employers. If no such place exists, or the competition is too fierce, look for large construction sites and ask for work directly from the foreman. There's also plenty of factory work; the nastier tasks usually come with a higher wage. If they don't, don't do them. Possible jobs include: house renovation, road building, landscaping, shrimp peeling and fish packing.

A few solid tips for creating your own independent job

Money-making opportunities for the creative entrepreneur are almost endless. You could sell cool drinks on a hot beach or cheap umbrellas on a busy street when it rains. And if you have a trade that allows you to work independently, even better. But unless you have a work permit, be sure to find out about the penalties, assess the risk and keep a low profile. If you're looking for a street to perform on, think about good acoustics, an original act and a place where the police are kind (northern Europe tends to be popular in this regard). Often small towns with

6

Teaching English in Madrid

I didn't have a job lined up before I arrived, but it didn't take long to find work with a private agency. I just browsed the phonebook for English schools and then paid them a visit. They meet you and make a judgment call. I was mainly working with students on their conversation skills, so my lack of formal training wasn't an issue. The setup was ideal. I had flexible hours – about five to fifteen hours a week – which brought in around $600 a month. This was enough to cover my $300 rent in the apartment I was sharing and gave me enough extra time and money to enjoy the city and my newfound friendships.

Amy Schrier
Editor, *Blue Magazine*

pedestrian streets and few buskers bring good fortune. Also, keep an eye out for festivals, which attract ready-to-be-entertained crowds with ample pocket change. Possible jobs include: street musician, masseuse, au pair, private cook, private music instructor, street juggler, house cleaner, gardener, window cleaner, language tutor, jewelery street-seller, T-shirt designer and peddler, and distributor of flyers for local bars and hostels.

The scoop on teaching English

If English is your mother tongue, you have a university degree of some kind, can dress smartly and carry yourself with confidence, you'll be likely to find a teaching job just fine without a TEFL (Teaching English as a Foreign Language; ⓦwww.tefl.co.uk) certificate or similar (such as Celta or TESOL). If you do have a teaching certificate, though (see p.294), you'll probably land a better job or beat unqualified competition, and find it easier in the classroom than if you were winging it. Is it worth $1500–3000/£945–1890 and a hundred hours of classwork to make that "liveable wage"? Or $350/£220 for a weekend introductory course? Your call. But factor this in: a certificate is more valued for the higher-paying jobs in Asia and less valued in Latin America and Eastern Europe. The pay could be anything from $20/£13 to $1500/£945 a week. In a country with a strong economy, an elite school or big company might pay upwards of $4500/£2835 a month. However, most require a six- to twelve-month contract to prevent you from skipping out and leaving their students with verbs unconjugated and participles dangling.

Teaching diving

With a Divemaster certification (ⓦwww.padi.com), you can find work throughout the world. Landing a job is another thing. Most certified instructors have success making personal contact with dive shops and get paid under the table for their work. Or they return later, once the proper work visa has been processed back home. You might try applying directly to some of the larger, more professional resorts. Among the major diving centers are: Airlie Beach and Cairns along Australia's Great Barrier Reef;

Belize and Cozumel in the Caribbean; and Sharm-el-Sheikh in the Red Sea. But you may have more luck at many of the lesser-known dive sites you stumble across on your travels.

Journalism and photography

Travel writing and travel photography are very competitive fields, and in both cases your chances of supplementing your income or supporting yourself while traveling will be greatly enhanced with well-honed skills from a course or formal education. No matter, however, how much skill you may possess, selling your material without an established track record is extremely tough.

But that's only if you go the traditional route. If you have a Facebook or Twitter account or are keeping a travel blog, you're already a travel writer. Several writers have launched themselves this way. The competition is tough so standing out from the crowd will take a good deal of effort (and possibly some decent programming, video and photography skills) but it can be done.

If you're serious about going the more traditional route, writing your way around the world, you'll want to give yourself a **head start** by making inroads in the industry before you go: get some articles or photos published (no matter what the subject), build a relationship with one or more editors and start putting your portfolio together.

Another popular approach, especially for photographers, is to document your trip and try to sell the images on your return. This can certainly bring in some money, but generally very little, and you're not likely to get it until long after you return. Cold-calling an editor just before you leave and asking if you can, despite your complete lack of experience, report your way around the globe is a textbook example of how not to go about it.

Before you look for a "real job" overseas

If you want to work professionally abroad, you'd do well to set up a job before you go. For most foreign companies to obtain a work visa on your behalf, they need to demonstrate that you have a skill that they can't find domestically, which might include web designing, specialized mechanics, commercial diving or language teaching. Or they need to demonstrate that the country is in short supply of your skills, for example in the fields of teaching, medicine, dentistry and veterinary medicine. One of the best places to get information is in your local trade publication or larger national one, where foreign companies may advertise for workers. Or, if you already work for a multinational company, you might start out by enquiring from within. Also try ⓦwww.monster.com, a site that specializes in foreign-work placement.

6

Some work practicalities

If you satisfy the **requirements** of various countries (nationality, age, marital status, student status), you may qualify for a **work visa**, or a limited version of one. Typically, it's for a set period or for certain job sectors, but it's definitely worth looking into. Just make sure you obtain it before you arrive in the country so you can receive the correct stamps when you pass through customs. Arranging for a work visa once you've arrived is, depending on the country, anywhere between difficult and impossible. You can find just about everything you need online at the immigration or work-visa section of the country's embassy website.

Primarily aimed at students or very recent graduates, international placement organizations (Ⓦ www.ciee.org, Ⓦ www.alliancesabroad.com and Ⓦ www.interexchange .org) help travelers slice through the red tape and find minimum-wage jobs in select countries. The fees range from almost nothing to about $500/£315 – in some countries you may also get insurance thrown in. It alleviates much of the hassle, but you have to decide if that's worth the price.

Once you get a job offer you plan to accept, ask for a few days to fix housing arrangements. Look into family stays, university-room rentals and enquire at various hostels to see if they'll offer you a long-term deal.

If you work abroad and declare your earnings there, knowing that the amount is too small to be taxed in that country, bear in mind that you might be taxed for the amount in your home country, depending on reciprocal agreements and any other income sources.

There's a load of red tape involved in getting this sort of work set up, but much of it is taken care of once you have an employer providing the necessary invitation and paperwork. You should have it all arranged before arriving so that you can clear customs with the correct visa. If you have to travel abroad for an interview for the job, you may need to return home and wait for your work papers to clear immigration before you can re-enter and begin. Many countries have bilateral arrangements that will allow you to skirt much of the process, so it's worth investigating each country's immigration/visa website for the most up-to-date information.

Keep your job and telecommuting as you travel

No one says you need to work where you live. It's entirely possible to work while you're away for people back home (or wherever) by computer: consulting, designing, writing, photographing, editing and so on can all be done remotely. Maintain contacts where you work (or seek freelance work before leaving) so you can do perfectly legal work that's well paid and in your own currency. Have a look at *The 4-Hour Workweek* by Timothy Ferriss for additional insights on making this work.

Volunteering – not as cheap or simple as it sounds

Donating your time can be a tremendously fulfilling experience, but if you're not careful in selecting a project, your time contributed may feel like time wasted. Some organizations' definitions of efficiency and utility may differ substantially from your own. In certain cases, it can be fulfilling for you, but **little benefit**, if any, to the community. And many of the volunteer ventures are almost identical to English teaching or the labor-intensive work projects listed above – only, as the name implies, you're not getting paid. You might be moving boxes, doing dishes or shovelling cow dung, which is fine, provided you know what you're getting into. Before you sign up, make sure you get an exact description of what you'll be doing and what your employer expects you to accomplish during your visit. You'll want some local orientation before you're dropped off with your project, and a safety net (local contact) for emergency support, supplies and advice. You can ask for these things because you're not just going to be working there for free; you're helping finance it. And volunteering ain't **as cheap as it sounds**. First, there's the airfare. Then you often need to pay a fee that covers your lodging, food, insurance and the entire screening and orientation process. You might be looking at costs in excess of $400/£252 a month. As a guideline, the more exotic the project the more you pay to assist.

Most projects have specific dates for training and transporting new volunteers. Plus, the organizations prefer to screen applicants. So showing up to lend a hand, though well intentioned, can actually backfire. Your best bet is to make arrangements well before you leave. If you're already on the road, your best shot might be online contact at a nearby internet café. With a more web-advanced organization, you may be able take care of all the details before you arrive.

More and more families are taking volunteering trips as well. These tend to be short term, more expensive and better coordinated experiences (see Ⓦwww.metowe .com and Ⓦwww.globeaware.org for more information). For those who do decide to bring their kids, it can be traumatic, but you are the best judge of what your kids

WWOOF (World-Wide Opportunities on Organic Farms)

Not all WWOOFing experiences are necessarily about farming. My friend and I used it primarily as an enjoyable way to make our budget last a little longer. We chose to spend a week with a couple who had renovated a cottage on a tiny island in the Hawkesbury River, just north of Sydney. Although they had a lovely organic garden, our task was mainly to paint the outside of their house. All our expenses were covered and we enjoyed some fantastic organic food and wine. After our four hours of daily painting we were able to relax and enjoy the island.

Sally Schafe

6

Employment in Israel

Israel has traditionally been one of the world's most **popular destinations** for travelers looking for work. Not surprisingly, the market has been swamped with immigrants and travelers alike, and the wages absolutely stink as a result. Travelers are left trying to raise funds at an abysmal rate after living expenses are deducted. Still, they keep on coming.

On a **moshav farm**, workers live together and cook together in basic provided accommodation and put in ridiculously long and hard hours for molecular-size wages (about £200 pounds a month, or half that if the farm provides your food). There are generally trace amounts of social life, though, so the little that's earned is easy to save. On a **kibbutz**, it's typically less work, less pay ($15–20/£9–13 per week – often provided on a card that works only at the kibbutz shop) and more socializing. You typically "volunteer" seven to eight hours, six days a week. In return, you get room, board, some leisure activities (depending on what's available) and an allowance that buys you a couple of cokes or ice-cream cones per week (at the kibbutz kiosk) and probably won't begin to cover your bar tab.

There are 256 Kibbutzim around Israel (with over 100,000 Israelis living on them), but only 16 are religious. The rest are quite secular.

Volunteers and kibbutzniks (kibbutz residents) have increasingly grown further apart as the volunteers have demonstrated their ability to party and the kibbutzniks have responded with more distance and disciplined work conditions. But, again, this is not necessarily the case everywhere. In many places, volunteers are greatly appreciated and welcomed with open arms and assigned to various families. Jobs range from milking cows to working in a cement factory, picking fruit, doing dishes or preparing meals. You need a bill of good health signed by a doctor, about $300/£189 in cash, an onward ticket and you must agree to stay for at least two months. Placement can be made through a local booking agent, or by calling or visiting an individual kibbutz directly. See also Ⓦ www.kibbutzvolunteer.com.

can handle. Dr. Harold S. Koplewicz, president of the Child Mind Institute in New York, commented on this in the *New York Times* (Aug 14, 2012): "Generally, I think during the teen years, a time when most kids are very self-absorbed, it is not a bad thing to take them out of their comfort zone.

Not sure why you might want to volunteer? Here's a little reminder

- Choose a remote community where it's easy to make friends.
- Learn customs and language skills.
- Get to know volunteers from around the world.
- Get some hands-on practical experience.
- Use your professional skills to make a tangible difference to people's lives.
- Feel that you're striving to leave the world in better condition than when you arrived.

The best souvenir you can bring back – a new skill

Taking a course is one of the most enriching things you can do on your trip: it's a chance to learn a new skill that will remain with you long after you've returned. Education aside, many offer a nice break from the travel scene and provide a chance for you to meet up with some

6

Sample volunteer projects

There are literally **thousands** to choose from, throughout the year and around the globe. If any of the projects listed below sound intriguing and you want to find something similar, visit a search engine and type in a few of the key words regarding location or the type of work plus "volunteer", "help" or "assist". Meanwhile, here are a few **volunteer** sites to get you started:

Ⓦ www.yearoutgroup.org
Ⓦ www.travelersworldwide.com
Ⓦ www.volunteerinternational.com
Ⓦ www.workingabroad.com/organis/international.htm
Ⓦ www.worldwidevolunteering.org.uk
Ⓦ www.habitat.org
Ⓦ www.doctorswithoutborders.org/work/field/ (non-medical personnel are also wanted)

Nature conservation

Repair forest pathways in Spain • Survey Australia's Great Barrier Reef • Aid forestry conservation near Japan's Mount Fuji • Renovate hiking paths in the Black Forest of Germany • Construct mountain footpaths in Italy • Work on an organic "WWOOF" farm in New Zealand • Develop ecotourism in Ecuador • Build an "eco house" in Belgium • Maintain parks in Argentina

Wildlife

Patrol beaches to protect turtle eggs in Mexico • Catch lemon sharks in the Bahamas and tag them with transmitters • Catch kangaroos in Australia and attach radio collars to them • Swim with and collect data from dolphins in New Zealand • Track killer whales off the west coast of Canada • Bring wintertime food to reindeer in Finland • Dive to examine ghost shrimps in Papua New Guinea • Locate groups of howler monkeys in Venezuela • Record octopus behavior in the waters of Burma • Track orangutans in Borneo's rainforests • Monitor wildebeest migration in Kenya

Human aid and development

Build simple water and sanitation systems in rural Nicaragua • Teach and assist at an orphanage in Malaysia • Meet medicine men to discover medicinal uses of plants in Nigeria • Assist at a camp for children with learning disabilities in Australia • Volunteer at an orphanage with an organic farm in Cambodia • Build city parks in Turkey

Archeology

Excavate dinosaur bones in southern Australia • Restore fortified castles in France • Catalog dinosaur remains in the USA's Mojave Desert • Excavate Mayan remains in Belize • Analyse mummies in Chile's Azapa Valley • Preserve an unearthed town from 1537 in Mexico • Restore archeological and architectural sites in Italy • Sort and catalogue unearthed pottery in Fiji

6

Volunteer success

In northern India I was able to put my anthropology studies to use helping translate oral histories of women who communicate their cultural identity by song. The report I produced from the experience enabled charities to channel their involvement toward the village's specific needs and left me with the sense that I had helped put something back into the community – which isn't as common as you'd think. Finding a volunteer program and a situation that allows you to do this isn't as simple as showing up in a remote village with a good attitude and plenty of enthusiasm. I've met so many frustrated volunteers. They have images of working in a rural area, but when they arrive they are assigned a task that seems unappreciated or unbeneficial, have trouble with the language barrier, and don't have any other foreign volunteers nearby to help cushion the culture shock. The isolation can be overwhelming, especially for those who are starting their trip with such a project.

Those who asked loads of questions before signing up, however, seemed to find programs that allowed both them and the community to gain from the experience.

Beth Wooldridge
Author, *Rough Guide to India*

locals or other foreigners with similar interests.

Many courses can be arranged at the last minute, especially if you're traveling alone. But most often, the better programs require some **advance booking**. Look into this well before you arrive. In fact, well before you arrange any flights. Unless you're absolutely sure about the soundness of a program, don't pay the entire fee in advance. And pay with a credit card to help protect yourself. The courses listed below are not "recommended" by Rough Guides or the author, but are meant to provide a sample of some of the activities out there, and are only intended to be used as a starting point. Take a look at ⓦ www.golearnto.com for more ideas.

Studying a language along the way

"Hello", "please" and "thank you" won't take more than five minutes to learn, no matter what the language. If you want to move beyond a few words, a **language course** is a great way to start your travels in a new country. Aside from tools that will help you unlock the cultural codes of the country, you'll meet more locals, be able to get assistance when needed, keep your grey matter active and make your travels far more meaningful. You'll need at least three weeks to make real progress, no matter how intensive the course is. Two months should provide good conversational skills, depending on your study habits.

Many of the better-known language courses take place in towns loaded with English-speaking students – great for your social life, but lousy for language discipline. It's better (and cheaper) to select a smaller place where you'll get an experience far more intensive than the more expensive "intensive" courses offered in major language-learning centers. If you're set on a specific course, you may need to sign up in advance. Otherwise, you can walk in off the street and usually start the same day. And, naturally,

Learning Spanish

Spanish is perhaps the most popular language for travelers to study. It's relatively easy to learn, the courses are cheap and often include arranged family stays, and a little Spanish is extremely useful for travel around South and Central America. For some basic price and course information, try ⓦ www.spanishschools.org and ⓦ www.donquijote .com. Three weeks of room, board and instruction starts at $675/£425.

6

you can find inexpensive private tutors to teach you in nearly any city. Put up a notice near a university and you'll have a few offers within hours.

Improve your photography with a course

Even if you're just taking a pocket camera, learning how to compose your photographs is going to get you a lot further than expensive film and an overpriced lens. You may not learn anything more valuable than some basic tips on p.203, but you'll need to practice them and develop an eye for what works and what doesn't. That means taking oodles of photos, getting them developed immediately and having them critiqued. You can find community photography workshops for less than $100/£63 but the upper-end instruction doesn't come cheap. It does, however, often include a trip to India, Morocco or some place you may not feel comfortable venturing to on your own.

- **Close Up Expeditions** ⓦ www.cuephoto.com. Workshops in over forty countries concentrating on nature, landscape and traditional cultures; 5–17 days; $250–350/£151–212 per day.
- **Ralph Paonessa Photo Workshops** ⓦ www.rpphoto.com. Specializing in birds, nature, landscapes and travel, these five- to fifteen-day programs cost $2000–6300/£1260–3969 with lodging, some meals and ground transport.
- **Jim Cline Photography** ⓦ www.jimcline.com. Small group (7–10 people) trips mainly to Latin America, India and Southeast Asia. Sometimes in combination with workshops, sometimes with informal tutoring on location. Length: 2–14 days; cost: $240–300/£151–189 per day.

Pick up some survival skills

You don't need one of these courses to navigate the planet, but it certainly wouldn't hurt. Most **survival schools** are run by Americans these days, but many of the programs take place around the world. You can study general skills or take a specific course in jungle, desert, mountain, marine and Arctic survival. Some, such as NOLS and Outward Bound, place more emphasis on the group experience, while others are more technically orientated. Make sure you ask plenty of questions before making your decision. Most courses work out to about $120/£76 per day.

- **Aboriginal Living Skills School** Prescott, Arizona, USA ⓦwww .alssadventures.com. One-day to one-week courses on desert survival and winter camping with primitive camp craft skills.
- **Boulder Outdoor Survival School (BOSS)** Boulder, Colorado, USA ⓦwww.boss-inc.com. Desert survival courses in southwestern USA or Mexico.
- **Karamat Wilderness Ways** Edmonton, Alberta, Canada ⓦwww .karamat.com. Courses run from two to six days, specializing in the northern boreal forests.
- **LTR (Learn To Return) Training Systems** Anchorage, Alaska, USA ⓦwww.survivaltraining.com. Mostly two-day programs on a variety of topics. Aviation-oriented survival is the specialty, but there are also courses in Arctic survival, water survival and international travel survival.
- **NOLS** Wyoming, USA ⓦwww.nols.edu. Courses typically last two weeks to one month, and are held mostly in the USA and Canada, but also around the rest of the world. Transferable educational credit is possible with some universities.
- **Outward Bound** Garrison, NY, USA ⓦwww.outwardbound.org. Courses last one to eleven weeks, with focus on wilderness training and team-building; they take place in the USA, Caribbean, Europe and South America.
- **Randall's Adventure & Training** Peru ⓦwww.jungletraining.com. Jungle survival instruction in the Peruvian rainforest that lasts from six to sixteen days, with cooperation from the Peruvian Air Force school.
- **UK Survival School** Hereford, England ⓦwww.survivalschool .co.uk. Courses are taught in the UK, but expeditions to Africa and further-flung locales are also available.

Travel security and first-aid courses

You can learn the basics from the pocket-sized *Rough Guide to Travel Survival*, but if you're looking for a bit more information on travel security and first aid consider these:

- **Adventure Lifesigns** Aldershot, Hampshire, England ⓦwww .lifesignsgroup.co.uk. Expedition training, remote medical training and courses for independent travelers lasting from one to four days.
- **Objective Team** Daventry, Northamptonshire, England ⓦwww .objectiveteam.com. Specialized corporate training for hostile

environments as well as one-day gap year classes, taking place weekly in London and monthly elsewhere across the UK.

- **Wilderness Medical Associates** USA and Canada ⓦwww.wildmed.com and ⓦwww.wildmed.ca. Courses around the USA and Canada, ranging from two days to the month-long Wilderness EMT (Emergency Medical Training).

Mountain survival

6

If you're more interested in staying alive in the mountains and summitting in the process, check out this list of international mountaineering courses: ⓦhttp://dmoz.org/Recreation/Climbing/Guides_and_Schools, or one of the following:

- **Australian School of Mountaineering** ⓦwww.asmguides.com. Guiding and training in the Blue Mountains.
- **Bob Culp Climbing School** ⓦwww.bobculp.com. Rock- and ice-climbing trips to the French and Italian Alps and in the USA.
- **Colorado Mountain School** Boulder, Colorado, USA ⓦwww.totalclimbing.com. From first snow school to extreme alpinism, and from starter rock climbing to Big Walls.
- **Swiss Association of the Mountaineering Schools** ⓦwww.bergsportschulen.ch. Pick the region you want to climb and the site matches you up with a school.

Try a cooking course

Learning how to make one great local dish could very well be the best souvenir you bring home. **Cooking schools** can be found almost anywhere. If you find you're really enjoying a local cuisine, talk to the local tourist office about courses available. Most last from a day to a month, with widely varying prices. As well as the listings below, try ⓦcookforfun.shawguides.com.

- **Chiang Mai Thai Cookery Course** ⓦwww.thaicookeryschool.com. $25.50 per day.
- **Italian cooking schools** ⓦwww.cookitaly.com. Choose by regional cuisine (Sicilian or northern Italian) or let price dictate your choice.
- **Cooking with Mari** ⓦhttp://mari-cooking.p1.bindsite.jp. Japanese home visit and cooking class in the heart of Tokyo. $45 for a two-hour class.
- **Le Cordon Bleu French Cooking** ⓦwww.cordonbleu.edu. Schools in Paris (the original), London, Ottawa, Seoul, Kobe, Tokyo, Adelaide and Sydney with day-long workshops to full-diploma cooking courses.

Learn a martial art

Most of today's traditional **martial arts** come from China and Japan (with other popular disciplines in Korea, Thailand and Brazil), and it can be particularly inspirational to study and train with masters where the craft was developed. If you're already trained in one or more of the martial arts, then it's likely you'll already have a decent grasp of the working vocabulary. And what you can't follow verbally, you can certainly pick up by watching, as most explanations are accompanied by demonstrations. This does apply to newbies as well, though it can be particularly helpful to have English instruction if you're just getting started. If your local training center doesn't have such contacts, they can usually point you to someone who will, as it's always nicer to arrive with a personal recommendation.

Otherwise, you'll just have to find your own way in, either through website contacts or by poking your head in the front door and making enquiries yourself. Be forewarned: while you may be welcomed with open arms, some locals may be reluctant to spar with you. They may be afraid to lose face if beaten by a foreigner or find it boring if your level is too low. In other instances, locals may try to demonstrate their superiority by giving you a sound beating. Keep in mind that some dojos practice rougher training than you may be used to: it's better to observe before you participate. A few courses cater to international students:

- **Boxing** Kronk Gym ⓦwww.kronkgym.com. A classic American boxing gym in Detroit, USA.
- **Capoeira schools of Brazil** ⓦwww.capoeirista.com. A list of various training centers around Brazil, where you can try this rhythmic martial art.

Ever wanted to know how to...

No one says you have to **learn something** you'll ever use again. So long as it perks your interest, it'll be a nice addition to your collection of experiences. Here are a few less conventional programs:

Ikebana ⓦwww.ohararyu.or.jp. Also known as Kado, this is the art of Japanese flower arranging. Learn how to make a living sculpture in Japan.

International Car Racing Schools ⓦwww.racingschools.com. Here's a chance to burn rubber with someone else's car, from F1 racing outside Monaco or Vegas to drag racing in New Jersey.

Taiko drumming ⓦwww.wadaikoworld.net. Bang a drum in Japan.

Wat Pho Thai Massage School Bangkok, Thailand ⓦwww.wahanda.com (search for "Wat Pho"). Get the lowdown on sore muscles and pressure points.

Windsurfing school Hood River, USA ⓦwww.hoodriverwaterplay.com. Big wind plus big water equals big air. Hold on tight.

- **Kick boxing** Jitti's Gym ⓦwww.jittigym.com. Learn Thai kick boxing in Bangkok from the trainer of national champions.
- **Shao Lin Martial Arts Academy** ⓦwww.shaolins.com. Learn kung fu straight from monks who've passed it down for generations.
- **Kukkiwon Taekwondo Academy** ⓦwww.ktamn.com. Kukkiwon is the world Taekwondo center in Korea, and has training and competition facilities.
- **Tai chi** Hong Kong ⓦwww.hktaichi.com. Hong Kong's Association of Tai Chi can steer you towards courses and practice venues.

6

Learn to meditate

This is perhaps the ultimate remedy to fast-paced travel. Whether you're spending a week in total silence or taking a series of yoga classes, getting back in touch with your mind and body can be an invigorating pit stop – just what you need to continue on your physical and inner journey. Many courses are offered in English around the world, so a simple online search including the name of the country where you plan to take a break and "meditation" should yield numerous listings. Try also ⓦwww.dhamma .org, ⓦwww.kopanmonastery.com and ⓦwww.yogadirectory.com.

Documents and insurance

7

Getting your documents in order for a long trip isn't nearly as much of a hassle as it sounds – just a case of sorting out your passport, any necessary visas and travel insurance. Many countries either don't require visas or make it easy for you to pick them up in neighboring countries. But it is useful to consider the all-important departure countdown (see box, pp.110–111).

Passports

Without a passport, you're looking at a short trip. Probably to the airport and back. Even Canadians need a passport to enter the USA these days. You can supposedly travel without a passport within the EU, but bring it along anyway. Many hotels still want to see a passport, and besides, do you really want to risk finding out if the Portuguese immigration police will just whisk you through with a smile and wave of the hand?

Two or more passports

The important thing for dual or triple passport holders is that you pick **one passport** – presumably the one that grants you the most visa-free access into other countries – and only use the other for emergencies or to get around work-permit issues. Leave a third passport at home with your document copies so it can be mailed to you if a crisis should arise. It may be tempting to swap when you can save a little money on a visa, but, especially when traveling among neighboring countries, this isn't a good idea as you need to be able to demonstrate a clear travel history to customs officials. Any gaps will raise suspicions. To keep the customs process at borders moving smoothly, it's best if you avoid bringing up your multiple citizenship.

Visas

Visas are essentially stamps (but sometimes stickers or entire documents), inserted into your passport by immigration officials or embassies or consulates acting on their behalf, that grant you permission to enter their country for a specified period of time. There are other conditions that can be included as well – such as the right to work, the right to re-enter the country multiple times and the right to extend your visa – which may require special approval. Much of this depends on which passport you hold. Each country has its own set of agreements with other countries, with fees yo-yoing (with diplomacy) in the region of $25–135/£15–82.

Many countries require no visas for some passport holders, or simply hand out visas at the airport or border crossing for free or for a small fee. Otherwise, they can take anywhere between a day and a few weeks to process, but they can usually be taken care of within a few days if you opt to pay an additional fee to expedite the application.

The big question is whether you should arrange for these before you leave or at embassies and consulates along the way once you've started traveling. For shorter trips, you should try to get it all taken care of in advance. For longer trips it simply may not be possible. Some visas are activated the moment the stamp goes into your passport, and may expire long before you even set foot in the country.

Keep in mind that you may not want to disclose your real job on a visa application. Doing so could mean additional paperwork, higher fees and a shorter visa stay. A journalist or travel writer is often better off writing "editor" or "author" or "writer." Consider if there may be any sensitivity to your job before filling in the blank.

It's uncommon but not unheard of for some developing countries to issue 48-hour visas at the border that have to be extended in the capital, which may mean some unpleasant backtracking, depending on your itinerary. And those who are winging it with their travel plans should watch out for visa applications that require itineraries, with specific ports of entry and exit. If you want to keep your dates and itinerary loose for the moment, take care of the visa when you're in a neighboring country and have a better idea about your intended route. Plus, if you're turned down for a visa at home, you can certainly try again at a neighboring embassy.

Obtaining a passport

	Regular service	Expedited
Australia	32-page passport Aus$233. 64-page passport Aus$351; ten working days; can be done online or at post office, but you must be interviewed.	Additional fee of A$103 to process in two working days (case-by-case basis ☎131 232)
Canada	24-page passport Can$87. 48-page passport Can$92; up to four weeks (not including mailing time), ten days in person, no renewal available, new passport must be purchased, photocopies of identity documents (eg driver's license) must be signed by a guarantor.	Express: two to nine days; C$30. Urgent: same day or next day (only available on case-by-case emergency basis); C$70. Personal pick-up: ten days; C$10.
New Zealand	Ten working days: NZ$153	Three working days: NZ$306; call-out service, when urgent delivery falls out of working hours, NZ$664; ☎0800 22 5050.
UK	Three-week service at post offices: £78; two weeks if applying at certain Post Office branches	One-week service at passport offices £113 (not possible with first-time passports). Same-day premium service (£130; only when renewing to a 48-page "jumbo" passport) is technically not available for standard passports, but you can try calling ☎0870 521 0410 if you think your situation merits special consideration.
USA	All first-timers must apply in person. Four to six weeks $110; $110 for renewal.	Two to three weeks expedited processing can be requested, and will add an additional $60 plus overnight shipping both ways. Or make an appointment to visit one of the 15 regional passport agencies near you: $160.

7

Photo info	Valid for...	Website
Two identical photographs taken within the last 6 months, between 35 x 45mm and 40 x 50mm, good-quality, color, full-front view of your head and shoulders in front of a plain, light-colored background. Your eyes should be open and if you normally wear prescription glasses, you should be wearing them in the photo, but your eyes must be clearly visible and not affected by glare from the glasses. The back of one photograph should be correctly endorsed by the person who identified you with "This is a true photograph of [your name in full]" and signed by the identifier. Believe it or not, they have even more guidelines on their website; best to check it out.	10 years	ⓦ www .passports .gov.au /Web /newppt /index .aspx
Two identical passport photos, black and white or color, taken from the same roll or electronic file. Photo must be taken against a plain, uniform white or light-colored background. The face must be square to the camera with a neutral expression and with the mouth closed. Photo size: 50mm wide x 70mm high. The image must be centered in the photo, square to the camera and the face length from chin to crown of head must be between 31 and 36mm. Photos must show full head without glasses or headgear, except if worn for religious or medical reasons. The name and address of the photographer and the date of the photo must be written on the back of the photo. No stickers.	5 years	ⓦ www .ppt.gc.ca.
Two identical photos must be less than six months old, clear, sharp and in focus, approximately 35 x 45mm, with a light-colored background (not white), without hats or head covering or sunglasses, full-front view of head and shoulders, on photographic paper. The witness (and nobody else) identifying you must write your full name on the back of one photo, then sign and date it.	5 years	ⓦ www .passports .govt.nz
Two identical photos taken against a plain cream or plain grey background must be clear and good quality, printed on normal thin photographic paper, unmounted 45 x 35mm and full face. Must be in color, and taken within the last month. Photos must be validated by the same person who signs your application form; they write on the back of one photo (not both) "I certify that this is a true likeness of [Mr/Ms etc... followed by your full name]", then sign and date both the statement and the photo.	10 years	ⓦ www.ips .gov.uk
Two identical photos 2 x 2 inches (between 1 inch and 1³⁄₈ inches from the bottom of the chin to the top of the head), must be in color, taken within six months, full-face front view with a plain white or off-white background. Uniforms should not be worn, just normal street attire. No dark glasses or non-prescription glasses. If you normally wear prescription glasses, a hearing device, wig or similar articles, they should be worn for the photo.	10 years	ⓦ http ://state .gov/travel

7

Strategy for getting visas before you go

If you're planning to work legally in a country, apply for that country's visa first since it must be arranged from your home country. Next on your list should be the first country or two you plan to visit, if a visa is required at all. Then look at the country/countries you may plan to use as hubs, since extended and multiple-entry visas can sometimes be more difficult to arrange at borders, but only pursue these if the visas are activated on entry. After that, go for as many visas as you have time for, looking at the more "exotic" countries first (again, only if the visas are activated on entry – if not, they may expire by the time you arrive).

Getting visas once you're on the road

It's almost always possible to pick up visas at **neighboring countries** (or even distant countries, provided there's an embassy), but do some planning. Arrive before the office opens to secure your place at the beginning of the queue, which will invariably develop. With a small staff, all it takes is one person with a complex case in the queue ahead of you to delay the entire process for hours. Remember that granting visas is not compulsory, and appearance counts (more at some places than others), so dress as **smartly** as your limited wardrobe allows. A clean shirt and trousers should be fine, though you'd be advised to subtly cover any startling tattoos and remove conspicuous body-piercing for the visit. Also, you may be asked about where and when you plan to exit the country, so you should arrive with some idea: bring along a guidebook to help you figure things out if you need to make some last-minute decisions. **Bring plenty of photos** as well. It's likely you'll be asked to provide two to four identical photos. Most don't mind if they're color or black and white, but bring both just in case. Every major city has such photo facilities, but it's better to have plenty taken in advance, so you don't need to get more taken for every application.

Knowing the entry requirements – and how to get around them (a must-read for those buying tickets as they go)

Some countries require you to have an **onward ticket and substantial funds** to support yourself while in the country. A credit card or two plus the crisp notes of your emergency cash (see p.131) are generally sufficient for the financial aspect. It also helps if you look presentable. In fact, you should make a point of pulling out your backpack's best for border crossings and flights because officials can, even if you're holding a valid visa, deny you entry. As for the onward ticket, it may seem a little problematic if you're traveling overland or buying plane tickets as you go. There's an easy solution. As noted in the section on one-way tickets (p.52), you can simply make a fully refundable booking using your credit card on the internet at a reliable site, print out the confirmation of the ticket and booking and then cancel the ticket without penalty once you've entered the country. You can also do this at a major airline office, which can issue you the actual tickets. Just make sure to confirm (ask for a **confirmation in writing**) that they can be cancelled without fee from the city where you plan to cancel them.

Other important considerations

- Some countries will not allow entry if you have a certain stamp in your passport. **Israeli stamps**, for example, may mean refusal into some Arab countries. In such cases, consider getting the stamp on a separate sheet of paper, which can be temporarily taped to your passport. The other two options require substantially more effort: obtaining a new passport or altering the order in which you visit countries to avoid stamp conflicts.
- Be aware of **local holidays**, as visa-issuing offices at home and abroad are likely to be closed.
- Some countries don't have embassy representation. In such cases, find out if it was a former colony, and of which country. Then contact that embassy or high commission instead. It may not be able to offer you a visa, but they should certainly be able to point you in the right direction.
- Many countries require that your **passport is valid for at least six months** beyond your anticipated stay.

Insurance – why bother?

Here's the single most important thing you need to know about travel insurance for an extended trip: get some. Why? All it takes is one mishap – a drowsy bus driver, a patch of sand when you try to brake your rented scooter, a knee twist during a trek, a bite from a malarial mosquito – and your family might be stuck selling their home to cover your rescue by helicopter, air-ambulance ride home, surgery, plus ongoing treatment (which may not be covered by your home insurance policy). All this could easily top $100,000/£60,500, not including any ongoing medical expenses. A comprehensive health-insurance plan may cover some of your medical expenses, even those incurred overseas, but it's not likely to pick up some of the major rescue and repatriation costs. Even among countries that have reciprocal health agreements (such as those in the

Departure countdown

You could theoretically get everything together in less than a week. You might pick up an ulcer in the process, but you could do it. You'd also pay more, not be fully vaccinated (you'd have to look for places along the way to get the additional shots) and miss out on valuable pre-trip research. Better to start **six months in advance**.

Six months before departure

- Get a passport. If you have a passport, make sure it has several blank pages left, and will still have six months of validity left by the end of your trip, as some countries require this cushion for entry.
- Start thinking about the things you'd like to do and see.
- Figure out what sort of jobs, volunteer programs or courses you'd like to do (see p.87). Gather applications and apply for those that require advance submissions.
- Consider your budget (see p.71). If you don't have the funds for the trip you want, perhaps pick up some extra work before you leave.
- Start surfing the web for plane tickets (see p.292).
- If you want to get a hepatitis A and B combination vaccination that's good for ten years, you'll need six months to get the injections (see p.181). If you plan to travel for more than a year and hit many developing nations, this is certainly worth considering.

Four months before departure

- If you're going by yacht, check ideal times and places to start your trip (see p.55).
- If you're going by cargo ship, try to book passage (see p.56).
- If you're flying, book a plane ticket and take out insurance (see p.109) at the same time to cover you in the event of cancellation.
- Arrange visas for any extended stays due to work, volunteering or study, plus the first country of entry (if necessary) and any countries with complex visa requirements.
- Make arrangements for your apartment rental (see p.115).

Two months before departure

- Get a medical checkup.

EU), you will not be fully covered, and certainly not for repatriation. Not all travel insurance is created equal. Most of the best policies aren't cheap, but that doesn't mean the most expensive policies are the best.

If, at the last moment before your trip, you get terribly sick, called up for jury duty or robbed, you don't want to get stuck with cancellation fees on top of it. A good policy will cover this, which is why you should book some flight insurance at the time you book your ticket, provided you're booking more than a one-way flight to get an overland journey started. Also, if your trip is disrupted for an emergency, the insurers should assist with arrangements to continue your trip once you're ready.

Also, no one plans on defending themselves in court while abroad. But if it happens, it's unlikely to be cheap. Say you hit a local cyclist while driving a rented car on a difficult-to-navigate road. Or scuff a Mercedes. Travel insurance is about the only way to prepare for such an unfortunate event.

- Check the CDC website to see which vaccinations you'll need, then call around to find the best rates (see p.181).
- Get credit cards and bank cards (see p.132) and meet your banker to set up your finances (see p.117) so they can be handled while you're away, either with help from your parents or via internet banking. Try to set up a line of credit.

One month before departure

- Buy your travel gear. If you're bringing or sending ahead new hiking boots, start breaking them in (see p.120).
- Get any discount cards (ISIC, Teacher Card, Youth Card, HI Card) you need (see p.74).
- Sort out your mobile phone, if you plan to take one (see p.164).
- Visit a dentist.
- If you need to get more rugged glasses, order additional contact lenses or determine your prescription, visit an optician.

One to two weeks before departure

- Start taking anti-malarials if you're heading directly to a malarial region (see p.191).
- Leave parents or friends an envelope with photocopies of your documents (credit cards, passport etc) that can be sent to you in case of an emergency.
- Take care of any veterinary needs your pet may have before dropping it off with a caretaker.
- Arrange for your mail to be forwarded if your parents or roommate aren't willing to handle it.

Two to three days before departure

- Pack.
- Reconfirm flight.

Day of departure

- Run over this checklist one last time.

Finding a the right insurance policy – you need to check two things

1. Find out what you're covered for already so you can pick out an insurance package that covers the gaps. Without this knowledge, you'll most likely waste your money on double coverage. Unfortunately, this means digging through the fine print. You might start with your homeowner's insurance policy to see if it covers lost luggage (even your parents' policy, if their home is still your official residence, may have you covered). Airlines will reimburse international travelers for up to 1000 SDRs (Special Drawing Rights), which equals about $1500/£945 per passenger, but the process is time-consuming and potentially exasperating. Check to see what kind of travel insurance your credit-card company offers, and whether it is solely for tickets or goods purchased using the card. Some credit cards offer flight insurance in the event of a plane crash or other transportation accidents. Then take a look at your medical policy. Will it cover you for illnesses or accidents incurred overseas? If so, photocopy the list of activities it will cover you for (or ask your insurer to send you the list). Finally, check out your life-insurance policy. Will it still pay out if you die bungee-jumping in South Africa or mountain climbing in the Andes?

2. Check the fine print. Oddly, insurance policies have their own little fine print for what they will and won't cover. There are really no rules or reason to it. Most prefer to bury this information, knowing you'd rather hack off your arm with a rusty knife than dig through the fine print of their policy (instead they pad their list of benefits with things like "money transfer referrals" and "embassy referrals" – which is nothing more than a referral you could find in half the time with a search on the internet). So you need to do a bit of digging. But only just a bit. Click on the PDF outlining the details of the policy. It's typically three to five pages. Simply scan through it for a paragraph with a lot of exotic activities. Once you find it, check if it says you can or can't do these things with coverage.

It's hard to anticipate what opportunities may come your way while you're traveling. Even timid travelers work up considerable nerve to try new things after a few months on the road.

Rarely included

Base jumping, boxing, cliff diving, competitions, crewing on vessels between countries, cycle touring, endurance tests, free climbing, heliskiing, horse jumping, hunting, ice caving, ice hockey, martial arts competition, motor sports/rallying, mountaineering (free climbing), open-ocean yachting, parachuting, piloting a private aircraft, polo, scuba diving (below 30m), ski acrobatics, ski jumping, skydiving, solo sea-sailing, stunt flying, using weapons, yacht racing.

Sometimes included

American football, bouldering, bungee-jumping, canyoning, caving, football, glacier crossing, gliding, hang-gliding, high diving from platforms, horseriding, horsetrekking, jet-skiing, marathon running/triathlon, martial-arts training, mountaineering with ropes, mountain biking on trails, motorcycle touring, rock climbing with ropes, rugby, skiing (off-piste may require a guide), sledding on bobsleigh/skeleton/luge, snowboarding, snowcat skiing, snowmobiling, snowshoeing, speed skating, tobogganing, trekking (over a certain altitude), waterskiing, whitewater rafting, yachting in territorial waters.

Usually included

Abseiling, baseball, canoeing, cricket, cycling, deep-sea fishing, elephant trekking, fencing, go-karting, hiking, hot-air ballooning (commercial tour), ice skating, kayaking, mopeds, motorcycling up to 125cc, mountain biking, overland expedition, paintballing, parasailing (behind boat), passenger light aircraft/helicopter, quad-biking, safari, sailboarding, scuba diving (above 30m), sea canoeing, cross-country skiing, on-piste skiing, soccer, surfing, walking high altitude, weightlifting, windsurfing.

Other vital considerations

Some policies won't cover you if you get hurt or injured in countries that appear on your foreign office's travel-warning list. Some provide excellent emergency assistance, but little medical coverage. Best to get a few brochures or websites and **compare** (start with ⓦwww.insuremytrip .com, ⓦwww.worldtravelcenter.com, ⓦwww.travelexinsurance.com or ⓦwww.travelinsurance.co.uk). If you're checking the web, be aware that some policies only apply to certain nationalities. STA Travel's insurance, for example, has a strong package for UK citizens, but their policies for Americans and Australians are rather feeble. Find out who the underwriter of the insurance is (it's almost never the travel agency issuing it), and try to contact that company directly and make a deal. Again, check what you're covered for already. You might take a look at these popular policy providers if they don't appear in the comparison sites: ⓦwww .sosinternational.com and ⓦwww.travelguard.com.

If you're beginning your trip with an outbound ticket and no return ticket (you plan to wing it), mention this to the insurer up front as it can influence which policy you may be able to get. Some insurers allow you to give a "latest return date" instead of a precise date, and some allow you to extend your policy while you're away.

Many policies provide 24-hour emergency assistance – a reverse-charge phone number you can ring from anywhere and get access to an English-speaking operator, who will keep you on the line while you sort out your troubles. With standard inexpensive travel gear, you needn't bother with protection against theft unless it's either included already in the policy you want or you're carrying something expensive (very nice camera, watch, etc). But such items may be covered in your homeowner's insurance. Besides, in the event of a theft, replacing your backpack, some clothes, toiletries and a pair of sandals with items available locally is going to be quite cheap and a lot less hassle than trying to get reimbursed for every little well-worn item.

Find out if your insurance provider will **pay your expenses directly or reimburse you**. In either case (but especially the latter), ask for and hang on to receipts for everything.

7

In addition to the comparison sites above, here are a few other insurance providers worth checking out. Rough Guides – brace for propaganda – offers travel insurance via World Nomads. It's one of the easiest policies to understand and offers an upgrade for more adventurous types. For a quick online estimate, see ⓦwww.roughguides .com/insurance.

Documenting your possessions

Before final packing, shoot a short video or a bunch of still images of all your stuff. Date mark them and keep them in your camera in case any customs official accuses you of buying items (your iPod, camera, etc) in their country and tries to extract a duty fee from you.

7

Preparing your home for departure

If you have any possessions, it's always nice if they're still around when you return. Keeping plants green and pets alive is another trick, one you'll certainly have to face. This chapter will help with the arrangements you'll need to make before you can head out.

Renting out your property

The two best ways are renting to a trusted friend, who can take care of things for you while you're away, or to a company, which will probably be willing to pay more, and provide a guarantee of payments and the safe keeping of your property (of course, not everyone has an apartment that would appeal to an executive).

To avoid the hassles of dealing with tenants (or Airbnb guests), you may wish to work out an arrangement with an **estate agent or property manager**, who will not only lease your place, but also collect the rent and handle any problems that may arise. This service isn't cheap, but if you're less worried about turning a profit than having to deal with day-to-day problems, this could be the way to go.

Otherwise, you can take out an ad or put up a posting on Craigslist. Ask around before ringing your favorite newspaper. Often there are much cheaper alternative publications/sites that attract a much better-targeted group.

If you do rent out your place to previously unknown tenants, it's worth taking the following **precautions**:

- While you are with your tenants, take a video camera and walk around the property, videotaping everything with running commentary ("There's a small mark on the table already and one spot on the wall") so that they're protected against minor damage you may forget about during your trip, and you're protected against anything new that appears. If you are going with an estate agent, you may wish to do this before you leave anyway so you can prove any damage on returning.
- Agree on anything that requires maintenance, such as plant watering or garden care.
- Show the tenants that things are in working order (refrigerator, washing machine and so on) and make sure as many of these points as possible are listed in the contract.
- Remove and store personal treasures and anything that would cause the slightest emotional stir were it to break or grow legs and walk off. You might consider getting a safety deposit box at the bank.
- Have some family member or friend keep an eye on the tenants and deal with any emergency situations that may arise. And let your tenants know that someone will be watching them. For minor issues, let them know you should be emailed rather than phoned. Bring the number and email address of a trusted electrician and plumber with you, so you can take care of things that pop up with minimal effort.
- Arrange for your mail to be forwarded to parents or friends, who can sort out the junk and send on what you need to your next port of call. Or get a PO Box so letters don't pile up in your mailbox.

Reminder list for leaving an empty apartment/house

- Unplug appliances (set some lamps on timers).
- Cancel your newspaper subscription.
- Suspend accounts/memberships you won't be using (gym, clubs, cable TV).
- Have your phone turned off (if you do leave your phone switched on, change the message on your answering machine, although "Hi, I'm out of the country for five months, leave a message and I'll return your call in July" is probably not a great idea).
- Clean out the fridge.
- Hide valuables.

- Arrange for your mail to be forwarded to parents or friends, who can sort out the junk and send on what you need to your next port of call. Or contact the post office and get a PO Box.
- Make sure someone is coming by every so often to check on your property.
- Find a heat setting low enough to save money while keeping any pipes from freezing.

Finances

Pay everything ahead (or with auto-pay via your bank) if you can (health insurance, rent, utilities and so on). Most banks allow you to monitor your funds and make payments from any internet connection. If you're good at keeping track of such things, it's a great way to go. Don't forget to **call your credit-card issuer** before your trip. Tell them when and where you're going so they don't put a stop on your credit card when they see a sudden burst of expenses overseas. While you've got them on the phone, ask for a larger line of credit. You may need to buy a ticket or get a hotel room in an emergency (sickness, hurricane coming, riot, etc) when you've already put a month's worth of expenses on the card.

8

Plants

Don't just hand over your plants to a good friend, unless you happen to know they have an excellent track record with their own plants. It's more important to find someone who's good with plants. Just about anyone with green fingers will be happy to find some space for your horticultural assets, and possibly take better care of them than you do.

Pets

It's not always easy to find someone who will love your pet as much as you do. Your best bet is going to be leaving your canine, cat or fish with a friend or family member, which may involve some carefully chosen endearment opportunities. Think of your pet's most attractive qualities and try to coordinate those with visits from prospective pet guardians. If you have a dog which can catch a frisbee, play catch with the friend who would find that most appealing. If the pet is cute and friendly and successfully helps you line up dates, let your desperate friend see this in action. If it cuddles up on your bed and keeps you warm, ring your friends with poor heating. If it's sweet, but looks menacing, perhaps some security-minded women living alone might find this useful.

Packing

I f you open ten different guidebooks, you'll find ten different packing lists. Naturally, this is a matter of personal preference, and the only one that really matters is yours. The problem is it will take you a good six months to get a feel of what you actually use and what you can do without. Until then, it's better to bring less, not more. This may sound like twisted logic, but it's much easier to pick up additional things you realize you need than to throw away stuff you don't. In this chapter, you'll get the lowdown on selecting a pack, what to do with souvenirs, how to handle your digital photo back-ups, which clothes to leave at home and which medications come in handy.

Why take less

As Henry David Thoreau once said, "Even the elephant carries but a small trunk on his journeys. The perfection of traveling is to travel without baggage." The bigger the pack:

- The bigger the sweat stains, the more odour you emit, the more often you have to wash.
- The more difficult it is to run for a train, the harder it is to lift the pack over your head into a luggage rack.
- The more gear you have to lose, the bigger target you are for thieves, the harder it is to run away from them.
- The harder it is to walk around, the more desperately you need to find a place to leave all your stuff, the bigger the locker you'll need everywhere you go, the more you'll need to pay to leave it.

9

The crucial backpack test

1. You should be able to wear your pack (fully loaded) for an hour without suffering what feels like spinal compression.

2. You should be able to pack it in five minutes.

3. You should be able to lift it over your head easily.

4. You should be able to toss your pack across the room and then step on it without anything breaking – chances are this is going to happen. And count on the fact that it may get stolen, so leave your mother's pearls, your snakeskin cowboy boots and your collector's edition silver-plated backgammon set at home.

Why you should send souvenirs home

The best way to get your souvenirs home is to send them as you buy them. They have a better chance of getting **lost, broken or stolen** in your backpack. Check the local postal regulations first. Sometimes there's a certain weight or box size that's extremely cheap, and you can divide your purchases into a few separate parcels accordingly and save a mint. Overland shipping is cheapest, but usually takes a few months to get there and items may get roughed up a bit on the way. If you'd rather not take the chance, try registered mail. If you plan to stock up on trinkets on your last stop before heading home, simply buy a cheap duffel bag. If you're on your way from an expensive country to a cheaper one, it can be worth dragging your souvenirs with you for an extra leg to take advantage of much better postage rates. It's a bit of a trade-off – mail sent from developed nations has a better chance of arriving sooner.

Solving the memory problem

A digital camera or phone camera is handy, but what about backup? If you're carrying a laptop, you can back your photos up there, though you'll likely want more backup than that. The best option is to upload them – either to yourself or a friend/family member. With batches of files larger

What travelers are carrying

I spent a few days walking around Stockholm's central train station last summer with a survey and a scale. I interviewed every traveler I managed to stop, and weighed their packs. The average weight was just over 20kg. Some of the heaviest packs (over 25kg) belonged to women who weighed less than 55kg. It looked like they were going to be crushed at any second, Wile E Coyote-like, under their packs. Everyone I asked had something they wished they hadn't brought. The general consensus on the least-used item was formal shoes for going out. After that came textbooks and extra novels. The most-used items were sandals and a rain jacket. I asked a few people to open up their packs so I could have a look. If you're wondering what people with large packs are carrying around, here's what's taking up about seventy percent of that space: shoes, sleeping bag, souvenirs and dirty laundry.

Doug Lansky

9

Overpacked

It occurred to me on the flight over to Italy that maybe my pack was too big. The woman seated next to me, who was also signed up for my Italian course, had what looked like a day bag. Mine looked more like a hockey bag. I wasn't just carrying the pocket phrase book. I had the whole $50 dictionary. I was into photography at the time, so I had all the lenses. There were three pairs of shoes. After three months living with a family, I set off to travel Switzerland, Germany and Austria. Only now, in addition to the stuff I brought, there was now stuff that I had purchased, and stuff my family had given me, including a ten-pound bathrobe. The school chipped in with a lithograph print that I couldn't part with. I even picked up a fourth pair of shoes. It must have weighed at least sixty pounds. Sending it home never occurred. I'd sweat through my shirt a few minutes after I put it on. Fortunately, I had about twenty others in my bag. My pack started to affect my itinerary. At one point, I trekked two hours out of the way to get to Milan's train station, so I could find a locker big enough to hold it. I'll never forget when I arrived with it in England and dragged it to the Wax Museum and Buckingham Palace, even the other budget travelers were shooting me weird looks. Hey, check out the sweaty guy with the giant pack.

Jason Wilson
Editor, Best American
Travel Writing Series

than 25MB, you may need a file sending site like ⓦwww.yousendit.com or ⓦwww.wetransfer.com. You may prefer to upload to sites like flickr or print processor like kodak/snapfish/shutterfly so you or friends can have prints made. For additional security, you might also load your pictures onto a USB/SD drive just to keep an extra backup of your photos with you. There are numerous data storage sites available as well, with prices varying depending on levels of security and amount of space needed.

Resupply on the go – don't try to bring it all

There may not be toilet paper in every stall or ice in the drinks, but you can get sweaters, T-shirts, socks, toothpaste, soap, superglue, hats… nearly anything almost everywhere you go. Just take the smallest tubes and bottles from home, plan on buying replacements along the way and stop at an internet café and special-order something to your next destination if you can't find it.

Why should you send gear ahead?

If you're going to be trekking every other week of your trip, bring your favorite hiking boots. If not, they're going to take up thirty percent of your pack and make the other seventy percent smell. Tying them to the outside of your pack may be even worse: the dangling Christmas-tree look makes it tricky to run for departing transport, knocks people in the head as you enter and leave trains, and lets people smell you from a remarkable distance. It's better to send your boots ahead to the place you'll need them, or simply rent boots when you get there. See "How to pick up mailed packages" (see p.168). All major trekking centers have boot rental and cheap used ones for sale.

What to look for when picking a good travel backpack

No matter how big your backpack is, you will always manage to fill it. The single best thing you can do is start off by buying **a small rucksack** (40–55 litres). That's just slightly bigger than a day bag. Once you do this, it's pretty hard to go wrong. The stuff you don't need simply won't fit. Be forewarned: that's not likely to be the advice you'll get from the shop assistant. The bigger the pack, the more it costs, and the more stuff they can sell you to put in it. Plus, that should allow you to use it as a carry-on bag, which will help you get around those nasty checked-bag costs imposed by most budget airlines.

This is not the time to try to save money. Take an internal frame model for support. Couple that with a major brand name and you're looking at prices in the range of $75–175/£47–110. There are a few bells and whistles that are nice to have, but skip the zip-off daypack, since these don't make the best daypacks and they tend to unbalance the main pack when attached. Check out the rucksacks used by climbers. They keep the gear closer to your body for a fuller range of motion and better balance. Packs that extend wide with side pockets make it extremely difficult when you're getting on and off trains and buses. Packs that extend straight back (such as those with attached packs) force you to lean forward to counter the weight.

There should be some kind of alternative opening that allows you direct access to the inside or bottom of the pack so you can grab things like a rain jacket or first-aid kit. Make sure there are compression straps on the outside (usually, the sides) to keep the stuff on the inside from jiggling while you walk and to make the pack smaller if you use it for a day-hike. Look for a top compartment that's completely detachable, because if you can raise and lower that, you can stuff things under it more easily. If you need to carry a bag of souvenirs to the post office, for example, the pack can temporarily accommodate the extra gear. Also, you could detach it completely, clip on a camera strap, and you've got a shoulder bag that makes an ideal daypack.

The most important feature is that it **fits comfortably**. This is not something you should buy over the internet unless you've tried it on first. The waist strap should not dig into your hips and the straps should be easily adjustable when you're on the move. Sometimes there's one strap that's meant to be sized to the wearer, and it's not that simple to find or adjust. Have the sales person adjust it for you and drop something heavy in before you try it out. Every pack feels great when there's nothing in it. There are now a number of special packs for women that are worth checking out, especially if you have a more curvy or petite body type.

9

These feature narrower shoulder straps, a shorter frame, more cant on the waist strap and a pack mounted lower on the frame.

Think twice about packs with wheels. You can roll them in some places, but in just as many you can't. In most airports (where they work best) you can find trolleys. For hiking trips, the extra weight of the wheels and plastic suspension isn't worth it. At the risk of sounding like a drill sergeant, if you can't carry it, you don't need it.

How to figure out what clothes to bring

Most people have probably experienced packing for shorter trips: a week in Mexico, Bali or Gran Canaria. On these trips it's perfectly fine to bring along a suitcase or two the size of an early-model Cadillac. They only have to be dragged into and out of the airport. The problem, you're thinking, is that it was difficult enough to figure out how to get a week's worth of stuff into just two enormous suitcases. How on earth are you going to get a year's worth into a tiny backpack?

To figure out what to bring, there's one important question you need to ask. What clothes do I need to survive a day that ranges from swimming

---

Clothes pack-list

- 1 T-shirt – women, if the T-shirt is a little longer, it can double as a nightshirt.
- 1 long-sleeve polypropylene shirt – one that looks nice enough to wear into a restaurant.
- 1 micro-fleece – if stylish, it can be worn as a pullover in a nice setting.
- 1 budget, breathable rain jacket – expensive Gore-Tex doesn't help much when it pours, and hurts your wallet if stolen.
- 1 plastic poncho – this covers your pack as well and will keep you dry if your rain jacket is on underneath.
- 1 thin beach towel or sarong – extra-large travel towels work well.
- 1 swimsuit – doubles as walking shorts for men, extra top for women.
- 1 pair trousers – not black (because dirt shows), but a good, dark, dirt-hiding color. Also, make sure they're lightweight, wrinkle-free, comfortable, fairly stylish and easily washable, with good, deep pockets.
- 1 wrinkle-free travel shirt – short- or long-sleeved is fine.
- 1 pair socks – for cool overnight bus rides and cold hostel floors.
- 2–4 sets of underwear – special travel underwear dries quicker and lasts longer.
- 1 pair of sports sandals. You don't want to skimp on these: they should be reasonably stylish (smart enough for a decent restaurant), have good support, stay on during a swim, not rot when they get out of the water and allow you to run for a train.
- 1 collapsible hat.
- 1 bandana – soak it with water to keep you cool on warm nights. Cover your mouth to protect your lungs from dust. Use it to dry off in the shower when you don't have time to let your towel dry.
- 1 wrinkle-free travel skirt or dress, mid-calf length (women).
- 1 pair shorts (women).

Just one outfit?

There are **two basic approaches to dressing**: stay in the same town and change clothes every day, or wear the same clothes and just change towns. When you travel you just have to accept that your general standard of cleanliness is going to be lower than you're used to. Also, you're going to have to wash your clothes daily, or tri-weekly – if you try doing it monthly, you're in for some strange looks, not to mention rashes.

Once you get the hang of this, you'll see you don't need more than one set of clothes. If you wash the clothes before you go to bed, hanging them on a clothes line outside, they'll be dry by morning. If you wash the clothes before taking a siesta in the afternoon and hang them in the sun, they'll be dry in about forty minutes.

in the ocean to tanning on the beach to a cool evening walk in the rain to a moderately nice dinner at a place where there's dancing, and be able to wash it all in the sink afterwards?

Let's start with the swimsuit. For guys (and possibly women), make sure it's quick drying and has pockets you trust enough to put car keys in while you swim – probably some kind of zipper-Velcro combination that will foil pickpockets as well. The shorts should cover your legs modestly so they can be also used for city exploring in appropriate countries – they're the only shorts you have along. Women, you may wish to bring a two-piece suit with a less-revealing "tankini" that can double as a casual top for beach settings. You'll also want a beach towel. It should be fairly thin, but long enough to stretch out on comfortably and wrap yourself modestly.

Later in the day, you'll want a hat and T-shirt to help ward off the sunburn after you've been on the beach for a while, and to cover yourself when you run over to the café for a snack. If you prefer to match, make sure all the items fit your color scheme (dark clothes – especially earth tones – hide dirt and help you blend in to the environment better) and try to pick multi-use items – pieces that fill at least two functions.

For a cool evening walk, you can get by with sandals or sandals with socks. You've got long, comfortable walking trousers. They should have deep front pockets that will deter thieves and not spill your valuables if you need to make a pit stop in the woods. On top you've got a long-sleeved polypropylene shirt that wicks away sweat, a micro-fleece pullover (not cotton!), a nylon rain jacket, and a bandana on your head to absorb any sweat. You're carrying your plastic poncho in your small daypack in case it really starts to pour.

For dinner, you can still get by in sandals, especially if they're black or brown solid colors. You've got a smart, short-sleeved or long-sleeved lightweight, wrinkle-free shirt/blouse. If it's still a little chilly inside, the micro-fleece should be stylish enough to wear. Men, your walking trousers will suffice, provided you didn't get "adventure travel" ones

9

with more zipped pockets than those of 1980s breakdancers. They should be dark enough to hide any dirt you might have picked up on your walk. Women might also elect to go with a long wrinkle-free skirt. Wash and repeat.

Winter gear is too bulky to travel with and too easy to pick up on the road to merit carting it along in warm climates. A cheap pair of warm shoes, gloves, hat, long underwear and a wool jumper can all be snatched up for about $50/£32 at a secondhand shop or handicraft market. Then give it away or send it home before you head on to warmer climes.

All of your clothes, minus what you need to wear, should fit nicely into a compression sack: one that holds a mid-weight sleeping bag will do nicely. With a few yanks on the cords, your clothes will be compressed to the size of a football. Crumpling is unavoidable unless the clothes are wrinkle-proof, and even then they won't look perfect. To minimize creases, try rolling your clothes first.

Toiletries

Start out by buying a toiletry kit with a built-in mirror and hanger since you may not have as much counter space in the bathroom as you're accustomed to. You could transfer perfume/cologne from a heavy, breakable, chic bottle to a small plastic or sturdy glass one with a tight, screw-on lid. Extended sandal-wearing takes its toll on your feet, so bring a foot file to help shed unwanted calluses and keep people from smelling you before they see you.

Major-brand contact lens fluid can be found at supermarkets, opticians and pharmacists in most cities and towns around the world. Bring a pair of glasses along just in case, plus your prescription in case something happens to your glasses. Pity to travel the world, then have to check your photos back home to see what it looked like in focus.

Outside the major cities in developing countries, tampons and pads can be hard to find. Even in the larger cities, they're likely to be low quality and expensive. Everywhere else, finding them shouldn't be a problem. To avoid being caught without, consult your guidebook. Another alternative (for those with a higher yucky tolerance) is the Mooncup, a reuseable diaphragm-like device made from soft silicon.

Again, only buy the miniature toiletry travel containers and restock as you go. Local toothpaste is especially interesting to sample and – there's at least one traveler doing this (me) – collect. Travel-size toiletries can sometimes be tricky to find, but there are a few smart ways to get around this. Instead of throwing out your small bottles when they're empty, refill them from big ones left in hostels. You can also buy a big bottle and portion it out with other travelers.

Miscellaneous gear

There are a few tiny items that, when you need them, you need them immediately. And they're not always easy to find. Keep the following items in a separate bag (preferably transparent):

- Ear plugs – don't leave home without them. Hostels have a nasty habit of occupying the space above nightclubs and next to busy streets. Plus, every dormitory seems to come with at least one snoring champion.
- Permanent marker – for making hitchhiking signs and other notices.
- Superglue – this fixes just about everything (keep it in its own plastic bag).
- Duct tape – this fixes nearly everything the superglue doesn't fix (wrap it around the marker to save space).
- Guitar string/wire – fixes whatever's left.
- Sewing kit – okay, that's a lie. This fixes whatever's left.
- Candle – power cuts are common. Here's a romantic way to save batteries.
- Lighter – you don't need a $60/£38 lighter that works on top of Mount Everest (besides, it's now illegal to carry them on many flights).
- Power adapters – you can pick them up at major airports as you go (see Ⓦwww.kropla.com for country requirements).

Toiletry pack-list

- Toothpaste
- Toothbrush
- Dental floss
- Cologne/perfume (in plastic bottle)
- Foot file
- Contact lens fluid (if needed)
- Lip balm
- Comb/brush
- Lotion
- Razor
- Sunscreen
- Mosquito repellent
- Mirror
- All-purpose soap which doubles as shampoo (container for it if not in a bottle)
- Conditioner (if needed)
- Deodorant
- Contraceptires/condoms

9

- Media storage device – good back-up for photos. Either a USB keychain or a larger mini-hard drive.
- Pocket knife – you can leave the Rambo survival blade at home.
- Spoon – just grab one for free on your first flight. It comes in handy for supermarket-food dining.
- Clothes line – you'll need about 10m of nylon cord.
- Mosquito coils – only carry when in malarial or buggy areas. They should be easy to find and cheap in those areas. No need to buy them in advance.
- Sleep sheet – you can sew a sheet in the form of a sleeping bag, or buy a pre-made model. The nicest are silk, which cost a fortune, but can be worth it, as they keep the bed-bugs out. In Southeast Asia, you can have one custom made for about $10/£6. Get it in white, so the cheap dye doesn't ruin your clothes.
- Rubber drain-plug – facilitates laundry washing.

Optional extras

Here are a few extras that you might want to bring along:

- Books/tablet: see the "Regional profiles" for suggestions.
- Small travel games: backgammon, chess and cards are the most popular. They can keep you sane on a forty-hour bus ride across the outback, and can be a nice way to meet locals.
- Musical instrument: a guitar can be worth the effort, especially if you're good and plan to earn money playing it, but a harmonica is better suited for transport.
- Frisbee: doubles as plate and soup bowl.
- Plastic container to use as plate or bowl and store breakables.

Extra stash

Consider keeping an extra (secret) stash of money separate from your passport pouch, perhaps in a pocket in your address book or taped to the inside of your backpack – $50–100/£32–63 should be fine, just enough to spend a night in the hostel, get some food or take transport to the nearest embassy.

First aid

Most prepackaged first-aid kits sold in outdoor stores aren't necessarily customized to your need. Make your own – to add on to a pre-packaged version. Start out with a Tupperware container large enough to hold about four muffins. Those nylon sacks don't keep your bandages and pills from getting wet or crushed. You should be able to resupply all you need (see p.128) on the road.

9

Travel with a seatbelt

Admittedly, it sounds like a warped idea. It sounds like something Kramer is trying to push on Seinfeld. But if you value your life and plan to **travel by bus in developing countries**, this is probably the single best thing you can do for your health (besides not trafficking narcotics across international borders). Buses crash. You'll see them flipped on their backs, tanning their rusted underbellies at the bottom of a ravine or bear-hugging the trunk of a tree.

For less than $10/£6 you can get about a metre and a half of webbing (the same material as the hip-strap on most backpacks) and a plastic clasp at any outdoorsy shop. It rolls up to the size of an ice-hockey puck. Then wrap it around the back of your bus seat and clip in. Will the people around you think you're nuts? Probably. But then again, you're a foreigner living out of a backpack and traveling around the world. They probably think you're a little nuts already.

A lot of travelers like to take antibiotics along, but it's not really necessary, or smart. If you're whacking your way through a rainforest for weeks or in a similarly remote location, it's probably a good idea to bring some. But the vast majority of travelers are never that far from a local doctor or hospital. If you get sick enough to require **antibiotics**, you should be going to a doctor, who can prescribe the right ones. Plus, antibiotics don't travel well. They expire, don't hold up well in heat and are often not handed out by doctors, who are understandably trying to prevent their misuse. If you do take antibiotics, take the full course, even if your symptoms abate after just one or two days. Otherwise, the few microbes that don't get killed off tend to mutate and come back stronger.

Bringing a collapsible daypack

That 50-liter internal-frame pack is not a joy to lug around the entire day while you explore ruins, museums and cities. Something smaller is a more sensible way to carry the few necessities you'll need.

Most travelers opt for small daypacks, such as the detachable ones that come with packs. If that's your preference – and for women who are getting repeatedly touched in crowds, wearing the pack on their front is an excellent idea – you can simply empty the laundry and toiletries from your main pack, tighten the compression straps and that should work fine. While it's on your back, though, it can be hard to protect it from quick-handed thieves. Some travelers prefer the comfort of a waist pack, but this is something of a thief magnet. A better idea is a **shoulder bag**. It's easy to tuck under your arm to protect from pickpockets, can be accessed more quickly while you're on the move and doesn't peg you as a tourist, especially in bars and nightclubs. If the top compartment of your backpack detaches, a camera or guitar strap can turn it into a decent shoulder bag.

9

Medical pack-list

- Plasters/Band-aids – take a box worth, but put them into a clear plastic sleeve that holds photos or credit cards to save space and keep them protected.
- Second-skin – modern science has created the wonder blister cure. Often called Compeed.
- Elastic wrap bandage – vital for twists and big cuts.
- Lidocain cream – works well on stings and bites.
- Antihistamines – you never know what will spark an allergic reaction.
- Hydrocortisone cream – cures most rashes and skin irritation.
- Aspirin/paracetamol – for minor aches and major hangovers.
- Laxatives.
- Anti-diarrhea medicine.
- Iodine – works for both water purification and cuts. Use 5 drops of regular (2 percent tincture) iodine per litre of clear water (10 drops for cloudy water). Let stand for 30 minutes. Not advisable for pregnant women, people with thyroid conditions or those allergic to iodine.
- Rehydration sachets – about four is enough to get you started (in a crisis, make your own mix: 1 litre water, 1 teaspoon of salt, 8 tablespoons sugar, dash of juice if available).
- Condoms – bring some from home, and try to use only major brands purchased in developed nations.
- Motion sickness pills – stale air and curvy roads make a lethal combo.
- Malaria pills – if you need them (see p.191).
- Thermometer – electronic rather than glass and mercury.
- If these don't fit in the first-aid container, toss them in the gear bag.
- Tweezers – find a good pair with a sharp point for removing splinters.
- Vaseline – prevents chafing and blisters during long hikes.
- Sports tape – it's mostly for blister prevention, but helps hold plasters on.
- Antiseptic wet-wipes – a great refresher when you're stuck in a bus seat for two days, trying to clean up before a meal or helping clean up a wound.
- Tiger balm – the all-purpose sports cream that also clears up clogged sinuses and soothes headaches.
- Optical prescription – just in case you need to get new glasses.
- Other prescriptions – in case you run out, but also because meds require that you have a prescription with you when crossing borders.

What to keep in your day bag

- Water bottle.
- Guidebook – you can lighten the load by ripping out unneeded sections (if you haven't gone for the digital version).
- Sunglasses – don't skimp on these as sunglasses without UV protection allow your pupils to widen and expose your eyes to more damaging rays.
- Journal, address book, pen – a necessity. Some photos of home and friends are also nice to include for letter-writing inspiration.
- Reading matter – there are sections on books vs tablets and how book swapping works (p.138) you might want to check out.

9

- Pocket knife – you don't need the Swiss Army knife with all sixty functions. One obstacle to consider is that, if you're thinking of taking all your luggage with you on a plane, the knife may not be allowed – so you might wait until you arrive before you buy one. Swiss Army, Leatherman and other popular brands are available virtually everywhere. In less-developed countries, you can get knock-off versions for about a fifth of the price.
- Flashlight – the little LED key-chain ones work well. The tiny LCD headlamp is even better.
- Pocket camera – you can get a good one for under $100/£63.
- Cell phone and charger – an extra battery booster (eg power monkey) can be a godsend when there are no outlets to be found.

Camping gear

If you plan to camp the entire time, **bring what you need**. If you're not sure, don't take anything. The gear will more than double the size and weight of your rucksack. You'll be forced to spend more on transport: getting in and out of cities on local trains and buses becomes a real headache. And you may worry about your belongings when your tent is unattended. If you're not dissuaded, make sure you have the right gear:

- Light, rainproof tent
- Cooking stove
- Pot with lid
- Cooking utensils
- Sleeping bag
- Sleeping pad
- Headlamp (when you need a light, you usually need your hands as well)
- Tarpaulin to lay under tent
- Water-purifying tablets (iodine works) or small water-purifier pump (don't forget drink mix to add to chemically treated water to improve taste).

What you don't need and why

- Shoes – this may come as a shocker, but with a decent pair of sandals, you can get by without shoes. If you find you're going out clubbing regularly, need shoes for work or it's just getting too cold, buy a cheap pair for $10–25/£6–16 and ditch them when you're done.
- Pro-camera set up – if you're a serious amateur or professional photographer, bring what you need. If not, this is probably not the

9

time to start. Forget the SLR, lenses and tripod. Stick with a pocket camera and you'll get more use out of it.

- Jeans – resist the temptation to pack your favorite pair, no matter how good you may look in them. They're too warm in hot weather, too difficult to wash by hand and take too long to dry.
- Sweatshirt – the comfort is alluring, but it will take up far too much room, offer no warmth when wet and require about two days to dry on its own. Microfleece is the way to go.
- Sleeping bag – nearly every hostel can produce a blanket for you as long as you have a sleep sheet. Beyond that, if you layer on all your clothes for a rare chilly night on a train or bus, you should be fine. If you're worried about a particular train ride, pick up a cheap hat and blanket before boarding.
- Travel pillow – bundle your extra clothes inside your fleece top.
- Laptop – there are PCs everywhere and it'll be easier to get connected with one of those than to try and connect your own computer. Hotspots aren't prevalent enough to be practical yet (though that depends where you're going). If you're trying to computerize your diary, carry a key-chain-size USB memory drive that you can plug in at various internet cafés. This works for backing up your digital photos as well.
- Appliances – it's a cliché to tell you to leave your hairdryer at home, but there's a reason for it. Better to find a hairstyle that works well without a dryer and hair product.
- Make-up – see if you can get by with just lipstick and eyeliner, or go for the natural look.
- GPS – if you're charting new territory, fine. If not, leave it at home – or stick with the one on your phone.
- Compass – the sun rises in the east and sets in the west. That sentence, plus your smart phone if you have one, should get you by. If you feel better having a compass along, take a tiny key-chain model. If you depart without one and regret it, you can always buy it along the way.
- Mosquito net – if you need one for a specific journey, you can pick one up on the spot. Otherwise, most hostels are equipped with them in malarial areas. If there's no net (and even if there is) use any combination of bug spray, clothing and mosquito coils – all of which are easier than carrying a net and stringing it up everywhere you go.
- High-absorption washcloth-size "travel towel" – a decent bandana will do the trick; you just have to wring it out a few extra times. Both will be damp afterward, but it's nicer to tie the bandana around your neck (keeps you cool) or outside your pack while it dries off. For toweling purposes, bring a full-sized thin travel towel you can lie on at the beach and use to keep you covered.

10

Carrying valuables

Passport pouches, also known as money belts, come in a variety of styles. Some go around the waist, just under the trousers, some hang around the neck and still others fasten to your leg. It's a combination of personal preference, how it works with your clothing, and how easy it is for thieves to spot. Try a few on before you make a purchase since this is something you'll be wearing round the clock.

Before you leave, remember to photocopy the cards in your money belt, leave a copy with your family or trusted friends and take a copy with you and store it separately from your money belt or with your travel partner. To save space, try to get all the vital information onto the front and back of one piece of paper.

Scan it as well and email it to yourself or upload it to a trusted online backup vault. There are many to chose from, including: Ⓦwww .myvaultstorage.com, Ⓦwww.digitalvault.bt.co, Ⓦwww.safedatastorage .co.uk and even file sending services like Ⓦwww.yousendit.com and Ⓦwww.wetransfer.com.

How best to carry your money

Once upon a time, travelers' check were a great idea. Today, with more vendors accepting foreign currency, most accepting credit cards, and cash machines almost everywhere, it makes more sense to carry cash (US dollars or euros), two credit cards and a bank card.

How much cash should you carry?

You'll want to carry your US dollars and euros (bring both and you can cover yourself in different parts of the world where one type is preferred) in a variety of denominations. The €100 notes are nice space-savers

10

and fine for changing at banks, but for an emergency stash (€300–500/£181–300), as well as some bills for hard-currency shopping, a good number of €50s, €20s, €10s and €5s are far more practical. If you've got a cash card and credit card, you can use those as your primary tools to pay for rooms, food and tickets and to get local currency, but you'll want some dollars/euros available at all times, which means either taking a large stack of bills or replenishing your hard currency along the way. If you can arrange to meet a trusted friend or relative just leaving home, perhaps they can carry some over for you. More likely, you'll just have to take cash out in a local currency, then exchange it for euros/dollars in a major city and take a bit of a beating with the exchange rate.

There's just one important thing to remember about **coins**. You can't exchange leftovers in other countries, so get them converted back to paper money and spend the extra that you can't convert.

Credit cards

Don't leave home without one of these. Two are even better. Visa and MasterCard are the most widely accepted; American Express is quite often not accepted. You should have codes for both to access cash machines, but in the event a cash machine can't be found, most banks will still allow you to use them for cash advances. That is, you can go to a bank window, let them swipe your credit card and buy cash (for a small fee, of course).

The benefits of credit cards

- You can access emergency funds and cover many daily expenses without carrying a thick bundle of cash.
- You can track your finances easily.
- Parents, relatives and friends can send funds to your account, which you can quickly and easily withdraw anywhere in the world.
- Cards can be replaced quite easily if stolen.
- You're entitled to additional insurance when you use the card to make purchases.

The drawbacks of credit cards

- Merchants who accept credit cards pay a small percentage fee to the credit-card company for the right to accept their card. Although they're not supposed to do this, many smaller companies make no secret about passing that percentage on to you (paying by credit card is still often cheaper than withdrawing money from a cash machine, especially for one purchase).
- Some credit-card companies have started tacking on little surcharges for purchases made abroad.
- You not only pay a fee to withdraw money from a bank machine (or bank), but you will likely have to pay interest on that

withdrawn cash until your next bill is paid. And the interest starts immediately.

- Not all credit cards are alike. They depend on the bank or financial institution behind them. When deciding on a credit card, make sure you ask about the surcharges for foreign purchases. More and more cards are adding a three-percent conversion fee. Try to find one that doesn't.

Setting up the card before you leave

- Try to increase your spending limit before leaving. Simply call the credit-card company and ask if you can get your limit raised. You may have more expenses on the card (or cards) than you're used to, and with an emergency purchase, such as a plane ticket or hospital bill, you might quickly be out of funds.
- Many credit cards or bank accounts can be set up for "Auto-pay"/"Direct Debit". Each month, your credit-card bill will be automatically paid from your current or savings account. That way you don't have to worry about missing any payments and getting hit with high interest rates. Of course, what you may have to worry about is having enough money in your bank account. To be safe, meet with your banker and set up enough credit to cover you in a pinch. If you get internet banking, all this can be easily monitored from any internet café.
- Make sure to tell your credit card company roughly where you're going so it doesn't freeze your card as a security measure when it sees a bunch of overseas expenses showing up.

Take a bank card (debit card) as well

You may still be slapped with a withdrawal fee (plus the local fee of the cash machine), but you won't have to pay interest on the money withdrawn, which makes them better than credit cards for this purpose. Shop around to make sure you're getting the best deal.

Because there's a fixed amount of money behind them, it's good for those who don't trust themselves with the spending limit granted on a credit card. But, if the card is stolen and used, charges may not be as protected as they are with credit cards.

Why travelers' checks aren't that practical

Many people still like the comfort of travelers' checks, which provide more security than the other options if used properly. Here's how they work: you buy the checks (typically, for a small fee), keep track of the serial numbers of the checks you use, then, if they're stolen or lost, you can report which ones are missing. Of course, in order to do this, you need to have a current list of the checks that were used, keep that

10

list safe yet separate from your checks, and hope the bag with that list didn't get stolen or lost as well. Some places accept travelers' checks as cash, but they're few and far between, and you're likely to have to encash the checks. Sometimes you can do this for free – you can cash American Express checks at AmEx offices for free, for example – but you may not be anywhere near the relevant office. So, you're more likely to be paying a fee to cash checks in addition to the cost of exchanging the currency (oh, and waiting in line at the bank for a teller). Understandably, some people find this to be a hassle – one that outweighs the security factor.

In general, places that take travelers' checks also take credit cards (or are not far from a cash machine or bank that allows cash advances). However, if you plan to spend an extended period in a rural area, and have read in your guidebook that cash cards and credit cards are of limited use, but that travelers' checks can be cashed, you can always pick some up in a major city if you're uncomfortable carrying the amount of cash you'll need to get by.

Visa, Thomas Cook and American Express issue the most commonly used travelers' checks. There are no real advantages in terms of acceptance. Remember to make sure the banker is watching you countersign the checks. Don't let them walk off while you're busy scribbling your name, or the whole thing may be void because you didn't have a signing witness. And shop around when buying travelers' checks.

AmEx also has a "travelers' check card", which you can load up with money, then use to withdraw funds from bank machines. When it's empty, simply toss away the card. However, if you've got a cash card from your bank or a debit card, this is unnecessary: you don't need both.

Other items you'll want in your money belt

Passport

Goes without saying (see p.104).

Driving licence

It's helpful to have an official photo ID besides the passport, especially since there's a good chance you'll end up driving a car at some point. The International Drivers' Licence (should you decide to pick one up) won't easily fit in your passport pouch, and you won't need it for many rentals, so before you pick one up, check if you'll be visiting many of the fifty countries where it's required. See ⓦwww.theaa.com for country listings.

Student ID card, under-26 youth card or teacher card

If you qualify for one of these, it's probably best to keep it close by. It's not as valuable as the other items in your passport pouch, but its size makes it easy to lose. See the section on specialty discount cars for more information (p.74).

Ten extra passport photos

10

Ok, ten photos seems like a lot, but there's a good chance you'll be using at least that many during a long trip. When you apply for visas and or transport cards, you often need two or three photos just for one application.

Emergency-numbers card

Just a card with list of important phone numbers in case of emergency... see if you can get it laminated. Family doctor, lawyer, travel agent, insurance and credit card hotline numbers (and account number), passport number, family contacts and a visible "emergency" contact just in case you get seriously injured and the authorities want to find someone to call quickly. Remember, your **mobile phone** may not be working or fully charged when you need it most.

Other licences

If you're a trained scuba diver or pilot, or hold other such licences that easily fit into a passport pouch, bring them along.

One anti-diarrhea pill

It's hard to predict when dysentery is going to strike. Inevitably, it'll happen while you're out wandering around town or on a long bus ride with your medical kit stored in the luggage hold below or back at the hotel. Best to keep one pill handy and on you at all times for such emergencies.

Guidebooks and other reading

This is precisely where you might expect to find a few sentences of Rough Guides propaganda. Happily, you won't. Not much, anyway. Naturally, the editors and writers at Rough Guides are proud of the guidebooks they produce, but they also understand it comes down to individual taste, trust and how you like your information gathered and presented. For that, you'll have to head to a bookstore and compare. Better yet, you might even "test drive" a few different guides out on the road and see which suits you best.

Specialists in the independent market are Rough Guides, Lonely Planet, Footprint, Let's Go, Time Out city guides and (for French speakers) the Guide Routard. For more mainstream travel, there's also Frommer's, Fodor's, the design-intense city guides by Dorling Kindersley and Rick Steves' self-guided tours.

At a bookstore, pick up a few guides on the same country and **compare a few paragraphs** on the same topic. Start with a city or town you're particularly interested in. Is the layout and writing easy to follow? Are the maps clear? Also take a look at the **author bios**. You'll want someone (or several people) who has spent considerable time in the country they're writing about. It's always helpful if they speak the language and have been able to get information by conversing with the locals.

How best to use your guidebook

For most, it's a revelation to find there are books that tell you everything you need to know to get around: where to stay, where to eat and what to do while you're there. However, this does more than just remove some of the adventure. It sends everyone to the same places. Not just the same towns, but the same cafés, hostels, bars and scenic spots. Ask nearly any guidebook writer and they'll tell you the book is best used as a **reference**, not a bible or substitute tour guide. The little maps are great for helping you navigate your way from the bus station to a hostel at 3am or to find a vegetarian restaurant in Scandinavia, but your best guide is still your own nose. Find your own unlisted restaurants and lodgings, and it's likely you'll have a much more memorable experience.

Here's another common misuse. The temptation is to sit on the bus or train approaching the city scrutinizing the hostel descriptions. Then you read them over and over until you get them into your head, and before you know it you've got the experience largely mapped out before you've even arrived. Save yourself the effort. It's not worth it. There's not that much difference between four recommended hostels. And if you don't like a hostel you can either change the next day after you've had a chance to look around, or just crash there at night and spend your waking hours elsewhere in town. You'll eventually find a system that works for you, but mine is something like this: if I'm tired out or staying a bit longer, I'll pick a place further from the center. If I'm just staying a day or two and feeling fresh, I'll go for the best rated of the flea traps in the center. If there are a few decent choices in these categories, I'll typically go for the ones that are the easiest to get to. But, whatever the case, I won't spend more than five or ten minutes deciding.

How many guidebooks to bring

Here's some good news. Just because you're planning to hit twenty countries on your trip doesn't mean you need to pack twenty guidebooks – or download that many on your phone, Kindle or tablet. Just take the one for the country or region you're heading to first and

---

Guidebook misuse

11

Should I treat my guidebook as a bible? Why not? Most guidebooks are like the Old Testament – full of fanciful inaccuracies and describing a mystical time in the past when everything was cheaper and more plentiful. The only difference is that not much "begetting" goes on in guidebooks. Unless you've got the second edition of Bill Dalton's *Indonesian Handbook*, that is.

You will notice in your travels a lot of the locals will exhort you not to treat your guidebook as a bible. They will cajole you into ignoring the price listed or the missing bathrooms. They encourage you to use the book only as a rough indication and argue that things change and prices go up. They are usually the owners of a hotel mentioned in a guidebook who, knowing that business is booming, figure they can charge pretty much what they want.

Peter Moore
Author, *Wrong Way Home* and
No Shitting in the Toilet

I always avoid the first hostel listing in the guidebook. Those places are too busy and filled with travelers who are too lazy to read.

Jason Cochran
Budget traveler

11

Putting the guidebook down

One day me, my wife and her sister decided to drive near the Swiss border to explore the countryside and find a small-town, mom-and-poppa restaurant for lunch. But for some reason, we couldn't find a place to eat. Hard to believe, but it was true. We were ravenous, but our timing was off – it was late afternoon, and we'd managed to miss the opening hours of what few rural restaurants we could find. The troops were getting restless.

Out of desperation, I pulled onto the deeply rutted driveway of a farm and drove a quarter of a mile to the main house where I asked in broken German if there was anywhere nearby to eat. Maybe the farmer and his wife who answered the door could see the hunger, for they invited us in and cooked up an unforgettable meal of ham (that I bet was squealing out back the day before), sauerkraut and boiled potatoes. Some sharp mustard completed the feast. I still remember the meal, as well as our host and hostess, fondly.

It was the kind of event that could never have been planned.

Rudy Maxa
TV & radio host (Ⓦwww
.rudymaxa.com)

buy, download or trade for the rest as you go. Relevant guidebooks (those for that country or city, plus surrounding ones) can be found in hostels, hotels, bookstores and airports – virtually everywhere (sometimes cheaper, sometimes more expensive). Someone in the hostel is sure to have a more detailed book you can borrow for an hour or two. Ideally, you'll be able to locate someone who's heading in the direction you just came from and make a straight swap. If you're trading with a hostel or secondhand bookstore, you may have to throw in some money or a novel to complete the deal.

Digital guides vs print

Print guides: Nicer to hold, not reliant on battery and easier to read in the sunlight.

Phone/tablet guides: More likely to be up to date, cheaper, take up less space, can be used in poor lighting, enable you to find what you're looking for quickly, have better maps and you don't look like a tourist when you use your phone in public.

What to read along the way

One of the very best ways to add richness to your trip and bring the locales to life is to read up on them. This entails getting beyond the brief guidebook descriptions and finding stories that explore cultural nuances and history easily missed while searching for your hostel or a better exchange rate. The series Travelers' Tales published in San Francisco offers diverse and well-crafted anthologies on the most popular destinations that do just this. And if you can find room (or manage to lift) any of the country-themed James Michener tomes you're in for a treat, with folklore and fiction woven into the locales named in the title.

But it would be a pity to miss out on some of the classics and modern hits, especially in the regions where they are set. Reading books like *Midnight's Children* or *White Tiger* in India, *Seven Pillars of Wisdom* in

Syria, *On the Road* in America and *Ulysses* in Ireland is one of the great joys of travel. These are among the most popular titles along the appropriate routes and can be bought or traded for quite easily. So, when you're starting out, one paperback will do. Pop fiction authors like Clancy and Grisham tend to serve as the strongest currency, but start with something you like and let your continuous swaps serve as a reading adventure that runs parallel to your trip.

Don't forget about the local periodicals. Magazines can offer some contemporary insights (eg India's *Stardust* magazine on Bollywood, Britain's *Heat* magazine for gossip). Newspapers in local towns will give you a sampling of the issues of the day, so you're better prepared for a more in-depth discussion with a local or to find out what's going on. Local flea markets, theatre productions or concerts are not likely to be found in your guidebook. If you don't feel like paying for print, most guidebooks have free online sites with a wealth of information as long as you can find a free internet connection.

Your city, country or regional guidebooks will provide a more complete reading list with descriptions; see also the "Regional profiles" at the end of this book.

Tips for using your tablet abroad

As long as you remember to keep it charged (and from getting broken or stolen), taking a tablet can be a great way to access any book you like. The Kindle's battery (two months on a single charge), daylight reading screen, lower cost and smaller/lighter body make it better suited to travel reading than an iPad. But here's an important setting to consider: if you don't go to the "manage my Kindle" page and reset your country to the one you're currently in, you'll get hit with an extra $2/£1.30 per purchase. You'll probably need to have a fabricated address in the country you are in to go with it, but that's easy to find in the phonebook). However, if you do this, some books may suddenly not be available in that country, so you may have to reset and pay the $2 after all.

If you are an iPad user, consider investing in a good case – something both solid (like the defender case from ⓦwww.otterbox.com) and that doesn't draw too much attention (like the bookbook case ⓦwww.twelve south.com) – and a portable battery charger like the power monkey (ⓦwww.powertraveler.com).

12

When you arrive

One of the best ways to take advantage of your time on the road is to vary the way you travel down it. How you get around, whether it be in the air, through the water, on wheels, or on the back of an animal, will shape the memories you bring home. And that doesn't just apply to transport. You can be adventurous or timid in your choice of accommodation, what you eat, even the bathrooms you decide to use. It's always going to be easier to travel in the style you are accustomed to at home, but making the choice (often several times a day) to try the local alternatives will ultimately enrich your trip. This chapter provides you with a little taste of what lies ahead.

Don't forget to take interesting transport

The thing to remember on this type of journey is that traveling is just as much about getting there as arriving, or maybe even more. This may not be apparent when you're sweltering on an Indian train that has broken down for twelve hours, so it's important to remind yourself regularly.

One way to do that is to take unusual transport. When you're sailing down the Nile on a felucca, it's a little easier to relax with the fact that you're moving barely faster than driftwood. The frustration comes when you're trying to get somewhere quickly, so the slower you try to go the less frustrating it is likely to be. In fact, the level of frustration may be directly linked to the difference between the speed you should be going and your actual speed. A four-hour delay on a nine-day trip up the Amazon by cargo ship won't faze anyone in the slightest. Sit four hours on an airport runway, and people's ulcers start to bleed.

If you have the chance, skip the air-conditioned bus and try… well, anything. Here's a guide to getting yourself around.

Aircraft

Check your email before flying to see if there have been any changes to your flight. While you're online, you may as well take the opportunity to print out a boarding card. Most carriers will have English-speakers manning the phones, but have the hostel receptionist or tourist office help out if you experience a language barrier. And remember to confirm your in-flight meals if you have any special dietary considerations.

On long flights, request a seat by the window if you plan to sleep, preferably near an emergency exit, and take anti-jetlag precautions so you don't sleepwalk through the first week of your trip (see p.191). Contact-lens users should either switch to glasses during the long flight or bring extra solution to combat the dry cabin air. If you hope to get bumped up to business class, make sure you dress smartly. Rather, try not to look or smell like an independent backpacker.

With local carriers, you may not experience the sort of professionalism you get on flights at home (if, indeed, you get such service at home). And the planes may not look that professional either. If you're nervous about flying with these companies, that's normal, but remind yourself that it's statistically safer than other modes of transport, including walking. Flying during daylight may help with some of your worries.

12

Bicycle

Bikes can be rented nearly everywhere, and in some cities, such as Vienna, they're actually free. And where they can't be rented, you can pick up a low-tech model for a trifle. Take advantage of this. It's an ideal way to get to know an area, particularly the ones set up to accommodate cycles: you can stop whenever you get the urge yet you're more inclined to venture further, well off the main tourist routes, which will afford you some of the most interesting views. For tips on longer bike journeys, see p.62.

Bicycle rickshaw

You can't ride in one of these and not feel like a hardened traveler. The problem is you may also feel like a slave-driver. Propulsion never looks easy for these malnourished pedallers, but they often throw in a few extra grunts to help justify the price. There's no meter, so always fix the price before you depart. In European city centers, modern bicycle rickshaws are appearing, and many of them are free (a trade-off for being covered in advertising).

Bus

You'll find some buses are as aerodynamic as a Formula 1 car, have spacious, fully reclining seats and attendants serving almost-edible food. Air conditioning and express routes are also options. (Beware of the movies, though, which are often loud and in the local language.) If you need to cover some ground and get a good night's rest, it can be worth the extra few bucks. When boarding older buses, choose your seat carefully if you can. Try to get a window seat near the front (but not at the very front) on the side that's not getting direct sunlight (take a moment to figure this out before you step onto the bus). That way you can control the temperature with the window, minimize the greenhouse effect, get a view of where you're going and still have a few rows in front of you to cushion any collision. And remember to ask if they have a *working* bathroom on board when buying your ticket.

Camel

Camels, though they conjure up Lawrence of Arabia adventures, are about as tempting to ride over long distances as they are to French kiss. As Jacqueline Kennedy said on her trip to India, "A camel makes an elephant feel like a jet plane." Sometimes there is just one rein, fashioned to a nose ring on one side, affording the rider an easy pull to go in that direction, but rendering it near impossible to make it go the other without a 359-degree rotation. In other words, be sure to ask for two reins.

12

Canoe

A convenient step up from their dugout brethren, the modern canoe can be rented affordably in an astounding number of countries, and provides an easy way to leave just a few footprints while you travel. From the Boundary Water Canoe Area in North America to the hippo-packed Zambezi River, you get the best possible views of the area with little more than a guide or a good map.

Car

Read the section on transport for car essentials (p.59) and see the "Regional profiles" at the end of the book for specific tips on buying, selling and renting cars as you travel.

Cruise ship

This doesn't fit the traditional traveler image. The cabins aren't conducive to drying hand-washed laundry, the staff don't appreciate people walking down the corridors in just a towel, and body art and piercing may frighten some of the other passengers. But this can be a way to connect certain legs of your trip at a decent price (see p.56).

Dhow

These wooden sailing boats are very similar to feluccas, although they're slightly more seaworthy. They're usually found hugging the coast of

Hitchhiking safety

In some countries, it's relatively safe to **hitch**, in others it should never be done. Your guidebook will help explain where it is and isn't an option, but there are several things you can do to minimize the **risk**, starting with your choice of hitchhiking spot. At petrol stations near the highway, you can simply approach the drivers who look most trustworthy – families, couples and single women drivers. Of course, to get rides with these people, you'll have to look presentable and trustworthy yourself, which means a shower, clean clothes, no sunglasses and a smile.

If you do have to stand on the side of the road, don't just hop in a car because it pulls over. That's only how it works in the movies. You want to go to the driver- or passenger-side window (you may have to open the passenger-side door) and ask the driver where they're going. Use these few moments to see if the person looks, well... normal. Scan for open alcohol containers and smell for alcohol on the driver's breath. If they look rough or drunk, just say thanks, but that you're actually headed to a different place and walk off.

Once in the car, if you sense that the driver may be drunk, over-fatigued, dangerous or is driving too aggressively, ask them to let you out at the next petrol station. If there aren't any around, have them drop you at an intersection (where cars are more likely to slow down), or just get out as soon as possible. If the driver turns off the interstate and starts heading in a new direction without telling you, ask to get out of the car immediately. If you feel you are in serious danger and the driver won't stop to let you out, try hopping out at an intersection when the car stops or slows down.

Hitching is never a good idea for women traveling alone, but especially so if you can't find a ride with a family, couple, or single woman driver. Simply put, make sure you're never the only woman in the car.

Digihitch (Ⓦ www.digihitch.com) is a good place to find rides with drivers around Europe, as well as info on world records in hitchhiking, while Autostop Guide (Ⓦ www .autostopguide.com) tells you exactly which local bus to take to the best long-distance hitchhiking spots all over Europe.

12

eastern Africa: trips are common in Lamu, Kenya, with camping along the surrounding islands, and near Zanzibar. They come in all shapes and sizes, from three-person dinghies to commercial fishing vessels. The faster ones employ a counterbalance beam. If you're allowed, crawl out onto it for an exhilarating ride.

Dugout canoe

They look and sound exotic, but most tip or take in water easily, and they're about as convenient to portage, weight-wise, as an automatic cash machine. Best if you have someone along who knows how to balance it and avoid crocs.

Elephant

You can ride these oversized beasts in Thailand, Vietnam, India and other selected tourist haunts. If you can get over the smell and bargain your way to a decent price, it's a pretty comfortable and regal ride. Unless, of course, you're riding bareback.

Felucca

These ancient wooden sailing boats are most commonly associated with the Nile. Most travelers book tours in Aswan for three-day trips north, sleeping on the boat's cushioned decks. They're among the slowest sailing boats you'll ever encounter, but the tranquility is unsurpassed. Don't forget to bring a good book.

Ferry

You may have a hard time trying to circumnavigate the planet by ferry, but they do connect a rather substantial part of the earth's shorter shipping lanes. Some are barely afloat and others are nearly as luxurious as their cruise-ship cousins, with hot tubs, saunas, movie theaters and discos, and all are more expensive if you try to bring along a car. For a website listing links of ferry lines around the world, try Ⓦwww.routes international.com. Those prone to sickness should make sure they're staying on decks well away from the engine room, where diesel smells can increase the chances of unwanted weight loss.

Horse

12

Equestrian travel can be incredibly romantic and exciting. You can take an African safari by horseback, cross mountains in the saddle or canter along the beach. But, in the words of Ian Fleming, "A horse is dangerous at both ends and uncomfortable in the middle." Make certain, therefore, you get a little practice before you head out on a longer journey, and spend some time getting to know your steed's signals before you need to interpret them in an emergency.

Jeepney

These converted 1940 US Army Jeeps are a little too unique to be lumped together with the other minibuses; they have become one of the Philippines' most recognizable symbols. The Filipinos stretched Jeep bodies to three or four times their original length, added rows of cushioned seats and about twenty kilos of glitz and paint.

Minibus

Better known, depending on the location, as a beemo, dolmus, dollar van, matatu or songthaew, these privately owned small vans or pick-up trucks function as city buses and inter-city transporters. They aren't always cheaper than city buses, but they run more frequently and can be much easier to locate. It's not uncommon to find eighteen people crammed into one designed to hold seven, with the tout still trying to take on passengers. Your best bet is to grab a window seat near the front, opposite the sliding door, just in case the oxygen levels start to drop. Too close to the sliding door and you'll have a buttock in your face for the duration of the journey, most likely that of the designated fare collector (also charged with the task of corralling as many people as possible aboard) who generally prefers to stand and hang out of the door.

Motorcycle

There are probably two hundred safer ways to navigate the planet, but few that offer the opportunity to do so in leather. Helmets and protective clothing are a must as road conditions and other drivers are often completely unpredictable. There's some advance planning necessary to drive across some borders, but we've got those details, plus overseas car and motorcycle-buying tips, covered (p.59).

Motorized rickshaw

Mate a scooter with a golf cart and then drive it across Asia, and you get a motorized rickshaw. You may recognize these yellow and black mini-transports from James Bond's *Octopussy*, and you'll certainly hear them coming. The mosquito-sounding engines get them going quick enough to somehow enter the flow of traffic. Meters exist, but they don't always work, or must be cross-referenced to some indexed price list. So consider learning the going rate and making a deal for the ride beforehand.

Ocean-going cargo ship

They come in all shapes and sizes, but few are appealing to the eye from the outside. The cabins can be another story, as more state rooms are being refitted for travelers. Getting on board can be no small feat, with advance planning and fees generally involved. If this seems appealing, you won't want to miss details on costs and what's involved in booking such a trip (p.56).

On foot

There's no better way to get around than with your metatarsals. Pounding the pavement gives you the pulse of a place. According to author Wendell Berry, "Our senses were developed to function at foot speeds." Put another way, if you move though a new place faster than a few kilometres per hour, your eyes, ears and nose won't be able to register all the information they're getting. There are two classic variants of hoofing it: pick up a map, or simply wander until you're lost.

Overland trucks

See p.58.

River cargo ship

Smaller than their ocean-going sisters, and generally much easier to get passage on, river ships are a far more casual affair. On Amazonian ships, you string up a hammock on deck and sleep elbow to elbow. Thanks to an extensive canal network, much of Europe can be navigated by inland boats as well. Some are overhauled luxury vessels for tourists, some are private mobile homes, and some are commercial barges. Look for passage on all three.

River kayak

These are short, rugged, and tip easier than a toddler on rollerblades, so it's best to take a course when getting started. Because handling is so sensitive, most kayakers prefer their own boats. However, on a long trip you'll probably just have to make do with what's available on site. If you stick to the rafting epicenters, you'll find there's good equipment on hand and, depending on your skill level, you may be able to catch free rides with rafting trips working as a safety kayaker.

Sea kayak

12

Both the hardshell and the collapsible variety have merits, depending largely on how you're able to transport them. They're increasingly available for rent, so enquire before you drag yours halfway around the globe. You'll also need to check with airlines to see what additional fees are involved when taking them on board.

Subway

No matter how little there is to see out the window, make an effort to try out the subway once or twice. It's an integral part of any big city's character. Some offer incredibly high-speed and efficient transport (Kuala Lumpur, Copenhagen and Dubai have driverless trains), some are overdue for repair and some are simply underground marvels. The lines in Moscow, St Petersburg, London, Tokyo, Hong Kong, New York, Washington DC, Singapore and Stockholm are particularly worth a look.

Taxi

At home you might order a taxi or flag one down for a personal and usually short ride. You can do that on the road as well. But in developing nations, some taxis function more like minibuses, and the driver will commonly supplement his journey by giving as many people rides as possible along the way without deviating from his course. These are known as shared taxis or collectivos.

In other cases, you may (particularly if you can arrange a group of three or four travelers) decide to hire a taxi for an entire day, maybe longer. It's surprisingly cheap, and may make the most sense if there's a border crossing where the alternative is to take a bus followed by a long walk, or if there are a number of interesting sights located just outside the city center. Check your guidebook to find out if the taxis are strictly regulated by meter or whether bargaining is necessary. If you need to bargain, arrange a price before starting out, but don't pay until it's over. Fuel should be paid separately to keep your driver from cruising along at an energy-efficient 10kph, refusing scenic detours, and trying to convince you that the air-con doesn't work.

Train

Remember to check that the train car you are boarding has the name of the city you are going to posted on the side, especially in Europe. If the individual car says "Hamburg" on it, that's where it's going. But that doesn't mean the entire train is going to Hamburg. In fact, there's a good chance it isn't. Trains drop off some cars and pick up others along the route, so you can easily end up someplace you hadn't counted on. It's tempting, especially with railpasses, to save money with a few nights on the train. But find out why that's not a great idea (p.76) and check out the "Regional profiles" at the end of this book to learn about supplementing your pass with other cost-effective travel.

Old locomotives are wonderful, if you can find any that haven't been turned into tourist rigs. They make you feel like a traveler, assuming they eventually get you where you're going. Some, like second-class Indian trains, give an excellent taste of the culture, while others, such as the rooftop rides in Ecuador, provide jaw-dropping vistas you can't get from the road.

With the high-speed models (China's magnetic levitation trains, Japan's Bullet Train, France's TGV, Germany's ICE, Spain's AVE), it hardly feels

Taxi thrills

A fight breaks out between the taxi drivers outside of my hotel in Cairo when they see me exiting. Eventually, I decide on one. I meticulously set the price before entering, though I still know I'm getting ripped off. The taxi takes off like a springbok with a bum full of dynamite. The drive is reminiscent of a computer game, only with bad smells. There are wall-to-wall beaten-up cars, five lanes of traffic (at least five) on a two-lane road. I can actually hear the taxi sucking in its breath as we pass between two other cars. Green means go in Cairo. Apparently so does red. And pedestrians are fair game. The driver tries to sell me a hubble-bubble pipe, demonstrating how it works as we hurtle through the city center. I find it difficult to pay, as my hands are shaking so much. I find one aspect settling, and I try to cling on to it as I count the bills and coins: a bungee-jump would have cost fifty times the price.

Craig Ayre
Nervous traveler

12

Are you a tourist or a traveler?

Why on earth should you go out of your way to try some sport or activity you've never heard of and will probably never do again? Why bother with the slow, less comfortable modes of transport? Why go anywhere near a squat toilet or, for that matter, a Vietnamese ear-cleaner armed with what seems to be shish-kebab skewers?

Because if you're not doing something new, you're doing something you've done before. If you're not taking **local transport**, you're taking Western-style transport. If you're not using the **local language** (or hand gestures and phrasebooks), you're probably speaking with professional guides and concierges. If you're not staying in places with local standards, you're staying in places with Western standards. If you're not eating **local food**, you're probably eating food you know from home. If you're not using the local toilets, you're using Western ones. The creature comforts (and language) of Western life are now available virtually everywhere, and if you don't go on a creature-comfort diet, you'll be getting a Disneyfied view of the place you're trying to see. It's often the inconvenient and uncomfortable elements that give travel its extra dimension, and separate the Sphinx in Las Vegas from the one in Egypt, the gondola ride in the Epcot Center from the one in Venice – and the tourists from the travelers.

like you're moving, never mind traveling. Until, that is, you catch the 300kph blur out the window. When high-speed trains are involved, it's almost always cheaper to get some type of railpass. (It may even be cheaper to fly.) There's a monopoly on the food, so plastic-wrapped sandwiches are priced like Michelin-star meals; fortunately, though, the rides don't last that long, so a few pack-along snacks should see you through. For worldwide rail links see ⓦwww.routesinternational.com.

Since most train stations have a tourist office (or are located just next to one) don't forget to pick up a free map before conquering the town.

Tuk-tuk

Thailand's answer to discount taxis. These enlarged high-powered golf carts appear to have been decorated by someone on an acid trip; judging from the typically rapid lane changes and high-speed U-turns, it's probably the driver.

Water taxi

Found everywhere from Venice to Stockholm to the Bahamas, they're usually priced for vacationing millionaires, so make sure it's a special occasion before you flag one down.

Accommodation

Bolivia is a little too far to travel to stay at a hotel that looks just like the one down the street. Besides, your budget is likely to suffer from even one night's plush rest at an internationally recognized hotel, which are typically priced for business travelers. It may take some time to get used to staying in budget digs, but it's more rewarding than it might initially seem. There's a sense of camaraderie that you simply won't find at the Ritz. You can swap tales at breakfast, make dinner together, play backgammon – it's a nomadic commune of sorts. The atmosphere changes from place to place, even day to day if enough new travelers pull in. You can also seek more interesting places from time to time: a hostel in a cave; a bed in a backyard tree house; an underwater hotel. Even if these unconventional digs cost a little more, it's usually worth the experience.

Camping

Traveler camping falls into two categories: free camping, which is usually illegal but pretty easy to do outside of big cities; and paid camping, at designated campsites with tickets and other amenities and **in people's backyards** (Ⓦwww.campinmygarden.com). If you plan to go down the free camp route, you'll probably need to give big cities a miss. Many of the city parks and beaches are too dangerous to sleep in, or too likely to be patrolled by police. Either way, you're in trouble. In smaller towns, you can usually find a field, perhaps even a remote part of a park, if you're discreet. Some designated campsites are quite extravagant, with a restaurant, supermarket and pool, but even the smaller ones can be surprisingly expensive – especially in Europe. For just a little more, you can often rent a walk-in tent with a "real" bed.

Farmstays

The name conveys the gist. You stay on a working farm where the family has made a few rooms available to those who are willing to pay for the experience. There's a significant range in comfort and price, but many of them dip well into the budget range ($30/£19 including breakfast). Some offer courses in riding or gardening; many provide family-style meals; and you can sample everything from grape-growing to a full cattle ranch. They're typically available in Australia (Ⓦhttp://aftagriculturaltourism .com.au), New Zealand (Ⓦwww.truenz.co.nz/farmstays) and Europe (Ⓦwww.eceat.org, Ⓦwww.farmhouseaccommodation.co.uk and Ⓦwww .responsibletravel.com), as well as other parts of the globe (Ⓦwww .farmstays.org).

Free accommodation around the world

Yes, this has appeared in other sections of this book because it affects so many things – budget, cultural immersion, etc – but the emergence of Couchsurfing may be the single biggest advancement in budget travel since the guidebook came along (see p.79).

12

Guesthouses/pensions/B&Bs

These are typically private homes or apartments with a few spare rooms or bungalows in the back yard. They're often run by older people whose children have moved out, and who are looking to earn a little extra money by letting travelers into their private living space. This means showing a little more respect and courtesy than you might employ at a hostel. Even if it is rather lacking in services, keep in mind you're living in someone's home.

With the emergence of Airbnb.com, everyone seems to be opening a pension in their house/flat or renting their places out while they're away to earn a little extra money (see p.80).

Independent hostels

Independent hostels come in as many different shapes and sizes as rocks, which, coincidentally, is what some of them seem to use to stuff their mattresses. You'll find some setups extremely professional, particularly in Australia and New Zealand, where they've either been taken over by franchises or all read the same youth-hostel-starter-kit handbook. Some have great bar scenes with cheap food and people dancing on the tables in the evenings; others feel like giant, anaesthetized dormitory-type buildings with concierges. Others are blissfully charming and serene with hammocks and sofas, and a chance to dine with the owners. They can be either centrally located or fiendishly remote, with little commonality other than being the cheapest digs in town. Special discounts cards (p.74) can help as well.

International youth hostels

No, you don't have to be a certain age to stay at a youth hostel. Being young at heart is enough. Official IYHs (all 4000-plus of them in more than 80 countries; ⊛www.hihostels.com) are part of an organization, which means there are certain standards, although it does not mean the standards are terribly high. Nearly all of these are well cleaned, some practically sterile, with dormitory-style rooms and separate quarters for men and women, self-service kitchens, common rooms and lockers, and a cost of $10–60/£6–38 per night. Some are equipped with pools, hot tubs and barbecues, while others are about as basic as their tree-and-hut logo. Even though they like to tout their lighthouse property in California and the tall sailing-ship *af Chapman* hostel in Sweden, IYHs don't usually earn many points in the architecture, cosiness or roaring-social-life departments. Most are located a little way out of the center of town – and don't be surprised to find that some have a curfew (they kick everyone out for a few hours during the day for cleaning and/or shut the doors around midnight). There are almost always other budget alternatives, but if this sounds like your cup of discounted tea, pick up the $28/£18 membership card. If not, you're still welcome, but will pay slightly more, eventually accruing enough stays to pay for membership. Try to book in advance if you know when you're arriving, especially in high season. IYHs can book for one another, so as you're checking out, you can ask them to book your accommodation for the following night in the next town.

In most hostels you can choose between a single room, double room, small dormitory or larger dormitory. The more people in your room, the cheaper it gets. It also means less privacy and more noise. You can assess the trade-off depending on how much sleep you want and how your budget is doing.

Sleeping rough

Ah, the last resort of the traveler, the safety net that leaves your back out of alignment, the experience that will help you overcome whatever was annoying you about hostels. At some point, it's likely you'll spend the night on a park bench or in a train station or airport lounge.

Even if you never do, it helps mentally to brace for the possibility. You probably won't be the only one doing this, so when it looks inevitable, start trying to secure a good spot. What's a good spot? You'll know it when you see it, if there is one. Not too hidden, not where people have to step over you, not right under bright lights. Corners are usually quite nice, and frequently coveted. You may be inadvertently borrowing the resting place of a "regular" – so be forewarned that many of them don't take kindly to this. Look for newspaper or cardboard to place under you; a cold marble floor will drain your body heat and make it difficult to rest. If you've got a travel partner, take turns staying awake. If not, make sure you're bear-hugging your backpack while you sleep. Alternatively, look for an all-night snack shop or bar and sip tea or coffee until the sun creeps up, then find a more comfortable place to sleep at a park or a beach.

12

Eating

No matter what level of comfort you choose to travel in, you don't want to circle the globe without sampling local cuisines. Check out the markets, or follow your nose into a tiny restaurant and discover anything from Brazilian *moqueca* stews to hand-rolled pasta in Sicily to tongue-sizzling Indian curries. There's no need to be paranoid about what passes your lips. If it looks truly vile (greenish drinking water), you might want to give it a miss. And, in developing nations, shellfish for sale anywhere but right off the fishing boat should probably be skipped. Otherwise, eat, drink, be merry, and pack somelightning-fast cures for diarrhea (see p.189).

Hostels

They know their customers' budgets better than anyone. Many hostels offer extremely cheap stews, sandwiches and plates of pasta. The ones that don't may provide cooking facilities. Team up with another traveler, or an entire group, head to the supermarket and make a meal together.

Restaurants

Eating at restaurants can run up your expenses quicker than almost anything else, so choose where you eat with care. As comforting as it may be to dine with other travelers, you'll often get a better deal ditching the guidebook, heading to the poorer parts of town and checking out places that don't take credit cards and are packed with locals. Here's one good tip: ask a construction worker for a recommendation. They're usually experts on cheap, filling meals.

Street vendors

Don't believe the intestine-quivering rumours. Not every street snack leads to a week in squatter solitary. In fact, buying food from street vendors is a wonderful way to supplement your diet; some travelers manage to exist entirely on these often exotic snacks. And since you can see the food getting thoroughly cooked, it can be safer than some restaurants. You can get fried grasshoppers and scorpions in China, which have more crunch than taste; delicious fried bananas with cinnamon in Indonesia; luscious pineapple on a stick in Thailand; salted cucumbers in Turkey; and warm and spicy bhajis in India.

12

Traveler cafés

You can't miss them. They're filled with travelers, plus the ubiquitous banana pancakes, mango milkshakes and toasted cheese sandwiches served to the beat of a Van Morrison song. These oases for the Western palate are what keep many travelers sane. They also keep many travelers from venturing into more interesting dining and drinking establishments.

McDonald's

On one hand, there's simply too much wonderful food out there to justify a trip to the **Golden Arches**. On the other, *McDonald's* has some rather exotic (albeit processed and chemically enhanced) dishes in addition to the old classics. For example, in New Zealand there's the Kiwi Burger, a quarter-pound cheeseburger with beetroot and eggs. In Uruguay, there's the McHuevo, a hamburger with a poached egg and mayo. India has the Maharaja Mac, a lamb burger. Turkey has the Köfte Burger, a spiced patty inside a bun enriched with yoghurt mix. The point is, if you absolutely must get your McFix while you're on the road (and these places are packed with travelers), you can at least give yourself a push to try something new.

Personal hygiene

Staying clean on the road is a challenge at times. The times it becomes particularly rough are during the back-to-back long-transit rides (an overnight bus ride followed by a long plane trip); walking in hot, humid cities; and when you're not feeling well. If you can't handle the toilets, that can be a problem too. Either way, relief can be found.

Airport wash stations

Many airports now have showers available for a fee (sometimes ridiculously high, but still worth it depending on your travel grime factor). Some have a sauna and gym as well. You may have to hunt around a little, as they're not as well situated as the duty-free items and postcard vendors. Even if you have to put your yet-unwashed clothes back on, a refreshing shower ($1–5/£0.6–3) can be an enormous boost. And you probably have some spare coins to get rid of anyway. If you don't take the opportunity during a long haul, the smell is only going to get worse. The budget route, of course, is simply to wash in the restroom, perhaps with a paper-towel shower, and swing by the duty free and take a squirt of perfume before the next leg of your journey.

12

The bus "shower"

On nicer bus rides, particularly around Turkey and the Middle East, don't be surprised if an attendant comes by and offers you a splash of unisex perfume or some fragranced towelettes. They're not as nice as the warm flannels distributed by many airlines, particularly considering they have the olfactory properties of toilet-bowl cleaner, but it's still better than having nuclear BO. Individually wrapped moist tissues function better since they also remove the dirt and odour rather than simply masking it. Bring some of your own just in case.

Turkish bath – the marathon sweat

A perfect remedy for travel grime – the accumulated film that covers your body after weeks with low-pressure showers. These medieval bath houses are mild steamrooms with washbasins, sometimes a hot pool and a steamier section. Most offer – for an additional fee – a joint-cracking, back-popping, skin-blasting "massage" that will leave you feeling like a boneless chicken. On exiting, you can cool down wrapped in towels with a refreshing yoghurt drink.

Japanese bath – boil yourself clean

No trip to Japan is really complete without a dip at a "sento" or its outdoor cousin, the "onsen." These public baths are sometimes as

12

Don't know squat

What gets lost, I think, amid all the fretting and complaining about toilets in the so-called Third World is this: it's just a hole.

A hole, and nothing more.

It's an undeniably elegant design, brilliant in its simplicity – a place to poop, I posit, that far surpasses anything we have in the United States.

This notion is reinforced on almost all my trips. Usually, the last place I use a bathroom in the US is at the airport. You know the type of stall – one where you have to place a sheet of what looks like deli paper on the seat, and then lower yourself gingerly down so the paper doesn't become a slip'n'slide, and then sit there while the electric-eye flush mechanism is triggered three or four times for no apparent reason, often dampening your nether regions, and then, of course, with all this careful hygienity, you have to grab the lock on the stall door – the one spot you can be certain that every unwashed hand has been placed – and then head to the sinks and hope the electric eyes work there, and then, finally, dispense yourself a paper towel by grabbing a lever that, once again, everyone has touched, thereby negating your hand-washing.

After I land – in Africa, in Asia, in Central America – my toilet facilities usually consist of this: a hole.

A hole, and nothing more.

A place where no fleshy parts make contact with any toilet parts.

Why it's not common knowledge that Third World toilets are superior to all other toilets comes down to one notion – we don't know squat.

That is, we don't know how to squat. We come from a baseball land – we squat like catchers, up on our toes. This is wrong. Proper hole-squatting technique demands a flat-footed stance. It's difficult at first, I'll confess, but if you work on it at home it'll soon become second nature.

So, first get the squat down.

Next, go travel.

And then you, too, will learn to love the hole.

Michael Finkel, Author

elegantly crafted as temples – or as commercial-looking as shopping malls. They offer scalding water, some with herbal mixes or stimulating electric shocks. It's as cultural as it is therapeutic, relatively inexpensive (the outdoor ones are often free) and will keep you clean in a country that practically demands it.

What you really need to know about toilets

Alert readers may notice this section is slightly longer than the ones above. That's because using a foreign toilet is rather more complex than catching a taxi or finding a traveler café. That said, you might want to check out these tips (p.189) to avoid visiting the toilet too often. Meanwhile, here's a look at a few of the more common models you may end up facing.

The infamous squatter

The idea with these is that you are supposed to squat over the hole and, like a B-2 bomber, hit the target. Place your feet on the small foot-size platforms provided and align your hole with the one in the floor, which usually means facing the same way you would on a Western toilet. There's rarely anything to hold on to, or anything you'd want to hold on to, so the obvious danger is simply losing your balance and falling backwards. The less apparent danger is that squatting causes your pants pockets to become somewhat inverted, so your valuables may go sliding irretrievably down the hole. And if this doesn't sound challenging enough, remember you may have to hold a flashlight in your mouth since these lavatories often don't have decent lighting or, sometimes, any lighting at all.

And by the way, **there's no toilet paper**. Most of the world goes without. If you look closely, you'll see there's a little plastic bowl and a water tap in every stall next to the hole. The idea is you wipe with your left hand (no, I'm not kidding) then wash it off under the water. There's probably no soap, so you can choose to wash with soap later, bring your own or do like the locals and just use the right hand for eating and shaking hands. Or just bring your own toilet paper. How to flush the hole is not entirely apparent. There's no little handle to push. No knob to turn. You have to fill up the plastic bowl a few times and dump the water into the hole and let water displacement take care of the rest.

The almost-Western toilet

This one looks like a Western model, but it was installed by someone who may not have fully understood the instructions that came with the assembly kit. Or lacked the necessary tools. If you're lucky enough to find one with a seat, you'll notice it's usually secured by something with the strength of chewing gum, so if you don't sit down exactly straight, the seat detaches and you slide right off the porcelain rim, which – take it from me – can be pretty painful.

More commonly, however, the plastic seat is missing altogether. This means that you're back to squatting again. Only now it's more difficult because you can't do a regular squat; you have to do a "standing squat" so you can clear the rim of the toilet. This usually entails bracing yourself with one hand on the wall behind you, which is highly exhausting for your arm and leg muscles and often makes them cramp painfully.

A few of these bathrooms do come equipped with paper, but it's usually the sort that Rambo would be afraid to use. Some provide strips of newspaper or a glossy magazine on a nail. So, while you're sitting there (or semi-squatting) use your time wisely by crumpling and uncrumpling the paper until it's almost tolerable. This takes about twenty minutes with the glossy stuff, so you may want to start working on it before you actually get to the toilet. (In an emergency, simply employ this technique with a few of your guidebook pages.) Whatever you use, if there's a little waste bin beside the toilet, fold the paper over to keep it tidy, then put it there. Don't even think of throwing your used paper into the toilet. These loos, though they may look vaguely like ours, have a violent reaction to toilet paper.

12

The high-tech Japanese toilet/bidet

Most of these models have more wires than Keith Richards' guitar, more features than a scientific calculator and the comfort of a beanbag chair. These commodes do just about everything but brush your teeth, although I'm sure technicians are working on that now.

The control panel is sometimes built in next to the throne and sometimes on a remote-control device attached to the wall with a Velcro patch, so you could conceivably remove it and flush the toilet from across the room. It automatically raises and lowers the seat with the press of a button. Another button creates a natural, camouflaging noise when you need it. A quiet vacuum under the seat continuously pumps any noxious emissions through an air filter and a dial controls the temperature of the seat. There are three separate buttons for the rinse cycle: one is exclusively for women, the second creates a gentle rinse of the backside and the third calls up a power spray. When you push one of these, a small plastic spigot creeps out from underneath the rear of the seat and commences cleaning. You can, of course, adjust the temperature to your liking.

Higher-end models also feature a pulsating "massage" spray. Then there's the built-in blow-dryer to complete the treatment. Whatever you do, don't jump up if you push the wrong button or the whole bathroom might be doused with water. Most are equipped with some kind of emergency stop button. Make sure you can find it before you begin your journey.

12

Culture shock

Culture shock is simply a dramatic way of saying that things aren't quite the way they are at home. It sounds dramatic precisely because it can be. When you change everything you eat, say, do, smell and hear at the same time, the effect can be overwhelming. Especially if amplified by sadness or apprehension about leaving home, fatigue from the journey or illness. The natural tendency is to return home immediately. But if you give yourself time, this urge will almost certainly pass.

Combating culture shock

Researchers in the 1970s and 1980s developed an idea that the individual traveler didn't need to embrace all or even most aspects of a society, just some key features to be able to operate within the culture. By simply being aware of **this phenomenon**, you're already a step ahead. Here are several practical things you can do to minimize culture shock:

- Recognize it for what it is: a reaction to sensory overload and unfamiliar surroundings. (Oh, that's just a bout of culture shock – I'll be fine soon.) Look at the upside of what it represents: you're getting new experiences, new insights and a new perspective. How bad is that?
- Start your journey in countries similar to your own.
- Read up on the place you are visiting before you arrive. You're going there to experience what that country has to offer, but a little knowledge can decrease the number of cultural surprises. It can be enough for some to just buy the guidebook a day before departure and start reading background information, but reading a novel set in the relevant country will do far more to get you in the mood.

13

First-night blues

Be prepared to be unhappy the first night or two. It can be a huge shell shock arriving somewhere on your own… and although you are excited about being in a new country, at the same time you suddenly realize you are on your own. Don't worry, it does get better very quickly, just make sure you get out and explore.

Becky Robinson, solo traveler

- Get some sleep on the plane (see p.191). Jetlag gets your trip off on the wrong foot.
- If you are making a large cultural jump early in your trip, ease yourself into your new location. Start by staying in a Western-style hotel for a day or two, and looking for cheaper, local digs after you've had a chance to acclimatize. Or simply spend some time just relaxing in a nice hotel lobby free of charge and don't return to your hostel until you're ready to examine the back of your eyelids.
- Speak to other travelers. Compare observations.
- Keep a journal.
- Allow yourself to get excited about your trip. It's natural to be a little nervous about what's ahead, but focus on converting that into positive energy.

Your travel philosophy

What you take with you on your trip will, to a large extent, determine the experience you take away from it. And in this case, I'm not referring to the dual-current hairdryer that you should probably leave at home. I'm talking about your travel philosophy: your approach to dealing with the cultures you encounter.

You'll face this the moment you begin your journey. People you meet off the "beaten track" tend to be more genuine, as they haven't been hardened by years of loud tour groups and tough-bargaining backpackers. If you're well off the trail, a situation common among independent travelers, you're in a more culturally fragile environment and should thus move about and interact with deliberate care.

Here are a few concepts to keep in mind:

- You are a guest in a foreign country. Be a gracious guest. Travel with an open mind and a desire to learn.
- Familiarize yourself with local customs and make an effort to learn at least a few words of the local language. Your efforts will make an impression on those you meet. (How would you react to someone who came to your country and asked you for directions in another language, then spoke louder and more slowly when you didn't understand?)

The four stages of culture shock

13

Everyone has slightly different reactions, so this may not provide a complete blueprint for your **adaptation**. The speed of the process also varies, and many people go through different phases more than once. Many travelers, for example, speak of the classic "three-month dip" when a spate of homesickness hits. And if you can just survive that, you can keep going forever.

1 Honeymoon

Cultural differences are intriguing and the new sites are fascinating. You are still comforted by the close memory of your home culture.

2 Crisis

After some time abroad, differences begin to affect you. Differences in language, concepts and values begin to create feelings of confusion and anxiety. (This is normal. It's a sign you're reconnecting with your own cultural values.)

3 Recovery

You begin to accept the differences and feel comfortable in new situations. Often the crisis dissipates as language skills improve.

4 Adjustment

Despite occasional bouts of strain, you're enjoying the new culture and able to make choices based on preferences and values.

- Be a sensitive photographer. Be discreet or ask permission. And consider the long-term implications before paying someone in cash or sweets to take their photograph.
- Bargain and resolve conflicts with a smile.
- Look beyond the tourist streets and resorts. Make an effort to meet and spend time with at least one local who is not trying to sell you any goods or services.
- Pay attention to the local dress. Shorts, vest tops and other revealing items often aren't appropriate. Better to choose styles and colors that help you blend in rather than display the latest fashions from your own country.
- Don't litter or waste electricity and water.
- Don't begin sentences with "Well, back home, we…" At least, not until they ask what you do back home.

Minimizing the impact of tourism

How about **the "shock" of your impact on other cultures**? In 2011 alone, the World Tourism Organization reported 980 million international arrivals. In other words, over half a billion people took a trip abroad. With high-speed trains connecting jumbo jets to quick-check-in rental cars, the world is now more conveniently, comfortably and cheaply accessed than ever

13

before. With a few clicks of the mouse and a valid credit card, travelers can send themselves around the planet. Yet just ten of the richest countries account for nearly sixty percent of all international travel. And hundreds of millions of these trips are short, packaged vacations to beaches and quaint, picturesque towns in comparatively poor lands, where visitors can enjoy comforts they couldn't or wouldn't pay for at home.

The travel industry obliges by creating an easy-to-navigate infrastructure complete with parking lots to handle dozens of tour buses; view-blocking, shadow-casting luxury hotels right on the beach; colorful costumes for evening cultural-dance programs; light shows with multilingual recorded voice-overs; and air-conditioned restaurants. The locals who travelers are most likely to encounter have been trained to accommodate: they speak the tourists' languages and sell items they desperately need (film, sun lotion, beer).

But is contact with visitors and their money making the lives of local people better? For some, yes. At least by Western standards. You see many driving more comfortable cars and living in nicer homes as a result. The

Giving to beggars

You learn a lot about yourself when you travel, and being confronted by **beggars** twenty times daily will certainly flex the bend of that learning curve. It's a vexing issue. You're walking around with more money than these beggars may ever possess, yet you'll have to return in less than a week if you start handing it out as you may like. Even if you give money to five people a day, you might be refusing it to fifteen. Or you give some coins to a starving woman and her two starving children and you walk off thinking that you could have easily done so much more.

It's common to **feel callous** – to the extent that you neglect to broach the subject with other travelers, including the ones you may be traveling with. Imagine you're walking beside a traveler who is emotionally touched by a beggar when you're not. They give and you don't and when you continue walking there's suddenly a little gap between you.

There's no right way to approach it. Some people hand out tiny coins to everyone they encounter. Some never do, but may contribute to a charity that can (hopefully) better distribute the funds. Most fail to adopt any sort of policy and just end up giving when they can no longer refuse, when they need an emotional lift (giving can be extremely rewarding), or when they've just spent too much on a meal and feel the pangs of guilt. Some try, with a look, to figure out if the funds will be used for alcohol or milk, and if they will be helping to support the truly bereft (or the mafia bosses many beggars must hand their earnings to). For this reason, many people prefer to carry tiny gifts or snacks to hand out, although this is not always appreciated.

Begging can get **aggravating** at times, so aggravating that it's possible to lose sight of the bigger picture: the beggars have a life harder than anything you can imagine. Instead, you begin to feel like the victim. You feel like you're viewed as nothing more than a walking money-machine. You think: "I'm spending my money in your country, trying to learn about you, and if you don't plan to get to know me in a genuine way, I'd really prefer to be left alone once in a while. Come to my country and see how you like getting hassled for change all day." Needless to say, try your best to keep things in perspective.

Breaking through the travel bubble

13

When you're caught up in the **excitement of traveling** in a foreign land for the first time, everything you see seems so different and wonderfully exotic, it's possible to miss the **travel bubble**. But after you notice it, you'll wonder how it ever eluded you.

Look around the traveler trail and you'll notice the Westernized biosphere, with cafés serving up banana pancakes, brownies and muesli on demand. Don't like to dine alone? No problem. You can watch the latest Hollywood movies on video while you eat. When it's time to shop, you can find a complete range of pirated products, from designer clothes to DVDs, at a fraction of their normal prices. There are reasonably priced laundry services that specialize in taking two months' worth of stink out of your clothing in one wash. There are henna artists, hair braiders with nimble hands and countless beads, discount body-piercers, and tattoo artists who can apply the most popular indigenous designs to any curve you offer up, and they're all anxious to help you look like a hardened traveler who has been changed by a rigorous journey on the road. In other words, budget travelers aren't as far removed from the hair-drying, luggage-wheeling, tour-guide-following, videotaping crowd as they once were.

You're not likely to **escape this bubble** by traveling longer or further or faster. Instead, go deeper. Learn a language, communicate with the locals, spend time with them (a lot of time), and form your own firsthand perspective.

One of the best ways to do this is to work for them or alongside them. **Volunteering** is another excellent path (see p.95). Joining a local sports club or choir will also create inroads. Since there's no membrane on this bubble, it's impossible to say when you've burst it. But there are a few signs. Can you describe the character of the local people to someone back home? Do you have the phone numbers and addresses of local friends you've made? Have you been invited over for dinner? These are certainly more worthy things to strive for on your trip than passport stamps.

---

money can also bring better drinking water, better schools and better medicine, but it doesn't always. How it affects the social fabric of a place is difficult to calculate.

On the other hand you can meet teachers who gave up their jobs to earn more selling postcards or bracelets. Oddly, the people who don't benefit much are the ones tourists are most interested to photograph: rug weavers, cloth embroiderers and donkey-cart drivers. They seem to be working like mad with little to show for it.

With good reason, travel publications have long asserted that mass tourism destroys the very things – quaintness, genuine hospitality, serenity, unique culture – that attracted visitors in the first place. Truth be known, we independent budget travelers contribute to this as well, probably more than we'd care to admit. Simply by being aware of your impact, though, you'll probably make more thoughtful decisions about where you spend your money and how you interact with people.

14

Staying in touch

Not long ago, staying in touch was a reasonably straight forward affair. Unreliable mail services, expensive telegrams and uncooperative pay phones that ate coins by the fistful were your only options. Now, perhaps the most difficult aspect of staying in touch is choosing how you want to do it. On a bare-bones budget you can get by with just about all international communication for free (or the cost of wi-fi).

The best way to keep your friends and family informed on a budget

With time zones and long-distance charges, **email, Facebook, Twitter and a travel blog** are going to be your best allies for almost-immediate contact. The bigger trick is getting used to not being quite as connected as you are back home – or paying more for that service. Naturally it depends on the country, perhaps even the city. Some hostels/hotels/restaurants/libraries offer free wi-fi, some don't.

Unless you're writing a novel or editing a movie along the way, the cons of bringing a laptop may outweigh the pros. You can get internet access virtually anywhere. And by anywhere, I really mean anywhere. Nearly all hostels are now equipped with a connection (often with their own computers), and if they're not, you shouldn't have to walk more than five or ten minutes to find an internet café or library. You can plug in USBs and SD cards to send photos and back-up files. Expect to pay anything from 25 cents/15 pence to $4/£2.40 for fifteen minutes of surfing if you can't find free access.

Safe surfing

Surfing on the road is not like surfing at home. The connection may be fine, but you need to be aware of a new breed of pickpocket – the kind who watches you type in your various passwords, or logs on to your machine after you're gone and accesses your private accounts with the info that you've unknowingly left in the far reaches of the computer's memory. There are a few things you need to do to adjust the browser settings every time you sit down at a terminal so that improperly set-up computers don't accidentally remember all your passwords.

Before you start

- Turn off password and form remembering (found under "Tools" or "Preferences").
- Check that file and printer sharing are disabled (found in "Control Panel" or "System Preference").

During

- Beware of those watching you type your passwords.
- Always log out of websites that require a password.

After

- Delete important downloaded files. Use "shift-delete".
- Delete "temporary internet files, history, and cookies" (found in "Tools" then scroll to "Internet Options" then under the "General" tab.

14

VoIP: the cheapest way to phone home

The technical name is VoIP… you may know it better as **Skype** or one of the other services listed below. Set up a free account with one, set your friends and family up with free accounts and then test it with them so everyone is comfortable using it.

There are connected computers everywhere, and many of them have headphones you can use. But it's not a bad idea to carry a little wire headset/mic (like the type that come with most smartphones) that you can plug in.

A free Skype account (you only pay for calls made to phones) should get you by just fine and will connect you with most. If not, Google Voice (also free) is a solid bet. There are a few others to check out as well:

- **Vbuzzer** Like Skype, but with cheaper rates if you plan to call to phones.
- **Viber** Much like the others, but a bit easier to use on your smartphone. With the free app, you get free smartphone-to-smartphone calls over 3G and wi-fi connections.
- **ooVoo** Free multi-user (when you have a group video conference call) – something that costs extra on Skype.
- **FaceTime** Apple's own video chat app comes preinstalled and can be found on Macs as well. The video quality is high but may take more bandwidth.

How to manage your mobile phone so it doesn't cost you a fortune

Warning: if you get email on your mobile phone or are used to surfing or updating social media, and you don't turn off the data roaming function while abroad, you can get slapped with high international fees worth hundreds or even thousands of dollars.

14

Benefits of changing your mobile habits

The easiest and cheapest workaround to traveling internationally with your mobile device is changing your habits. First, shop around for a service that offers as good as possible global phone deals (just in case you do need to use it in an emergency), then keep your phone in airplane mode (or at least turn off data roaming). In airplane mode, you can still use downloaded digital guidebooks and other useful apps that don't require a web connection (see p.291). If you're keeping the same phone number you've had before and don't want a bunch of expensive "I'm on the road" explanations for friends who forgot you were away, just leave a voice recording that you're traveling and that people should email you instead of leaving a message.

Keep the phone's data off during the day, then turn on wi-fi when you get to a hostel or free wi-fi hotspot and download/upload what you need there. Then don't forget to turn it off again. (You can find several free wi-fi finder apps for iPhone and Android phones in their respective app stores.)

Benefits of a local SIM

If you have an unlocked phone (or can get your provider to unlock it for you), you can take advantage of local SIM cards. If you're in one country for a few days or more and want to do some on-the-move surfing/calling, you can buy a local SIM card (you can fill it up as needed) – these local cards are always cheaper than a global SIM. If you want to keep your main cell number for emergencies, you might just pick up a cheap extra phone for these local calls/surfing. Some SIM cards offer special deals for calling internationally and some have better surfing – just check with a local mobile shop for a deal that best suits your needs.

Benefits of a MiFi device

If your phone is locked in with a specific provider or you'd just rather keep your main phone number for emergencies, this could be a solid alternative to the SIM card. You even have the choice to rent or buy a MiFi device that will give you a hotspot for up to five devices. Some of these can be rented or bought before leaving, but will likely cost you more

(15$/£9 and up per day) and are therefore only realistic options for much shorter trips. With MiFi, you can use VoIP for your regular calls and then use your phone for basic online communication.

Benefits of a global SIM

The global prepaid SIM card option isn't all that cheap, but is likely far better than using your current plan while traveling. It works cheaper in certain countries and is aimed more at sending/receiving SMS and receiving phone calls. Data roaming is still crazy expensive. Here are a few options to compare (remember: prices can change at any time, so please look at the websites for up-to-the-minute rates):

14

- **WorldSim** (ⓦwww.worldsim.com) Plans with SIM from $60–150/ £38–95. Free incoming calls in 90+ countries, $0.50–2.50 per minute in others; data roaming is off-the-charts expensive.
- **Sim Card Global** (ⓦwww.simcardglobal.com) $73/£46 SIM option includes $25 credit; $250/£158 SIM option includes $250 credit. Free incoming SMS globally and free incoming calls in 65 countries, the rest are 10 cents–$4 per minute for incoming calls, $0.5–4 per minute for in-country calls and $0.5–3 per minute for calls to the USA). Surfing/email is possible, but they say rates aren't available yet and they are trying to bring down costs.
- **One Sim Card** (ⓦwww.onesimcard.com) Cheapest outgoing calls ($0.60–2) but uses callback service. You dial a number, get a call back, then dial. Free incoming SMS globally, free incoming calls in 135 counties – unless they are using one of the local numbers you set up, which adds $0.20. Plans are $30–37. Seems to work best on jailbroken iPhones.

More tips to minimize mobile costs

- **Use SMS-to-email** One such service is ⓦwww.ipipi.com. With pre-loaded funds, you can send texts to your friends' email addresses for 10 cents/6p a piece. For your friends to email-to-SMS you back, they have to fill in their message on the ipipi.com site.
- **Use offline maps and other apps** iPhone users can try Skobbler's ForeverMap app. Android users can pre-download Google maps within a 10-mile radius (enable the "Download map area" feature via the Labs tab in the Google Maps app). In fact, we have a list of other great offline apps (p.291) you may want to have with you.
- **Compress your data** Onavo (ⓦwww.onavo.com) offers this service as an app. It will at least help minimize the data you are sending.

Are those special international mobile phone service budget plans a good option?

There are crop of companies that offer "amazing deals" for international calling. They may be cheaper than your current service plan, but they aren't nearly as cheap as just using VoIP when you find wi-fi hotspots or a cheap internet connection. Check the websites of the major providers in your area to see what special deals they may have around the time of your departure.

Speak with your service provider about any **global data roaming deals** they may have. Often these are prepaid arrangements, but you maybe be able to top them up online as you go.

14

How to stay connected when you're off the grid

If you're planning to be in the middle of nowhere on your own for a while and want to be able to call in the cavalry, or if you're on a guided trip and you want to be able to update your social media continually, you'll probably want one of the following palm-sized gadgets:

- **Spot Satellite GPS Messenger** You can send out an SOS to local emergency services, or send "HELP" or "I'M OK" to a preset list of contacts. You can also make a custom message that goes out to your contact list as well. All messages include your current coordinates. Rugged, good for check-ins and emergencies. Cost: $119/£75 plus $99/£62 a year.
- **Delorme inReach** This two-way GPS communicator pairs with your Android or iPhone via its Earthmate app and allows you to send SOS beacons and text messages, lets people follow your every move on a map and even posts messages on Facebook/Twitter. Better for sending personal messages, social media. Cost: $250/£176 for the device and $10/£6 per month to stay linked up.

Try the lost art of snail mail

Sadly, letter writing has dried up. There's still nothing quite as nice as receiving an actual letter from abroad: the stamps, the smell and knowing it had to travel around the planet to get to you. The proliferation of email simply makes the occasional postcard or letter all the more special. It's easy to forget this while you're on the road hopping from one internet café to the next, but it's worth the effort and is likely to strengthen friendships and ensure you'll be getting mail from your traveling friends in years to come.

14

The trick to sending packages as cheaply as possible

Depending on the place, sending a package can take anywhere from two minutes to two hours. There are a few tricks you can use to simplify the process, but they all revolve around the same concept: scout out the **sending requirements** before you try to mail (or buy) something. In some countries, there are special postal boxes you can buy that will speed up the shipping process. More often there are package weight limits in various price categories. (It's a drag to show up with your carefully wrapped package, only to learn you're 20 grams over a price cut-off, which will cost you an additional $15/£9.) Sometimes you can get good bargains within a lower weight range, so if you divide up a larger package into two or three smaller ones you can actually save money.

Before you start wrapping (or shopping), swing by the post office and find out about the rates and any wrapping requirements. In some developing lands you may need string, cloth, forms and a wax seal, but bear in mind that you may end up having to open packages for inspection. Consult your guidebook for local tips.

Surface mail – the slowest, cheapest way to send packages

Surface mail is fairly reliable, cheap and slower than a snail with a hangover. It's perfect for sending home items you realize you no longer (or never did) need: inexpensive souvenirs, worn-out clothing you simply couldn't part with, and so on. Just about the time you've forgotten you sent it, it'll arrive, prodded and shaken by countless customs officers, like a gift from the heavens.

Registered mail and major couriers

If you're sending anything of value, such as jewelery you purchased or a filled diary, it's worth spending the extra money for registered mail to make sure it arrives. If the local mail

---

Over-communication

I spent my first thirty minutes in Asia standing outside an internet café waiting for my friends to finish writing to people back home about the trip over. Even in remote areas, net access was cheap and easy to find, making it a painless way to stay connected to home... and with the nearest familiar place an ocean away, feeling connected became something I found myself wanting more and more.

From internet cafés in northern Thailand, I was moderating roommate disputes, checking sports scores and typing out relationship advice to friends back home more often than I did when I lived there. Pretty soon I was less focused on my adventures in Asia than I was on finding a high-speed connection. And I wasn't alone. Internet connectivity has become a common addiction on the travel trail.

Eventually, I learned to check once a week, limit myself to one good mass email a month, and cheerfully neglect the day-to-day stuff, which gave me enough distance to experience the culture I came for. No one back home seemed to mind. When you're living in villages and sleeping on trains, nobody expects you to be plugged in 24/7.

Jonathon Werve
Traveler and researcher

service has an especially shoddy track record, go straight for a private delivery company such as DHL or FedEx.

How to pick up mailed packages

If you're organized enough to plan an itinerary, it's a good idea to send yourself bulky gear you'll need later in your trip. The old school method was to address it "Poste Restante, Central Post Office" or send it to an American Express office. With shoddy Poste Restante service and few AmEx offices, a better route is to figure out when you'll be passing through a town. Book a night in a hotel and write them to say you'll have a package arriving just before you get there and ask if they would please take care of it before you arrive; tell them you will compensate them for the service. If you're using a private delivery firm (DHL, Fed Ex etc), you can let them know when you want the package delivered.

How to get your mail forwarded

You may just want to switch as many bills as possible to online payments and then ignore your mail. If there are mailings you don't want to miss, check with your national mail carrier to see if your post can be forwarded for free or for an additional charge. The **Royal Mail** (⊛www.royalmail .com) charges £15.50 for one month for an address in the UK (£52.05 for six months and £78.10 for a year). For £29.40, it will hold your mail for up to two months. **Canada Post** (⊛www.canadapost.ca) offers international redirection for C$69 for three months and C$23 per month thereafter. Holding mail services cost C$15 for the first ten business days and C$7.50 per additional week. In **Australia** (⊛www.auspost.com.au), a year of forwarded mail to the Asia/Pacific region costs A$393, A$200 for six months, A$107 for three months, and A$41 for one month. (Prices for forwarding to the rest of the world are A$550, A$278, A$146 and A$54 respectively.) Mail holding rates are A$12 for the first week and A$4.50 for each additional week. In the **USA** (⊛www.usps.com), they'll hold your mail for up to thirty days, but won't charge for it. **New Zealand Post** (⊛www.nzpost.co.nz) will redirect mail for two months for NZ$20, for four months for NZ$30, for six months for NZ$45 and for a full year for NZ$85. Holding mail costs NZ$5 per week for up to twelve weeks. Best, of course, is if you can have a friend or relative filter out the junk mail and send stuff on.

Security

Most of the world is peaceful, though this can be hard to tell from the media. Television coverage of riots, wars, terrorist incidents, volcano eruptions, hurricanes and famines may keep you up to date with unfolding world affairs, but won't do much to awaken your wanderlust. Nor will it convey an accurate picture of the level of danger abroad. Cancun's bar bombing made front-page news in 2010. The city has moved on, but for many the images lingered and kept visitors away. In this chapter you'll find out where to get good information, how to determine if a place is actually dangerous, how to take precautions as you go, how to avoid some basic scams and what to do if things actually do go wrong. The best protection you can pack along, however, is a small survival guide (something like – warning for small promo – *The Rough Guide to Travel Survival*, available as an iPhone app), which has lists explaining exactly what to do when things go awry: you get separated from your tour group, are in the path of a hurricane, stumble into riots or need to survive for a few days or longer in the desert, jungle, mountains or at sea. It also lists all emergency numbers around the world and has global embassy hotlines for Brits, Americans, Canadians, New Zealanders and Australians.

How to figure out if the destination is safe

Start by getting the official position of state departments. But keep in mind, a country can be very safe but for a single, remote border dispute. The UK Foreign Office (Ⓦwww.fco.gov.uk) is more likely than the others to specify the volatile area when they place an entire country on warning; crosscheck with Canada's Consular Affairs Department (Ⓦwww.voyage.gc.ca), Australia's Department of Foreign Affairs (Ⓦwww.dfat.gov.au) or the US State Department (Ⓦtravel.state.gov). Pakistan, for instance, has a consular warning as a "terrorist-supporting nation", but travelers have been visiting safely for years. So a travel warning does not necessarily mean you should not go – it just means you should investigate a step further. That step is checking your guidebook. Nearly all the major guides have security information. They may very well explain that the country has had a strong travel advisory for years, yet remains extremely popular with travelers and is quite safe but for a single easily avoidable region. However, even recent editions get out of date quickly, especially when reporting political unrest, so check guidebook websites as well.

If you're still uncertain, surf the web for tourist bureaus. You can almost always find an email address of a specific office. The people who staff the counters meet travelers all day and generally have a good feel for travel conditions. Tell them your nationality, when you're planning to travel and roughly where you hope to go. Ask if there are any security issues you should be concerned about. Lastly, check with other travelers. Visit internet chat sites to hear directly from travelers who've been there in recent weeks, or are still in the country: try Let's Go's Forum(Ⓦwww.letsgo .com); or Lonely Planet's Thorn Tree (Ⓦthorntree.lonelyplanet.com).

What to do if the political climate changes

If the political conditions take a turn for the worse, you probably won't want to stick around to check out the mass riots, no matter how exciting it may seem. And if you're American, you probably don't want to go to the US embassy either (often a prime target, so they shut their doors when the going gets rough). The Australian embassy, Canadian embassy, New Zealand embassy, UK embassy and others should be fine – even for American citizens. The other option is to **get out of town** immediately (it's rarely a country wide riot). If you hadn't picked up some discreet local clothes yet, this would be the right time. Keep an eye on the local news, and head to an internet café if necessary to find English updates.

How to avoid being robbed

The basic trick here is to blend in, keep out of areas where you're likely to become a target, stay alert, carry your gear discreetly and provide yourself with a quick exit when you need one.

Start by removing all jewelery (if necessary covering a wedding ring with a band-aid or tape). Wear a cheap digital watch or no watch at all. Keep your camera concealed (not in a case that says "Nikon"). Then you'll want to wear clothing that blends in, the more discreet (think earth tones) the better. A little tip: safari pants with zip-off legs and a photo-journalist vest are generally not what the locals are wearing.

It's a bit like outrunning a bear... you don't have to be faster than the bear, just faster than the other people around you. Show that you don't have much to steal – or that you have less than other potential targets. With just a backpack and no carry-on bag, you have both your hands free and can remain mobile for a quick getaway, so robbing you looks like more of a challenge. The small padlocks and wire mesh pack-covers will do little to protect your pack, but they will draw attention to the value of its contents. Plastic rice bags are easy to find, dirt cheap, decrease the perceived value of the pack's contents and make great rain covers. It takes five or ten seconds more to access your pack's interior, but it can make you less of a target. Cut two slits for your shoulder straps, then sew or use duct tape to fasten the rice bag around your pack.

If you're traveling with a partner, make sure one person isn't carrying all the cash and valuables. And at ATMs, have one stand back a bit to guard against someone who might grab and dash.

And remember: put nothing (you can't afford to lose) in the overhead compartment on overnight trains. Your pack is your pillow (or at least spoon with it).

15

Pack to prevent theft

Don't keep your money and passport in a handbag or daypack, or even in a wallet. **Use a secure travel pouch.** A waist pouch kept under the waistline of your trousers is quite effective, and similar pouches that hang around your neck (under the shirt) or fasten to your ankle are also available. Just make sure you don't access it in busy areas like train stations and markets. Walk over to a more discreet spot and, if you have a travel companion, stand between them and a wall so that your actions are hidden.

To protect your slightly-less-valuables, **wear your backpack on your front in crowded places** and don't use a backpack for a day bag. Because it's inconvenient to wear a backpack on your front all day for city exploration, **use a shoulder bag** and keep it tucked tighter under your arm in crowded places. Try to find a model with Velcro flaps, which are difficult to open without you noticing, or a double-entry system (eg a zip plus a clasp). "Bum bags" (waist packs) are thief magnets and are best avoided. If you must use a backpack as a daypack, make sure it's packed carefully (valuables at the bottom, away from the zippers).

And finally, **don't keep all your money in one place.** Stash some emergency funds in the secret compartment of a belt, or tape some (in a small plastic bag) to the inside of your backpack. Another trick is to **keep a decoy wallet in your pocket.** Empty your wallet except for $5–20, a non-essential ID and a few random photos or business cards.

Avoid dangerous urban areas

Often a hundred metres can be the difference between a completely safe street and a dangerous one. And these boundaries may change after dark. Ask your hotel clerk or tourist-office staff to mark the **dangerous areas** on your map (both day and night). No matter where you are, get in the habit of checking over your shoulder and across the street every now and then. Even in crowded markets, you can see if you're getting followed after a few turns. But be particularly aware after dark. Muggers can easily hide in doorways, so the closer you are to the street, the less chance they have to surprise you. If you spot one or more suspicious characters in a doorway up ahead, cross the street. Or **hop in a taxi** if you've got a bad feeling about the area. Trust your gut feeling and always keep enough change ready to pay for a short cab ride. For less than $1, you can quickly get yourself back to a safer area. When you're in an area you're not sure of, resist the temptation to pull out your map on a street corner. **Walk purposefully**, even if lost, and duck inside a coffee shop or store to study the map or ask directions.

Take a few extra precautions in bus and train terminals, where many pickpockets lurk. If you need to pretend you're a secret agent to stay alert and pull this off, so be it. One simple method is to walk around the perimeter of the station instead of crossing it so you can keep a wall on one side and your eyes on anyone approaching.

Also, get in the habit of avoiding the tables near doors or bordering sidewalks in cafés. A quick thief can grab your gear and run. Keep your bag under your table while you eat, with the strap around your leg. If you need to use the toilet, take your bag along. You can't expect someone else to guard your bag as closely as you do.

Accommodation safety

It's not just local thieves – travelers steal as well. Sad, but true. There's not much threat to your dirty laundry, but your valuables still need to be guarded. At night, **cameras** and suchlike are better left at the reception desk in a safe, in a hostel locker if provided, or behind the counter if there's someone keeping an eye on it. Some places also offer the reception safe to travelers who need a place to keep their passport pouch while at the beach – which is better than taking it along. Otherwise, **treat your passport pouch like your spleen**: sleep with it (or put it in your pillow case) and take it along when you shower – you can hang the pouch on the hook, just under your towel inside the shower stall.

Some hotels require your passport for a few hours to gather information. They should not require it any longer than that. Ask for it back as soon as they're done.

Getting out of a dodgy situation

I went to Lebanon in 1984, as a tourist, in the middle of the civil war. I especially wanted to see the ancient cities of Sidon and Tyre. But the Israeli army was occupying the southern third of Lebanon. The only way into that part of the country was through a checkpoint in the Chouf mountains at a little village called Betar. When I got there I found about a thousand Lebanese, mostly women, children and old people, trying to get through the checkpoint to join their families in the south. It was 90°. There was no food, no shelter, no toilet. Little boys with plastic jugs were selling water by the paper cupful. The checkpoint was not actually manned by the Israelis but by Christian Lebanese from the South Lebanon Army. The Lebanese civilians were all yelling at them, and they were yelling back. I asked someone "How do I get through?" and the person just pointed at the milling, furious crowd and said, "That is the line."

I was wearing a coat and tie. Everyone was looking at me as if I were a CIA agent or something so I decided to go with it. I pulled out my blue passport and waved it over my head and shouted, "American. American, American, coming through!" To my complete surprise the crowd parted and the South Lebanon Army stepped aside. I walked into Israeli-occupied territory.

I had no idea what to do next. Then I realized that, on a hilltop about fifty yards away, there was an Israeli gun emplacement. A .50 calibre machine gun was pointed at my chest. The Israeli soldier behind the machine gun made a "come here" motion. I had to walk up the hill. The machine gun was trained on me the whole time. I was thinking, "Wait a minute. My tax dollars paid for that machine gun. That is my machine gun." But of course I didn't say so.

I asked the Israelis if anyone spoke English. The company commander certainly did. He was from Santa Barbara and had gone to UCLA. He said, "What the f– are you doing here?"

I said, "I'm on vacation."

And he began to laugh. He said, "Actually, I'm a reservist, and as a matter of fact this is my vacation. Have a good time." And he let me through. I walked away from the Israeli military positions and found a taxi cab. I told the cab driver, "I want to go to the ruins."

The cab driver stared at me. "Lebanon", he said, "is all ruins."

P.J. O'Rourke,
Author, *Eat the Rich*, *Holidays in Hell*, *Give War a Chance* and others

15

What to do if you have everything stolen

Fortunately, this is not as much of a hassle as it used to be. You could very well have everything you need – credit cards, passport and cash – in one to ten days. But act immediately to get the process started. Your first job is to **file a police report**. Go to the nearest police station nearest to where the robbery occurred, report the robbery and ask for a numbered copy of the police report. Presenting this at your embassy will speed up the issuing of a new passport. You will be waiting a while at the police station for the forms to be processed, so use this time to make phone calls. Have someone look online to find reverse-charge numbers. Start with a call to your **travel insurance company** (assuming you have one). Most good insurers accept charges and keep you on the line while they cancel your credit cards and have new ones issued. Otherwise, you'll have to cancel them yourself by phone or email. If your insurance or credit-card provider doesn't supply emergency cash, Western Union (UK ☏0800 833 833; USA ☏1800 325-6000) can assist, if you have someone at the other end put money in. It

15

can even provide this service online (ⓦwww.westernunion.com). Expect to pay a fee of four to eight percent, depending on location. Its "Money in Minutes" scheme charges $40/£25 to send $1000/£630 from New York to Belarus. To Canada it's $79/£50. If you don't have ID, you can make arrangements to pick up the money with a code word.

Put a stop on your mobile phone if you've had it stolen. Then call your embassy, tell them what happened and that you'll be on your way over as soon as you get the report. Ask for an appointment or a specific name you can request at the gate. Make sure you have a few passport photos before you show up. If you don't have copies of your documents or haven't emailed them to yourself – you can keep renewing the email so it stays in your mailbox, but do not label it "Visa card" or "Passport number" or include any of that info within the email – or haven't left a back-up disc with a trusted friend or relative and you don't have any ID, find a fellow citizen who has their passport and ask them to come with you to the embassy and vouch for you. The embassy can help make arrangements for your friends and family to fax or email photos to help confirm your identity.

Fighting back

It was dusk. I was walking back to my rented room in a house on the outskirts of Dharamsala, India – the Dalai Lama's home in exile – with an armful of mangos and basmati rice and dahl [lentils]. I had just been to the market. I noticed there was a man following me. When I turned around again, he was gone. The next time I heard him he was behind me. He didn't attack me from behind. It seemed he just wanted to make conversation. He started by asking if I wanted a *beedie* (hand-rolled cigarette), then he wanted to know if he could carry my bags. I said no to both. I was nervous. But he was also nervous. And short. He just came up to my shoulder. We chitchatted a few moments, then I said *"namaste"* and turned down the path to my house. Just then he threw both his arms around me in a bear hug. I dropped my groceries and shoved him. He fell down. I yelled *"Jaow, joaw!"* (Go away!) and ran down the path. He didn't try to follow.

Sara Hare, intrepid traveler

How to avoid sexual harassment

Most harassers get information direct to their libidos via their eyeballs, so let's start with appearance. Dress conservatively. Even if your clothes aren't racy by your own standards, they might (coupled with the general loose image many Westerners have) send out the wrong signals. Shorts, short skirts and tight-fitting clothes are likely to denote you as promiscuous. While you're at it, pick up a cheap, simple ring. You'll need a story to go with it – something about your husband coming to meet you in a day or two.

That should take care of much of the harassment, but count on some rude remarks, catcalls and pinches anyway. Do your best to ignore them and keep walking. Or, alternatively, react with clarity and confidence and tell them you don't like it. If you get followed, head into a nearby busy shop and tell the owner.

> Check out this vital info on hitchhiking safely (see box, p.143).

If you're alone and see a crowded or well-lit area in sight, consider running (note: make sure you have shoes that allow you to run). If the harasser chases or grabs you, **scream for help**. This is, in fact, how most women escape rape. Pleading and stalling are not very effective. Kick in the knees or privates and don't think twice about jabbing him in the eyes. Feel free to use any objects nearby to aid your fight: pen, car antenna, rock or camera.

How to avoid scams

15

The best trick, really, is to learn some of the most common scams. Con artists are hatching new plans all the time, but they tend to be slightly mutated versions of the ones you'll read about here. Keep your guard up, but not too high. Not all locals are out to scam you. Many of their gestures, although odd, are genuine acts of hospitality that you wouldn't be likely to experience at home. You'll have to trust your instincts.

Border-crossing scam

You become an unknowing drug mule when a seemingly innocent person asks you for the small favor of helping deliver a package, carry a suitcase, or push a buggy across a border.
How to beat it: never, never, never carry anything over a border for anyone, even if it's just a postage stamp for a nun in a wheelchair.

Credit-card scam

A store owner takes your credit card to a back room to swipe it, then swipes it again for another price. You sign one, then he forges your signature on the other.
How to beat it: keep a close eye on your credit card and ask the person to run it through the machine in front of you. Take a business card from the shop when you make any purchase so you can better alert the credit-card company in case you later learn you were robbed.

Hotel pay scam

Okay, this isn't really a scam, but it can result in a rip-off. You pay up front for your hostel accommodation, then when you check out you don't have proof of payment and the new person at the desk doesn't believe that you already paid, so you get charged again.
How to beat it: if you pay in advance, get a written receipt and keep it.

Spill/bird shit scam

Someone "accidentally" spills something on you (or bird shit lands on you); nearby helpful locals start cleaning it off and rob you in the process. Variation: small children thrust cardboard or newspapers in front of you while their mates pick your pockets, or someone thrusts a baby at you which you practically have to catch, or someone tries to teach you a football move.

How to beat it: keep a firm grasp on your belongings and walk off immediately.

Scooter scam

You rent a scooter/motorbike, park it, and someone from the rental agency with an extra set of keys shows up and "steals" it leaving you to foot the bill for an entire scooter.

How to beat it: bring your own lock (or buy a cheap one at your first stop) and make sure you're not followed when at out-of-the-way locations.

15

Repair scam

You rent a car/scooter/motorbike. It's almost guaranteed to break down. The rental agency helps you get it to a garage where they can hit you with hyper-inflated repair fees. Or they suddenly notice small damage that as there before and want you to cover it.

How to beat it: Take several photos of the vehicle before you leave, making sure to get close-ups of any scratches… and do this together with the person who is renting out the vehicle to you.

Scratch card scam

A local offers you a free scratch card. You accept and start scratching and – big surprise – you win. Just need to follow him to collect your prize. Often this is well out of the way and what you get is splitting the tiny "prize" of the local bringing you to some store or a long timeshare sales pitch. It's not so much about robbing you… just wasting a lot of your time.

How to beat it: say no to free scratch cards or anything that involves a journey of more than a minute.

"Drug-buy" scam

A dealer approaches to sell you a small amount of drugs in a very discreet location (like the bathroom of your hostel). He then tips off his buddy the police officer, who demands a fee for not taking you to prison.

How to beat it: obviously, the best way is not buying drugs. If you absolutely must, make sure other travelers have bought from the person previously.

Exchange scam

You get a good price on moneychanging from an unofficial street dealer. He counts out the money with painstaking slowness and finds – in a show of false honesty – that it comes up a few notes short. So he adds a few new notes on top. However, while he's adding the new notes, he's discreetly pulling off even more from the bottom. Before you have a chance to double-check (not that you would, as you've just watched the world's slowest count), he's off.

How to beat it: avoid unofficial moneychangers, have the person put the money in your hand as they count it and always re-count (even at official booths where employees have been known to try to skim a little off the top from time to time).

Fake police scam

15

A kid comes up and asks for change for a small banknote. Not long after (most likely in a city park or on a quiet road), a man approaches, flashes a badge quickly and tells you he's a police officer. He explains that the note you just received from the boy was counterfeit and that he needs to take it back to headquarters and you will be fined for your involvement. At this point, just as you are starting to wonder if it's real, a large muscular "colleague" arrives and pressures you to pay up.

How to beat it: take a good long look at the badge and tell him that, although he is certainly a genuine officer, there are many impersonators and that, according to their own tourist ministry, you're suppose to make all such spot payments at police headquarters, and you'll be happy to follow him there on foot. Under no circumstances should you get into their "unmarked police car".

Fake travel agent scam

You buy a ticket from a travel agency you found on the web or on a direct mailing. The ticket never arrives and when you try to call you find the place has gone out of business.

How to beat it: make sure you're signing up with an accredited agency. In Australia, check with the Australian Federation of Travel Agents (Ⓦwww .afta.com.au); in Canada, the Association of Canadian Travel Agencies (Ⓦwww.acta.ca); in the UK, the Travel Association (Ⓦwww.abta.com); and in the USA, the American Society of Travel Agents (Ⓦwww.asta.org). And pay with a credit card so you can stop payment if necessary.

Free transport scam

You're met at the train or bus station by a tout who is offering free transport back to his hostel. You follow him onto a city tram and notice that it's not free – he just didn't pay the fare.

How to beat it: ask how you'll be getting to the hotel. If it's by public transport, make sure the tout is willing to cover your fare.

Claims scam

A merchant gives you a "great deal" on some uncut gems that he says you can resell back home for several times the price. He even offers to throw in the postage and help you mail them. You watch him mail the parcel at the post office but the gems never make it to you back home, or they arrive but turn out to be worthless glass.

How to beat it: there are great gem deals, but knowing how to find them takes a professional eye and knowledge of world markets. Don't get involved unless you know exactly what you're doing. If you decide to mail gems, do it yourself, and don't be surprised if customs officials extract a fee on the way into your country before allowing you to claim them.

Pay-it-later scam

Your taxi driver tells you not to worry about the price, or the meter, that you'll work it out later. Then, on reaching your destination, they sting you for many times the actual fare.

How to beat it: always agree on a price before getting in the taxi, or make sure the meter is on. If it's too late, do your best to bargain, try to attract the attention of a nearby policeman and take down the driver's ID number and name so you can report him. Tour guides have been known to practice this technique as well.

Taxi-dash scam

You've paid your taxi and the driver leaves before you can get your bag out of the trunk.

How to beat it: leave the door open or don't pay until you've got your bag.

Help from your embassy or consulate

If you think of your government's **embassies**, **consulates** and **high commissions** as a safety net, you're liable to slip through one of the holes. They can't do much if you've been arrested for violating local laws, and they won't help send you home or give you a place to sleep if you run out of money. But they can help you in the event of a lost or stolen passport. They can also provide contact information during emergencies; give you the latest travel advice; allow you to register your travel plans if you're heading into treacherous areas (remember to check back in); and assist with overseas marriage and birth documents. And most of them make excellent cocktails, should you manage to attend one of their functions, so consider swinging by if you're in the neighborhood during a national holiday.

Health

There's no need to place your health under a microscope when you travel. The things you should concern yourself with are actually quite basic: get your pre-trip health details in order before you leave (including all the necessary immunizations); take some fundamental precautions while you're on the road; keep an eye out for some specific symptoms; and get yourself to a doctor if you encounter any of them. Despite the tales you may have heard, many of the common illnesses are avoidable or easily curable with some of the basic information you'll find in this chapter. If you want more details, there's always *The Rough Guide to Travel Health*.

Where medications are listed in this section, you'll only find the generic medical name. These are known by various commercial names in different countries. Simply check the label or consult your pharmacist or doctor.

16

If you do get sick

Here's the basic approach: with high fever, loose stools or vomiting – anything very painful or unusual – get to a **doctor** and have blood and/or stool tests conducted. It's generally quick and cheap and far better than trying to wait it out. With a quick diagnosis and the right medicine, you may be feeling fine within a day or so.

This is also a great time to check into a decent hotel with a private toilet and phone. You owe it to yourself and your fellow travelers. Hostel dormitories are not meant as recovering wards (beyond temporary alcohol-related afflictions). When you check in, tell the desk clerk that you're not feeling well and see if they have a doctor who can pay you a visit. You can always ring for an ambulance or taxi if things take a turn for the worse.

If things seem serious, don't take chances. Get yourself to a hospital and contact your family and travel insurance company. If you're in a remote area, get to a major city immediately.

Fixing your pre-departure medical details

Far too many travelers neglect basic pre-trip medical arrangements and suffer needlessly as a consequence. It's not a bad idea to get a check-up before leaving, especially if something has been troubling you a bit. Don't make the common mistake of putting this off till the last minute. A month or two before departure is a more sensible time to schedule an appointment. If the doctor finds something during the check-up and wants you to come back for a second consultation, your next-day flight is buggered. Besides, you'll want to get your check-up before you start the vaccinations. Some vaccinations should not be given if you have so much as a cold, or if you're taking other medications. Make sure to ask for a copy of your clean bill of health to take along (this may require an additional fee if an official certificate is required), so you don't have to pay for one again if you end up working on a kibbutz or volunteering for an organization that requires one.

Schedule a visit to the dentist as well. It would be a serious setback to get a gnawing tooth problem while you're in a country not known for dentistry.

Make sure you have enough contacts and fluid to keep you going (you can always send some lenses ahead as well). Glasses are important backups even if you never wear them at home: you may find yourself in dusty environments where contacts don't function well. If you're trying to decide between two frames for your glasses, take the most durable, even if they're not the most flattering. Make sure you bring along a copy of your prescription and your optician's telephone number in case you need emergency replacements on the road or ordered from home.

You should carry the following **items**:

- Your name, address and phone number
- Emergency contact's name, address and phone number
- List of immunizations
- List of allergies
- List of any chronic health problems
- Family doctor's contact information
- Name of health-insurance and travel-insurance provider with phone number and policy number
- List of current medications, plus copies of prescriptions with pharmacy name and phone number
- Prescription for glasses or contact lenses

16

For information on the vaccinations required in each region, see the "Regional profiles" section (see pp.213–288).

Which vaccinations do you need?

This part is surprisingly easy. Simply visit the **Centers for Disease Control and Prevention's (CDC's) website** (Ⓦ www.cdc.gov) and select the places you're visiting. The website has the latest information and will tell you exactly which immunizations to get. Then call around to make sure you get a good price. A full course of shots might set you back $250/£151. If your country has a national health plan, a number of the shots (eg hepatitis A and polio) may fall under that policy and can be received free from your GP.

Confirm the information you get from the CDC with the doctor or clinic administering the shots, and be sure to inform them of any medical conditions (including allergies) and medications (including the pill) you're taking. Also, explain where you'll be staying and how long you'll be there. Even in a malarial region, for example, if you're staying in the main cities where mosquitoes are rare, there's often little risk. These risk-free oases are not usually mentioned on the CDC website, so be sure to ask.

Some vaccinations require **several shots** over months to take effect, so don't leave it until the last minute, or even the last month. If you're getting several jabs, bear in mind that you may not be able to get them all on the same day. They may conflict with one another, require more than one course or take time to become effective. However, if you're not entirely sure where you're headed, you don't need to get every needle in the cabinet. Vaccinations are all available on the road. Just make sure the clinic looks clean and professionally run and uses sterile needles. If you have the option, try to get this taken care of in more developed countries. And it's not necessarily a good idea to get "the works" just in case – lots of drugs can take their toll on your body and you increase your chances that you'll experience some side effects.

Get a **vaccination record card** and keep it with your passport while traveling. You may need to demonstrate that you've received certain immunizations to enter a country or obtain a visa. And, let's face it, with all these mega-syllabic names, it's hard to remember what you got, what you didn't want to get but got anyway, and what you were going to get but decided not to get at the last moment.

Cholera

How you get it: This serious diarrheal disease is caused by consumption of contaminated water or shellfish. When there's an outbreak (it seems

16

to follow natural disasters and wars), avoid the area if possible and be very careful what you eat (no ice, only bottled water, no raw food unless peeled).

Symptoms: Profuse vomiting of clear fluid and diarrhea (10–20 liters per day!), which may help convey the risk of fatal dehydration.

Vaccination: Until recently, there was no good vaccination for cholera. The old injectable vaccine was ineffective since it didn't provide resistance against the majority of cholera strains. Two new oral vaccines (Dukoral and Mutacol) have proven more effective (85–90 percent immunity within six months of taking the vaccination, decreasing to 62 percent immunity after three years) and should be considered if you're heading to areas where the disease is prevalent. Because the vaccine is new, it may not be available everywhere. Avoid antibiotics and malaria prophylaxis with Proguanil one week before and one week after cholera vaccine.

Full course: Two oral doses.

Booster: One week apart (killed vaccine) or one single oral dose (live vaccine).

Time before effective immunity: One week after the last dose.

Hepatitis A

How you get it: Contaminated food, water and people pass this bowel blaster along.

Symptoms: Flu-like with diarrhea, possibly itchy skin and jaundice.

Vaccination: There are two basic types: one (Havrix) lasts a year, but takes a month to become effective, while the other (gamma globulin) lasts two to six months, but is effective immediately. In the UK there is a combination Hep A and Hep B vaccination that will also give you ten years of immunity and is available free from GPs. But you'll need half a year to get all three shots taken care of. Or ask your doctor about Hepatyrix, fifteen-year protection against Hep A and typhoid in one stab.

Time before effective immunity: One month to one minute depending on which type.

Getting Hep A

On one of my trips to Ho Chi Minh City for a Hong Kong art magazine job I landed, a large group of Vietnamese artists organized a large dinner in honour of my visit. They asked me if I liked seafood… which of course I do. They ordered, among other things, an enormous platter of oysters. I had never seen oysters so big – they were larger than my hand – and this purplish color I didn't even know existed on the color spectrum. And they were delicious. However, the next day when I traveled to Hanoi, I felt like I was going to die. I mean I literally thought I was going to die in Hanoi. I was freezing cold, running a fever, puking and expulsing out the other end as well. I tried a few local concoctions, but they didn't do much. Then two Swedish expats recommended a doctor at their embassy. I managed to get over to the Swedish Embassy in a haze, shivering on my cycle. Once I took the prescribed antibiotics, I was fine in half a day.

Amy Schrier
Editor, *Blue Magazine*

16

Hepatitis B

How you get it: It's transmitted like AIDS (most commonly via unprotected sex, foreign medical treatment and tattooing) but it's about a hundred times more infectious.

Symptoms: Often a "silent disease" that doesn't necessarily make you feel sick, but symptoms can be flu-like, with loss of appetite, fatigue, cramps and vomiting. In extreme cases skin and eyes may be jaundiced.

Vaccination: Three jabs over six months. For those who have put it off to the last second, it's possible to get three jabs in three weeks with an additional booster, but it's slightly less effective. As previously noted, in the UK there's a combination Hep A and Hep B jab that will also give you ten years of immunity, available free from GPs.

Time before effective immunity: One month after third dose.

Japanese encephalitis

How you get it: Mosquitoes carry this brain-attacking virus around rural parts of Asia.

Symptoms: A stiff neck and intolerance to light. It's both life-threatening and neurologically damaging.

Vaccination: You'll need three shots over a month and the jabs should last you three years, but you may need an additional booster before then.

Time before effective immunity: Ten days after last dose.

16

Meningococcal meningitis

How you get it: Coughing and sneezing spread this much-feared disease in central Africa.

Symptoms: Most recognizable by a rash that starts as pinprick blood spots on ankles and armpits, buttocks or groin, and matures into purplish bruises that do not fade or disappear when pressed.

Vaccination: One dose with booster every three years.

Time before effective immunity: Two weeks.

Polio

How you get it: From contaminated food or water or (if you have a weak immune system) contact with those who are taking the vaccine.

Symptoms: Of those who do contract polio, 95 percent will show no symptoms and, despite its reputation, paralysis occurs in only 0.1 percent of cases. In five percent of cases, people experience flu-like symptoms.

Vaccination: If your parents were against the vaccination or your government was, now is the time to get your shots: a full three-dose course administered at monthly intervals. Otherwise, make sure you've had your lifetime booster.

Time before effective immunity: Two weeks after the second injection.

Rabies

How you get it: It's transmitted by animal bites, scratches and licks (mainly dogs).

Symptoms: Begins with loss of appetite, fatigue, headache and fever; then nervous-system damage appears with hyperactivity, hypersensitivity, hallucinations, seizures and paralysis.

Vaccination: Three doses over one month with a booster after two to three years.

Time before effective immunity: Two weeks after completed course.

Tetanus/Diphtheria

How you get it: Diphtheria is passed person to person quicker than an email chain letter. Tetanus spores enter the body through open wounds as small as a pinprick, and can be picked up through contact with dirt, manure and – the classic – rusty nails.

Symptoms: Typical diphtheria unpleasantness includes fever, chills and a sore throat. Eventually it can cause heart failure and paralysis. With tetanus, you won't get the symptoms for five to twenty days, but the one that should get your attention (and any doctor's attention) are spasms of the jaw muscle. Those will spread across your face and into your torso, and that's when things get really nasty. It is potentially fatal. And those who have it are highly infectious for ten days. Seek medical help if you suspect it: a quick throat swab can determine if you've been exposed.

Vaccination: Check your booster records, because you definitely want to make sure you're vaccinated against this bacterial illness. You need one after ten years.

Time before effective immunity: A few days.

16

Tuberculosis

How you get it: By breathing the same air as those who are infected by it. Sneezing, coughing, speaking, etc.

Symptoms: Cough that is worse in the morning, chest pain, blood in spit, night sweats, breathlessness.

Vaccination: One dose, no booster required. Not routinely recommended for travelers; to be considered for infants and health workers, as infection usually requires prolonged exposure to infected individuals in closed environment.

Time before effective immunity: Unknown.

Typhoid

How you get it: Areas with poor sanitation and poor health standards attract the most typhoid. This bacterial illness is picked up by ingesting contaminated food and water or by coming in contact with the faeces of an infected person.

Symptoms: High fever, increasing daily for the first week and accompanied by weakness, stomach ache, coughing and deafness. It's cured by antibiotics.

Vaccination: One dose (with booster every two years or oral every five years). Recommended, but not overwhelmingly effective (eighty percent).

Time before effective immunity: Two weeks.

Yellow fever

How you get it: Ticks, flies and mosquitoes carry this fatal viral infection primarily just north and south of the equator in Africa and South America.

Symptoms: High fever, vomiting and abdominal pain, which will abate on its own after a week. For fifteen percent of those infected, there will

---

Traveling with immune issues

This applies not just to those with AIDS/HIV, but post-chemo patients and many prescription-drug users. If you have special health considerations that render you **immuno-compromised**, keep in mind that the bacteria and bugs that affect all travelers may have a more profound effect on you. Developing countries in particular pose significant risks for exposure to opportunistic pathogens. Your consulate or the International Association for Medical Assistance to Travelers (🌐 www.iamat.org) can provide English-speaking physicians trained in Europe or North America.

16

Vaccinations

The CDC currently recommends that live-virus vaccines (except the measles vaccine) be avoided by people with immunodeficiency. "Killed vaccines" such as tetanus/diphtheria, hepatitis A, rabies and Japanese encephalitis are okay, and recommended for "healthy" HIV-infected travelers. However, the immune response to these vaccines might be reduced and is largely dependent on the degree of immunodeficiency. For more information, visit 🌐 www.cdc.gov.

Medications

Discussing an emergency plan with your doctor prior to departure is an excellent idea. The CDC advises all HIV-infected travelers heading to developing countries to bring an antimicrobial such as ciprofloxacin (500mg twice a day for 3–7 days) for empirical therapy for diarrhea, although alternatives (such as TMP-SMX) should be discussed with a doctor. If the diarrhea does not respond to this treatment, there is blood in the stools, fever and shaking chills, or dehydration, get to a doctor.

Going through customs

If you are carrying a full array of HIV drugs, or just the virus, be aware that some countries have vague restrictions preventing those with "communicable diseases" from entering. So, faced with an inquisitive customs officer holding your medications, you might offer other half-truths about the things you're suffering from first (such as liver/heart/kidney problems), and delay mentioning HIV. If you're staying for an extended period to work or study, you may face a serological screen in many countries. Check out the unofficial list compiled by the US State Department on 🌐 www.travel.state.gov.

be a lull of a day or two after this first wave before it kicks in again with more severity, with symptoms including jaundice.

Vaccination: Full course one dose, should be avoided if you have severe egg allergy or compromised immunity; requires special consideration if you also wish to take Hep A immunoglobin.

Booster: After ten years.

Time before effective immunity: Ten days.

What you can't get vaccinated against

These are the ones you'll have to watch out for, and may just get anyway. Some maladies are more common than others and some more severe, so read through the descriptions to get acquainted with the symptoms and dangers you may face.

AIDS

You've probably heard an earful about this already. What you may not know is that in some areas of the world it affects over seventy percent of the sexually active population, and it's continuing to spread at a staggering rate. Among prostitutes and drug users, you may find even higher proportions with HIV. It's a pandemic poised to wipe out enormous portions of Asia and Africa, and you as well if you don't take precautions. Consider this before you have unprotected sex or share a needle.

Allergies

If you experience allergies at home, you'll probably encounter them on the road. Watery eyes, runny nose, sneezing… you know how it goes. Pack an antihistamine (chlorpheniramine or loratadine) to relieve the symptoms. If these don't help, visit a doctor.

Altitude sickness

This is more dangerous than most people believe, especially when others who don't have it are egging you on to keep going up. If your head feels like it's about to implode or you're dizzier than a wino trapped on a Ferris wheel, that's your cue to head down the mountain. Continuing up (or even staying where you are) can be fatal. It doesn't mean making a beeline for the base camp (unless it has reached a critical stage). Usually, the symptoms will abate after just a little descent, and you may even be able to continue once your body has adjusted at its own pace.

Fitness is only one factor: you could be a competitive triathlete and still get altitude sickness. Other factors are your rate of ascent, elevation, and how well your body happens to cope with it. At higher elevations, do what climbers do: don't go up more than 300m per day once over

3000m and hike up past the camping spot to acclimatize, then return and sleep. Follow a careful acclimatization plan and, most important, listen to your body. If you want to try a short cut, the drugs Acetazolamide and Nifedipine have been known to help combat the sickness. As have coca leaves (chewed or in tea), which are readily available in parts of South America.

Bed bugs

These are not merely bedtime-story myths. They're out there, typically in the cheapest hotels, and they do bite. The bites aren't serious, but they seriously itch. And you'd have a better chance of spotting Elvis than some of these critters. Your best defence is a good sleep-sheet: make sure it's big enough to cover the pillow as well. A tight weave should keep most of them out. The bites look like two or three little red dots in a row. Treat with hydrocortisone or antihistamine cream and refrain from scratching.

Bilharzia

Truly exceptional spellers may know it as schistosomiasis. These micro-worms live in freshwater lakes, canals and still sections of rivers: the larvae penetrate your skin, head to your liver and lay eggs. You could get the disease by drinking the affected water or eating food washed in it. Without going into the full graphic detail of what these critters do in your body for one to ten weeks before you notice the symptoms (such as blood in the urine), you should know it is also called the disease of the "menstruating males". It mainly affects the urinary tract and gut and can be treated quickly once diagnosed. It's best prevented by avoiding stagnant water, especially in Africa (perhaps most commonly in the Nile, Lake Malawi and Madagascar). It can also be found in Southeast Asia, South America and the Middle East. If you suddenly realize you may have exposed yourself, hop out of the water and rub yourself thoroughly and abrasively with your towel in case your skin hasn't been fully penetrated yet.

16

Cold sores

Don't kiss people with lip sores or blisters. Don't share water bottles with them either. There's really nothing cold about these sores, which are actually herpes picked up by oral contact (fellatio and cunnilingus included), and are most likely triggered by too much direct sunlight. Once you've got the virus, you've got it for life. To keep the sores at bay, keep your lips well glossed while exposed to the sun and apply aciclovir cream as soon as you feel the tingling sensation coming on (apply five times a day for five days; it may require prescription). Once the sore breaks open, the medicine won't help.

Will eating the "wrong" food give you the shits?

There's a **travel-health** mantra that if you can't peel it, boil it or cook it – forget it. Only one problem with this approach: in practice, over the long haul, it's basically worthless. You can't travel around the world in a hermetically sealed suit, and you're going to be taking some culinary chances at some point whether you want to or not. Some rules of thumb are wise, like avoiding shell fish in developing countries especially when you are not right on the coast (it's very temperature sensitive while shipping and storing). But other things can be deceiving, such as "fine dining" being safer – depends what you get… a four-star buffet can actually be more risky than a small, cheap restaurant because so many people handle the food for a buffet and all it takes is one non-hand-washing offender to contaminate one dish. There's simply too much **interesting food** out there to painstakingly investigate its biological properties three to five times a day. Rely instead on your own good judgment. Are the locals drinking the water? Are there bugs visibly swimming in it? Does the meat look like it has been cooked long enough? Is it dead? Are flies laying eggs in the fruit? Is the street vendor jamming his hand down his pants between servings? On a long trip, you're almost certain to entertain an occasional spell of travelers' diarrhea. Accept it and don't worry about it. The cure is usually quick and painless (see opposite) and your stomach will most likely get stronger as you travel.

Constipation

Because people are so worried about travelers' diarrhea, they usually forget about this one, which can be nearly as uncomfortable and troublesome. Travelers who are new to the trail are especially susceptible. They take one look at a squat toilet (or one of its unsanitary hybrid cousins) and suddenly they don't have to go any more. A few days later the mental block has become an intestinal block. This can be solved by simply carrying some laxatives (senna) and not waiting too long to use them. Better yet, force yourself to go when you have the urge, no matter what the loo looks like. And a little diet altering won't hurt: more fruit, bran and fluids.

Dehydration

The trick here is to drink before you get thirsty. For a full day of walking in a hot climate, you should be drinking about four litres of water. In dry or high-altitude terrain, you'll need even more, and wind masks the amount you're sweating away. Once you're dehydrated, you'll experience a dry mouth, dark urine, headache and, in extreme cases, fainting. Find some shade, take it easy and mix your water with a rehydration mix so you get your salt balance back, and if fluid can't be taken orally, get to a hospital for an IV.

Dengue fever

Here's another great reason to use mosquito repellent. This viral infection is not typically fatal, but it hurts like hell for about a week and there's

> Check out our list of basic medical supplies you don't want to leave home without (p.128).

little you can do to treat it. It's most commonly found in subtropical Asia, the Caribbean, Central America, South America, Australia and the Pacific islands. These white and black mozzies tend to bite during mornings and late afternoons in shaded areas of the body. Once bitten, the incubation period is about a week. Then you're looking at high fever, joint pain and backache. As if that's not enough, you'll probably see an itchy rash develop on your torso and experience bleeding from your nose, mouth and rectum. You want to be in a hospital for this one, preferably in your own country, as weeks of depression may set in after the severe symptoms are gone.

Diarrhea

It has plenty of colorful monikers, from Delhi Belly to Montezuma's Revenge. Whatever you call it, you'll probably get diarrhea at some point, no matter what precautions you take. The good news is that it's most often extremely treatable and the troublesome symptoms can be cured in less than a day. This may be the single most valuable thing you get out of this book, and if it saves you a week of traumatic toilet dashes, the book will have paid for itself a few times over. You'll meet numerous travelers suffering from dysentery for days or weeks. The typical reason is that they're trying to ride it out. You want to do exactly the opposite.

The moment you start to "go liquid", drink a bottle of water mixed with a packet of rehydration mix that you should be carrying in your first-aid kit. And keep drinking. The biggest danger with dysentery is dehydration. Then, the next time you have to go, bring a little plastic container with you and put a stool sample in it. Either take the sample to a nearby clinic yourself or have a trusted fellow traveler do it for you. With a quick look under the microscope, a doctor will most often be able to identify the cause. If so, they'll write a prescription on the spot, which will likely include the pharmaceutical equivalent of a cork. Less than a day after you start taking the medicine, you may feel back to normal, or at least better. While recovering, stick to simple, unspiced foods like rice for a day or two just in case. Little tip: carry an anti-diarrhea pill (loperamide) in your passport pouch. If you're on a long bus ride or walking around town, it will come in handy more than you can imagine. Women travelers should be aware that diarrhea can reduce the effectiveness of the Pill.

Hepatitis C

Less common than Hep A and Hep B (but with no vaccination) this one requires contact with contaminated blood. Which means stay alert

16

where any needles are concerned. Always make sure they're opened from new sterile packages while you watch. If you get taken to a hospital in an emergency, ask for screened blood.

Hiking blisters

Nepal's Annapurna circuit is not the ideal place to try out a new pair of hiking boots. If you buy or rent some, give yourself at least a day or two for your feet to adjust (especially with new boots). For serious treks, make sure you bring a skin-like blister cover (such as Compeed), sport tape, petroleum jelly or a silicon spray, and scissors (with antiseptic to sterilize) to cut the dead skin from blisters. Puncturing used to be the way to go; now professionals recommend cutting away all the dead skin so the tender skin underneath gets exposed to the air and hardens and heals quicker. Tape should be applied in advance to trouble spots, then sprayed with silicon. Two pairs of socks are advisable, neither of them cotton. Polypropylene or silk (next to the skin) and wool make an excellent combination.

Hookworm

16

This one doesn't sound like much fun. And it's not. These tiny worms live in the soil, so avoiding them is simply a matter of wearing shoes. Otherwise, they enter the foot, make their way to the lungs and lymph glands, and eventually end up in your gut, where they will probably cause you to be nauseous and generate loose stools, and you'll experience general abdominal discomfort while they go about laying eggs. A simple stool sample can identify the worms. Once identified, it's easily treatable and there are a number of drugs suitable for the task, including mebendazole. Iron tablets should also be used if anaemia is detected.

Hypothermia

A lot of people say they're freezing, but hypothermia is the real thing. The medical definition of loss of core body temperature starts at 35ºC. The condition begins with uncontrolled shivering and is followed by slurred speech and mental confusion and, eventually, stiff muscles, abnormal heart rhythms, coma and death. Sufferers should be gradually warmed (not rubbed, as that can cause the skin to come off) and given sugary drinks (not a St Bernard-style shot of whisky). Alcohol, exhaustion and illness all weaken the body's ability to keep warm.

Infected cuts and scrapes

In tropical environments, cuts don't tend to heal like they do back home. They're easily infected and can actually grow in size. Use antiseptic ointment or powder and try to expose the cut to direct sunlight so it has a chance to dry out. Visit a doctor if you're unable to stop the growth of the wound on your own.

Jet lag

An alarming number of travelers don't take simple steps to combat jet lag, and are then plagued by fatigue for days (typically, one day per time zone), starting off their trip on the wrong foot. If you can sleep on the plane and sleep well your first night in the new time zone, you're not going to experience much jet lag, if any. Sleeping on the plane, if you're not naturally gifted at the art, can be achieved with an over-the-counter or prescribed sleeping pill.

According to all studies, drinking alcohol is exactly the wrong approach. The next worst thing you can do is stay up late watching a movie and eating. There's no reason to eat dinner at 11pm, then watch a movie at midnight simply because you're at 30,000 feet. Eat a meal in the airport, pop the sleeping pill when the plane leaves the ground and drink plenty of water when you wake up. Then refrain from naps until bedtime and take another sleeping pill if you wake up during that first night or pop a Melatonin tablet (only available over the counter in the USA) before bed to ensure you sleep a little longer. If you can't resist the meal on the plane, order a special meal (doesn't cost extra, and chances are it will be as good or better than the standard fare) and you'll get served first so you can get to sleep sooner.

16

Malaria

The reason this mosquito-carried disease gets so much press is that there's no simple fire-and-forget jab in your arm that will prevent it.

You have to take pills regularly. And which pills you take (or don't) depends on where you're headed, how long you'll be there and how your body reacts to them. Lariam (mefloquine) is the most common, and gets the most complaints for side effects (typically panic attacks and nightmares), though your chances of getting these are minimal. Chloroquine, once the all-purpose prophylaxis, is now only used in places where mosquitoes haven't become resistant to it. And doxycycline is typically used just in places where chloroquine and mefloquine no longer work. Therefore, it's vital that your information is up to the minute. For long-term care, the chloroquine/proguanil combo can be used for up to five years provided you get frequent eye checks. Otherwise, Lariam is prescribed for up to a year. None of the prophylaxes are one hundred percent effective. And because of the side effects, some travelers (especially those living or traveling in a malaria region for a long time) opt not to take them.

Symptoms typically take one or two weeks to develop and involve three stages: cold shivering and shaking; high fever with rapid heartbeat; then sweating and a drop in temperature. You can also expect coughs, joint pains, vomiting and general unpleasantness. If you suspect it after one day (even if you're feeling okay the next day) get to a clinic, even if you're already back in your home country. You can come down with malaria up to two years after your trip. A simple blood test will reveal if you have the disease, and the treatment is best administered under medical supervision. In an emergency, if you're unable to get to a doctor for days, you strongly suspect malaria and you have mefloquine, take 20–25mg per kilo of bodyweight as a single dose.

Anti-malarials aren't enough when the bugs are out in force. Use mosquito spray or lotion containing DEET at all times. At night or when you're relaxing in your room, burn mosquito coils (easy to find anywhere there's a risk of malaria). And use mosquito nets when provided, or buy your own if you arrive and find they are not regularly provided in that area.

In the end, how you prevent malaria is up to you. What's important is that you make an informed decision. If you do decide to take prophylaxes, make sure you also use mosquito repellent and take other precautions. And remember, the drugs take time to become effective (one week for choloroquine/proguanil, two weeks for mefloquine, two days for doxycycline), so you will need to start taking them before you arrive in an at-risk area.

Getting malaria

I was a ball of twine and the malaria was a great big frisky cat. It started batting me around about a month after I got home from a protracted stay in the swamps of Indonesia. One hot summer day, I started shivering intensely, shaking so badly that my teeth rattled. Later, I found that the convulsive first stage of an attack usually lasted about two hours. It was exhausting. After shaking myself asleep, or at least half conscious, I'd doze while a fever soared. White-hot dreams bloomed and detonated somewhere in the back of my mind. The final two-hour segment of my typical malarial attack involved sweating. I could go through two or more thick terry-cloth robes and leave them sopping. At first the disease hit me every week. Gradually, it subsided to once a month, then once a year. I haven't had an attack in over three years, and while it is very exotic to be treated for malaria in Montana, where I live, the price of celebrity, in this case, is intolerable. And I don't miss it, not even a little bit.

Tim Cahill
Author, *Hold the Enlightenment: More Travel, Less Bliss*

Motion sickness

It's not serious, but it's bad enough to ruin a day or two of your trip. On a winding bus ride, try to sit near the front (although not at the front, where you'd be the first one through the windscreen) and next to a window or air vent. Make sure you get out to stretch your legs whenever the bus stops. On a boat, stay above deck and try looking at the horizon. Take deep, relaxing breaths or simply try to stay busy. And, in any event, have a motion sickness pill or a skin patch (hyoscine or scopolamin) ready just in case. It takes at least an hour before the effects of these pills are noticeable, so you may need to take them in advance of boarding.

Rashes

You'll be encountering plants, fruits and bugs that your skin has never been exposed to before. It's common for travelers to experience a host of new body art. Try applying topical antihistamine, calamine lotion or steroid creams (hydrocortisone) to the area. If it persists, visit a local doctor.

Snake, spider and scorpion bites

If you're not a professional snake handler, don't approach snakes. Follow this essential strategy and they'll almost certainly leave you alone: if you are walking in tall grass in a known snake area, wear high, protective boots and carry a leafy branch to keep any you meet at bay. If the snake that bites you is dead, bring it along for identification so the proper antivenin can be administered if necessary. Otherwise, try to get a good description without getting bitten again. Do not suck on the bite, apply ice or make an incision. Place a firm bandage (not tight) on the torso side of the bite, just a few inches above the wound. Wash and apply cold compresses if possible. Otherwise, just keep the limb immobilized while you get to a medical facility. Antivenin is the only direct treatment, and it should be administered only by a medical professional.

16

Spiders are less likely to be dangerous, but apply the same guidelines for bites from unknown and poisonous ones (black widow, redback and brown recluse). Scorpions are found in arid regions; the treatment is the same as with spider and snake bites. To help with the severe pain, administer painkillers and antihistamines liberally while en route to a medical facility. And get in the habit of shaking out shoes and sleeping bags before using.

STDs

Just because you're choosy about who you have sex with doesn't mean they were. And once is all it takes to wake up with syphilis, gonorrhea, chlamydia, chancroid, trichomoniasis or herpes. Symptoms include: unusual vaginal or penile discharge, pain when passing urine, itching, abnormal vaginal bleeding and genital ulceration. There's only one thing to do if you get any of these: go to a doctor. With chlamydia it's a little trickier. Most women don't notice they have it. Some never find out. Some only learn of it at an infertility clinic while trying to find out why they can't get pregnant.

Sunburn

Sunscreen keeps you from burning, but it also keeps people out in the sun longer with more UV exposure, and the long-term effects of this are yet to be determined. Still, burning is bad. So get in the habit of using SPF 25 sunblock and reapplying it frequently. Note that some medications reduce your skin's ability to fend off the sun's powerful rays: ciprofloxacin, tetracycline-group antibiotics, sulphonylurea (for diabetes) and thiazide (for high blood pressure).

Vaginal thrush

Warm climates, tight nylon underwear and increased sexual activity are among the factors that lead to higher incidence of thrush on the travel circuit. Men who carry the fungus do not usually show any signs of it. For women, soreness, discomfort during sex, pain while urinating and passing a white or yellowish discharge are among the symptoms. It's easily treated by an antifungal preparation that should be easy to find in most countries, but you may want to carry one just in case. In a jam, try applying regular plain yoghurt (at night with a pad for three to seven days) and altering your diet briefly: no sugars, bread, beer, wine, mushrooms, Vegemite or other yeast-containing or yeast-encouraging foods.

16

Special considerations

For many, conquering street food, crowded bus rides, aggressive market touts and squat toilets without lighting are challenge enough. But there are some groups who must also cope with a number of issues, from a medical condition to sexual-preference discrimination. This chapter focuses on the concerns these travelers face and offers a few tips that will hopefully smooth out their journeys.

Discounts for seniors

There's enough material to write an entire book on senior discounts. In fact, several people have. One of the things that seems to get better with age is the amount of rebates available. Seniors might get anything up to fifty percent off museums and other sites, and local transport. Look for notices at ticket windows, check your guidebook, and – most importantly – **get into the habit of asking**.

Budget flights

On airlines, the magic discount age is usually 60 or 62. Rates vary, but you can typically get ten percent off "the lowest published fare". And that's exactly how you should phrase it when you ring a travel agent. Not only that, but you're often allowed to bring someone of any age along at the same rate. Several struggling airlines have cut back senior discounts lately, but it never hurts to ask, since they are still available, if only for select destinations or times.

17

Budget accommodation for seniors

There's **nothing that says you have to be a youth to stay in a youth hostel**. In fact, in many of the calmer hostels, senior travelers far outnumber the youths. International Youth Hostel cards (Ⓦwww.hihostels.com) cost just $18/£11 if you've turned 55. There are also special organizations, such as the non-profit-making Elderhostel (Ⓦwww.elderhostel.org), which runs trips around the world for those aged 55 and older. For roughly $130/£82 a day, you get a room, food, educational classes on a variety of subjects and the chance to meet plenty of like-minded, interesting people. Seniors may also be offered ten to fifty percent off normal rates at major hotels (and some minor ones) across Europe. Always enquire when you book.

Travel agents

- **CARP** Ⓦwww.50plus.com/travel. Not the most inviting acronym, CARP is a travel agency for Canadians over 50.
- **50+ Expeditions** Ⓦwww.50plusexpeditions.com. Adventure trips for the over-50s who are ready to hit the road.
- **Senior Women's Travel** Ⓦwww.poshnosh.com. They ditch the "old lady" image, with adventures for the 50-plus set with a thirst for active travel.
- **Wired Seniors** Ⓦwww.wiredseniors.com. Under "Travel guide", they have lists of "senior friendly" travel agents and hotels.

Senior gear and gadgets

There are a number of specialty items available these days, from lightweight canes that can be collapsed and stored in hand luggage to inflatable back-support rests, that can make a mild trip comfortable and rough ride tolerable. Browse senior-travel websites such as Ⓦwww.seniorsuperstores.com for ideas.

Considerations for travelers with special health conditions

When planning your itinerary, think about the medical facilities of the country you're visiting. The Netherlands, for example, will have a more modern health-care system than Pakistan. But also keep in mind that many developing countries have at least one world-class, English-speaking hospital, which often supports the large number of expatriates working there. Guidebooks list such facilities where available. You can also find them online before leaving home at Ⓦhttp://hospitals.webometrics.info.

17

Consider also the **temperature** of the places you're headed. Even if you've experienced such sweltering heat before, it can be another thing entirely if you're out walking in it most of the day or staying in places without air conditioning.

If you're concerned about pre-existing ailments, discuss them with your doctor before leaving and keep an eye out for symptoms. Depending on your case, it may not be a bad idea to bring a copy of your medical file along, or at least the relevant pages. Check your medical insurance for travel coverage and supplement it with any special travel insurance you may need (see p.109).

How to bring your meds

Bring your prescriptions if you want to get refills, but ask your doctor to include the generic name since some brand-name prescriptions are not available abroad. Keep medicines in their original labelled container to avoid problems at customs, and have the prescriptions handy. (The label on the plastic bottle is not always enough, especially if you're transporting stronger pain medications which may require a special permit obtained at the pharmacy.) If you need medication refilled in an emergency, a good travel-insurance plan will assist. And keep the phone number of your doctor and pharmacist with you for backup.

Travelers with disabilities

Don't let anyone tell you that you can't travel around the world. There's going to be more planning than an able-bodied person may face, more hassles and you may have to give up more independence than you'd prefer at times, but if you're prepared to accept this, the rewards are immeasurable.

No matter how much planning you manage, you'll still need to prepare yourself for the unexpected: unstable or missing handrails, faulty ramps, narrow passages, and assigned assistants with little training and even less enthusiasm. Greet them with good humor and look for ways to solve the problems on the spot.

Prepping for the trip

Much depends on your degree of disability, and no one has a better grasp of that than you. Stay in control of your options. An activity that may not be a possibility for someone else could be fine for you. But if a travel agent or tour operator hears that you're disabled first, they may decide which things are appropriate for you and present you with an inappropriately limited selection. In other words, look into things you'd like to do, then ask questions to find out if you can be accommodated. Don't simply look for "activities for the disabled".

17

Before you begin your trip, whether you're joining a tour or doing it alone, think about ways to enhance the experience of travel and remove potential obstacles. For example, a deaf traveler may wish to purchase a railpass in advance to avoid the hassle of buying individual tickets at a station counter, and a sight-impaired traveler might pick up souvenir replicas of the famous monuments once they arrive to help get a better understanding of the structures they're standing in front of. Consider activities that can be done on an equal level. For those in a wheelchair, a cultural show, garden and recommended restaurant should take minimal preparation beyond confirming that they can accommodate you where stairs and doorways are concerned.

Brace for what you'll face

In most wealthy countries you'll find a mix of excellent accessibility and complete lack of it. However, there should be a fundamental infrastructure in place and your requests for assistance will often find an experienced ear. In less developed countries, expect to find little infrastructure, if any at all. What you may experience, however, is a refreshing abundance of helpers with an enlightened indifference towards disability. On the other hand, you may feel like a novelty act at times. If so, keep in mind that you may be one of the first independent disabled people that locals have seen.

Several of the world's great attractions are still **inaccessible**, or at least extremely difficult for manoeuvring, such as the tombs in Egypt's Valley of the Kings, the ruins of Machu Picchu or the trail down the Grand Canyon. At such times, you'll either have to content yourself with a view from afar, have a traveling companion videotape it and replay it on the spot, or find alternative activities.

It's not impossible to find accessible toilets, but it may not be easy. Make sure there's one at your hotel. Access-Able (ⓦwww.access-able.com) has a database of hotels that accommodate those with disabilities, plus listings of places to rent special medical equipment and get it repaired.

Help for transport with disabilities

Whether you're traveling around the world or around a vast country, flying may just be the best of a sorry selection of choices. The toilets may be impossibly narrow and the seats painfully uncomfortable, but at least it's generally the quickest option. Always call the airline well in advance if you need any special assistance. If you have a wheelchair, let them know which kind and be prepared for a transfer to a special aisle-sized chair. At All Go Here (ⓦwww.allgohere.com), there's a list of airlines that cater to those with disabilities, with detailed information on what they do.

On the ground, taxis are usually the most convenient, most comfortable option for getting around a city, but also the most expensive. In some enlightened cities (Vancouver and Wellington for example), there are local discounts for the disabled. More buses and trains are equipped for wheelchairs, but taking the time to find out where they're available will be a big budget saver. With assistance, the transport possibilities are as limitless as your imagination. Take a ride on a dhow, rickshaw, hydrofoil or elephant.

If it still seems a bit overwhelming, or you'd like some help just getting started, there are a number of organizations set up for this very purpose:

- **Accessible Journeys** Ⓦ www.disabilitytravel.com.
- **Can Be Done Travel Agency** Ⓦ www.canbedone.co.uk.
- **Flying Wheels Travel** Ⓦ www.flyingwheelstravel.com.
- **Moss Rehab Hospital** Ⓦ www.mossresourcenet.org.
- **The Society for Accessible Travel and Hospitality** Ⓦ www.sath.org.
- **Travel Eyes** Ⓦ www.traveleyes-international.com. Pairs sighted travelers (who get a discount) with blind travelers.
- **Trips Inc. Special Adventures** Ⓦ www.tripsinc.com.

Considerations for gay travelers

It's certainly much easier for gay travelers than it was twenty years ago, but some parts of the world are far less enlightened than others. In Pakistan, for example, where it's normal for straight men to walk hand in hand down the street, homosexuality is still illegal and punishable by flogging and imprisonment. In India, though, laws criminalizing gay sex have recently been overturned by one court at least.

Public displays of affection – know the local laws

Unless you're trying to make an active protest against an intolerant government, learn the social and legal conditions before you display any behaviour that may land you in a foreign jail – and this applies to heterosexual behavior as well. If you're not sure, simply avoid displays of public affection. Take special care in Muslim countries, where "inappropriate" or revealing clothing may cause problems. A good place to start is the International Lesbian and Gay Association's database on treatment of gays and the legal status around the world (Ⓦ www.ilga.org).

Tips for vegetarian travelers

It's one thing to organize your diet at home, and quite another to maintain your eating habits in places where being vegetarian is a little-known

17

concept. But it can be done. And it doesn't even have to be stressful. Naturally, your chosen destinations are a major factor. Knowing where to look is another. A number of supermarkets, restaurants, resorts and B&Bs around the world cater specifically to vegetarians.

In terms of where to go, India is a vegetarian's paradise. So is Thailand. Delicious non-meat Italian pastas and pizzas can easily be found. Japan's food is lovely, especially for fish-eating "vegetarians". New Zealand, Spain and Spanish-speaking South America, on the other hand, don't offer quite the selection. In general, the ethnic vegetarian food you eat at home will be offered in wider variety in the country it comes from. There are a few excellent online resources that will lead you to a vegetarian restaurant anywhere in the world: Ⓦwww.vegetarianguides.co.uk, Ⓦwww.vegguide .org, Ⓦwww.vegdining.com and Ⓦwww.happycow.net.

The International Vegetarian Union (Ⓦwww.ivu.org) lists foreign phrases to help you explain, or at least state your dietary requirements. Most good guidebooks suggest vegetarian alternatives where available.

18

Documenting your trip

Just because you're traveling with your best friend, or an entire overland group, doesn't mean you're going to collectively remember everything. When you're going solo, it's even harder. A journal, camera, tape recorder, video camera, color pencils, paints and watercolors (or a tablet with a sketching app) are the most common tools for recording your journey and its impact on you. Taking along all these is overkill, but keeping some record of your trip is an excellent idea.

Why you should keep a journal?

Many travelers say this is the single best thing they brought on their trip. Or **buy it when you arrive**: hand-pressed paper from France, India or elsewhere gets you off to a good start. If you've kept a journal before, you'll be bringing one anyway. If not, this is the perfect time to start. It's not easy to process, or even remember all the places and people and stories. And simply putting your thoughts down on paper can have a soothing, therapeutic effect. It can be a friend when you're alone or provide structure for your day. If you have some artistic skill, spend a little more and get paper that will soak up your watercolors or hold ink better.

For those who are prepared to share all their innermost thoughts with the world, perhaps a travel blog, Twitter or Facebook provide a better option.

Thinking of setting up a travel blog? Here are your best options

The following three template-based blogging tools are among the most popular and easy to use and will let you customize the site and add the widgets you want (maps, calendars etc). And they're free.

18

- **Wordpress** (Ⓦwww.wordpress.org). Most plug-ins, huge range of templates.
- **Blogger** (Ⓦwww.blogger.com). Best for multiple bloggers, easiest to get started.
- **Tumblr** (Ⓦwww.tumblr.com). Best for images and simplicity; has most artistic feel.

If you want to use a special travel-blog setup, here are a few popular (and free) online travel diary sites that let you post diary entries, photos and videos as you go. Plus they'll help you list out your itinerary and plot your trip on a map. They're all quite same-same-but-different. Take a look and see which seem to gel best with your taste:

- **TravelPod** (Ⓦwww.travelpod.com). One of the originals, now owned by TripAdvisor. You can upload via your mobile and even turn your trip into a printed book. Ads inserted into your content, which some may not appreciate, can be removed for an annual subscription ($40/£25).
- **Travel Blog** (Ⓦwww.travelblog.org). Bit simpler with less (but enough) features than TravelPod.
- **Travellerspoint** (Ⓦwww.travelerspoint.com). Flashier than Travel Blog, still as easy to use and blog entries feel more like your own independent site, less part of a network.

Have a look around. There is plenty of competition here, with new sites popping up you may like better.

The easiest way to take good travel photographs

Bringing along a camera is pretty obvious. Which kind – and how to use it – isn't. The temptation for many is to get a "good camera" – that is, one above their level of expertise. Or to not bring one because they like the one on the mobile phone… also a mistake (many stop taking pictures when the battery gets low or memory fills up). If you're a professional or exceptional amateur, bring what you need. Just be aware of the security risk of carrying valuable gear. Remove the brand names from the bags, try to select a case that doesn't look like a camera case, and minimize your lenses and accessories.

If you're not a pro, go for a relatively inexpensive digital pocket camera. Keep size in mind. The smaller it is, the easier it may be to get to it quickly or even keep in your hand a while. And that's going to help you catch those gone-in-a-heartbeat moments. Besides, if it's easy to carry and access, you'll probably use it more often and – here's one of the oldest photography tricks in the book – the more photos you take, the better your chances of getting something amazing.

If you're buying a new camera, consider skipping on the **zoom**. On pocket cameras, it jacks up the price, runs down the battery, brings down the quality and is not very powerful. If you take one to three steps forward, you'll get the same effect for free. Plus, if the moving zoom parts get so much as a grain of sand in them, kiss the camera goodbye for a month or two while it gets sent back to the manufacturer.

18

If you're using your phone as a back-up camera, you might consider getting a lens attachment set for it. There are now several, like the "Dot iPhone Panorama Lens" ($49/£32) or iPhone Telephoto Lens (8x zoom, $25). ⓦwww.photojojo.com sells specialty photo accessories for iPhone. Limited memory means backing up pictures can pose a few problems – check out this section for a few tips (p.119).

Five essential photography tips for pocket-camera/smartphone users

1. Don't worry so much about the postcard shots. Just buy the postcard. Those photographers used the best equipment, found the best vantage point and waited until the lighting was perfect. Nothing will put your friends and family back home asleep quicker than endless landscape shots.

2. Photograph things that show your life on the road. It takes some effort to remember to photograph them (doorways, weird meals, freaky buses,

When not to take photos

There's a reason it's called **taking a picture**: rarely is permission requested. It may be your camera, but it's their image or holy site and either of those trumps whatever you've got in your hand, even if you're holding a Nikon with a Swiss lens. The path to pictorial enlightenment involves respecting local bans on photography and asking all subjects for the right to snap their photo. Everything else – including the zoom-lens sniper approach – is nicking pictures. That sounds a bit dramatic, but for many, photography is their only interaction with locals, and it's a relationship largely based on selfishness and insensitivity (the author has been guilty of this as well at times). For some cultures, our swinging lenses can feel as intrusive as if someone walked up and took your picture while you were lying on the beach half-naked or stuffing your face at a restaurant. To get those great portraits you see on guidebook covers and in magazines, simply **ask permission**. Or go one better and try to initiate conversation. Make a few friends or even a small connection and it will add another dimension to the picture. Then, if you can, get an address and send them a copy. Giving photos has a much nicer ring than taking them.

18

Capturing the moment

In college I spent a year abroad in Southeast Asia. I didn't have a camera. At the time I believed that you shouldn't travel with a camera because you'd bring back pictures instead of experiences. I'm sad to say I probably pulled the idea from some Richard Bach novel. Now I carry a camera when I feel I've got the space, but I still try to avoid that stereotypical tourist thing: spending so much time choreographing pictures that you miss out on the place.

During that year without a camera I discovered I had a good memory for visual things. I could close my eyes and give myself a slide show. I recorded the stories that went with those slides in my journal: the Chinese guy in Laos who fed me fried bugs for dinner and wanted to marry his daughter; the Mekong whisky shared with three Danes on the train ride from Laos to Bangkok; the experience of watching captive orangutans repatriated to the wild in Sumatra. I still fill my journals with such encounters. A recent favorite is the Turkish submarine commander who showed me Gallipoli, the battleground where his grandfather died. Keeping a journal also gives you something to do when you're traveling solo. Eating alone can be especially depressing. But with a journal you feel like you're reporting, even conspiring. And it lets you focus on the little things in front of you. That's when I noticed that the cats in Thailand had broken tails. I've since heard they're broken intentionally – otherwise the felines would be too perfect to strive for Nirvana. I like a medium-sized journal with non-lined paper in case I want to doodle. I'm not particularly gifted artistically, but I want to draw if I'm in the mood. That's part of the beauty of a journal: it's more personal, more private. With pictures you often take them for other people. The journal is my trip, just for me.

John Hoult, radio producer

scary toilets, charismatic taxi drivers and so on). Also, resist the urge to photograph your travel companions posing. Catch them off guard and you'll get a more honest, interesting photo.

3. With scenery, and often even with people, try to compose the photo so there's something very close, something mid-range and something in the distance. If you want to photograph someone standing in front of a waterfall, for example, try positioning yourself just behind a texture-rich tree branch and allow it to appear in a third of the picture.

4. Think your picture as a grid of three by three, like tic-tac-toe. It often works well to position the center of your subject on one of those for crossings, instead of just placing the subject in center. When the subject is moving, you want to position it on the side so it appears to be moving towards the center of the photo, not off the frame.

5. Shoot when cloudy or try using a flash in daylight. Despite the fact that things seem brighter, midday sunlight actually flattens images and provides unappealing photos. For people, animals and objects, you want overcast skies or indirect light. A cloudy day is the perfect time to get great pictures. If you must shoot people in the middle of a sunny day, use your flash to eliminate unattractive shadows or (this may sound counterintuitive) have your subjects step into a shaded area. You can get some great silhouette shots by having the sun behind your subject, but unless you're intentionally trying to do this for visual effect, you'll do well not to shoot into a light source.

Recording sound

If the sounds of a place conjure stronger memories for you than photos, or if you'd prefer to dictate your journal, you can easily save them on your smartphone or bring along a small digital recorder (there are microphone attachments for iPhone that will help you collect ambient sounds better and others that will improve the sound of interviews). This can be a nice addition to any blog posting and help encourage your reader to close their eyes and try to imagine the scene.

Two basic tips for shooting video

Like photography, video has spawned stacks of books on method and technique. If you're going to shoot, here are two simple tips. The first is to hold the camera very **steady**, even if it's equipped with an electronic stabilizer. That may mean leaning against a tree or lamppost. If you're serious about getting good footage, however, bring a tripod. Nothing induces headaches like watching shaky footage. The second tip is to resist letting the camera follow your natural head or eye movement all the time. For example, allow someone to walk across the field of vision – entering on one side and disappearing on the other. This will make editing much easier once you return home.

Drawing and painting

Watercolors, color pencils and sketching charcoal are relatively cheap and

Carrying your gear

The biggest challenge with carrying camera equipment in any situation is to be constantly aware without being suspicious. The gear is valuable, but you have to remember that it's just gear and it's replaceable. For example, I'm often in remote places and find myself in the middle of a group of kids who want to see my camera – look through the lens, take a few pictures. Some photographers freak about that. My feeling is that some kid has never seen a camera, really wants to, and I'm not going to deprive them of that. I'll keep a hand on the strap, but let them play with it.

That doesn't mean I make it easy for professional thieves whose full-time job is trying to figure out what people have and how to get it. First, I try to be inconspicuous. Camera bags attract too much attention. I currently use a regular bike-messenger bag. I wear dark clothes and my camera is dark, so that works as camouflage while it's half tucked under my arm. Then I think about the picture before I take it. I don't compose my shots through the viewfinder, so I'm not keeping my camera visible for long.

This doesn't always work though. I was in the Central African Republic going through a crowded market. I was carrying my gear in this utility belt around my waist. I call it my batman belt. It's so close to the body, I can feel if anyone touches it. And it's not easy to cut through or open. Plus my shirt flops over it so it's not easy to see. Anyway, I thought I felt something. So I turned around and there was this guy holding my light meter. The reporter with me said that it looked like there was some kind of silent agreement between us. I just fixed his gaze. Then calmly removed the light meter from his hand.

Chris Anderson
Photojournalist, *New York Times Magazine, Magnum Photos*

18

> ### Mementos of your trip
>
> Most of the best are free and easy to carry. You might collect small, flat items that catch your eye and evoke a memory: concert and train tickets, a beer label, fortune-cookie prediction, even a sample of the abrasive toilet paper that once gave you some trouble. Scan them or cram them into your journal for safe transport.

18

extremely easy to transport. Even if you don't have much artistic skill, or much that you're aware of, this is an ideal time to give it a shot. It's a nice alternative to reading or writing when you're stuck somewhere for a long time. Which, invariably, you will be at some point. Pick up a "how-to" paint/draw book and learn as you go.

What to do with souvenirs you buy

Send them home! Few travelers need any help selecting souvenirs, but most seem to need some help carrying them. No matter how small, lightweight and space-saving the items may seem individually, the best thing you can do – unless you're at the tail end of your trip – is a big round of shopping when you get to a market you like, then **ship everything home the same day** (see p.167). Your glass turtle earrings, Dutch windmill decanter and fake Ray-Bans from Vietnam will have a much better chance of getting broken, stolen or lost under your care than that of a postal service. Naturally, there are several levels of security available (as well as private couriers) at a range of prices. Consider the reliability of the postal service (are you in Denmark or India?), the weight of the package and the value of what you're sending, before you ship. There's no magic formula, but it's not uncommon to pay more for postage than for the actual item enclosed. Keep that in mind when you're about to buy that set of traditional fire-walking rocks in Fiji.

Watch out for illegal souvenirs

Another thing to consider is the legality of exporting **antiques**. Just because a vendor in a market is willing to part with it doesn't mean you're allowed to bring it out of the country, so the authentic fifteenth-century porcelain spittoon you bargained for may not be getting off the plane with you when you land back home. Nor is it likely to arrive in the mail. If it looks old and valuable, consult your guidebook. You may need to get a certificate of authenticity from a museum. Shopping caution also applies to plants, seeds and items made from wild animals, which may be removed by customs officials. You won't be reimbursed for any of this, but you may get fined.

Returning home

t probably feels a bit premature to be thinking about coming back home already, but this information may affect your planning, so best that it's addressed now. Let's assume you've circumnavigated the planet. You've fended off wild animals in Africa, hitchhiked across Asia and blowgun-hunted with indigenous forest-dwellers in the Amazon. You've learned to eat rice with chopsticks, dhal with your fingers and meditate with monks. You have new friends on every landmass, a new global outlook and even a few new parasites. All you have left is to **return home**.

But here's where things can get problematic. With a comfortable bed and fresh set of clothes in sight, it's tempting to lower your guard. Instead, you're going to need to brace yourself for a potentially rough re-entry.

How to brace for re-entry shock

Many people coming home from a long trip experience a bigger shock on their return than when they first set foot abroad, and at a time when they're least prepared for it. The good news is there are a few simple things you can do to turn the experience into a smooth landing, and the most important of these is just **knowing what to expect**. The stages of re-entry mirror those of culture shock: honeymoon, crisis, recovery and readjustment.

The **honeymoon** is the initial exhilaration of returning home, and precisely what most are expecting: a warm welcome, familiar bed, inquisitive friends who are dying to hear your stories.

The surprise left-hook (or "**crisis**") is the reverse culture shock, which lasts until you acclimatize to your home surroundings and eventually return to your old self (with a bit more wisdom and experience).

The degree of the reverse culture shock you experience largely depends on how integrated you became into foreign cultures during your journey, and how different they are from your own. On returning, you may miss the regular and close social interaction you had with your foreign community and other travelers. You may find yourself revolted by the aggressive marketing campaigns you had previously learned to ignore. More likely, you may feel a distance has come between you and your friends and family because they can no longer relate to your "new" well-traveled persona – one that has grown and been shaped by your range of different experiences. Instead, they're treating you the same way and don't have the patience to hear the thirty hours of stories required to bring them up to speed. And if you're returning to a job, you may notice reduced responsibilities and little acknowledgement for your overseas accomplishments.

This is compounded by The Questions. If you've ever broken your leg and had to explain what happened to everyone you met for a month, you already have a good understanding of what it's like to be a human recording. But when you're trying to sum up a few months or a few years of life-changing experiences in one or two cute lines, it's even more frustrating. The Questions tend to be the same worldwide. They'll start with "How was the trip?", go on to "What was your favorite?", and quickly get to, "So what are you going to do now?"

Eventually you'll **recover** and **adjust** as you ease back into routines, accept your difference and apply your newfound approaches to various situations.

Making a re-entry game plan

Scuba diving and cultural immersion are similar in at least this one respect: a little decompression is a good idea. Before you return home, try to build in a little stop for **mental refuelling**. It needn't be a month of silence at a monastery: a beach will do fine. You just need a place with minimal stimulus. It can take a while to process the lifetime of experiences that you've just crammed into a ridiculously short period. And more important still, you need to begin to engage with the concept of returning home. You're going to have enough to worry about when you get back, so try to work out a game plan in advance: where you're going to stay, who you plan to visit and so on. So, if you do plan to stay at a beach, make sure it's a beach with a good internet connection.

Brace others for your arrival

The best single thing you can do in this respect is keep your friends and family up to speed during your trip with regular dispatches from the road… tweets, Facebook updates, email, travel blog. Your friends and family will have far more patience to read about your experiences in bite-sized chunks as you go than to listen to them all in one sitting when you get home.

19

Write a helpful last dispatch from the road

When you're just about to head home, take some time to sum up your trip in your last dispatch. Answer the questions they're likely to ask. List your favorite places, favorite experiences, craziest misadventure… things you expect you can spare yourself from having to answer one hundred times in person. Tell them what your plans are. Those around you will want to get that extra dose of info when they see you in person. Help them out. Give them something they can ask about. You might say, "I'll be carrying around a very small selection of photos I wasn't prepared to put online. For a beer, I'll be happy to show them to you."

Stay in touch with people you met

Stay in touch with the friends you made on your trip. It improves the chance you'll see them again, have a free place to stay (and a cultural guide) when you head abroad next time and gives you a free support network. Facebook makes this ridiculously easy.

19

Keep involved with the places

Join an organization that supports a place or cause you found on the road. Study that language you were dying to speak at the time but couldn't. Read fiction or non-fiction books on the subject. If you do eventually head back to any of these places, you'll be able to appreciate them on another level.

Seek out travelers in your area

There's probably a hostel in your area filled with Europeans (and Aussies and Kiwis and Americans and Canadians, if that's who you miss). Spending time with travelers, visiting students or an immigrant crowd can be just enough of a dose to remind you that you're sane after all.

Find patience

It's common to feel superior to those around you who haven't had such international experiences. Suddenly, their views may seem pedestrian and insular and you feel the continued need to "set them straight". Just remember: your own views may not be that popular, either. Time outside your own country tends to highlight its faults, and you may come off sounding like a born-again critic. Take heart. You will have enlightened perspectives, but don't expect others to come around easily.

Get busy

If you have the possibility to arrange your work/study schedule before returning, keep this in mind: a little down-time at home is wonderful, but too much can be self-defeating. Finding that right balance is up to you, but in general the less the better. One or two weeks is usually sufficient.

Revive the memories

If you need a quick fix, you might try escaping back into your travels for a brief tour. This is where a good scrapbook/pinterest board and well-kept journal come in handy (see p.201). Using your notes and images, it can often be helpful to write about your experiences more fully. Who knows? This may be the chance to release that budding travel writer within.

Treat your home city like a destination

Chances are you never fully embraced your town like those you visited during your travels. Hit those museums you never bothered to visit, try some new pubs, even stay in traveler accommodation for a night. Apply your spirit of exploration to your home turf and chances are you'll see it in a new light.

Start traveling again

If all else fails (except your finances), hit the road again. It doesn't have to be a long trip, or even an international one. Just taking some trains and buses, packing up your rucksack, sleeping in a few ratty hotels and meeting some other travelers can be enough.

19

First-Time
Around the World

Where to go

Africa

Africa is much less daunting than most travelers tend to think, and there are myriad sights, sounds and experiences to draw you to the continent. The Arab hospitality in the north can be overwhelming, the wildlife and landscapes of sub-Saharan Africa are unmissable, the music of West Africa is infectious and inspiring, and you'll be stunned by the continent's dramatic southern coast. In other words, there's a lot more to Africa than a bunch of wild animals stomping around outside your tent, although that can certainly be arranged.

Main attractions

● **Bazaars of Fes and Marrakesh** Morocco. You'll find 10,000 alleys to explore, with spice and handicraft vendors adding to the confusion, in streetscapes as surreal as an Escher painting. Open spaces brim with acrobats, snake charmers, storytellers and, at every turn, more interesting characters parading by than a Hollywood studio could cast with a limitless budget.

● **Cape Town** South Africa. You might expect something grand to happen where two oceans converge, and the tip of Africa does not disappoint. Cape Town is one of the most naturally stunning cities on the planet, with clouds regularly spilling over the kilometre-high Table Mountain like a candyfloss waterfall, white beaches strung along the rocky coast, and world-class vineyards maturing just a short bus ride away.

● **The Great Pyramids** Egypt. They're more than just the world's largest tombstones. The precision of their construction represents the highest level of science and craftsmanship and a remarkable understanding of astronomy.

And, what's more, they're really just a sample of what the ancient pharaohs left behind: a wealth of archeological treasures that stretch far down the banks of the Nile.

● **Maasai Mara** Kenya. The northern sister park of Tanzania's Serengeti, the Maasai Mara stretches for 3000 square kilometres and serves as the living room, kitchen and playground for elephants, lions, zebras, giraffes and other photogenic species. It's also the home of the Maasai, a tall and striking warrior people who still hunt on the grassy plains, though more recently many have been pushed into selling handicrafts and performing for video cameras.

● **Mount Kilimanjaro** Tanzania. Kili, as it's often called, is the storybook mountain silhouette you first learn to draw in primary school: the perfect heaven-scraping cone shape with a jagged snowline near the top. Whether you're climbing to the 5895-metre-high "mountain that glitters" (as the name means in Swahili) or simply having a picnic in its shade, the peak is mesmerizing. It's typically hiked in five or six days: good hiking gear, strong legs and pristine lungs make the task much

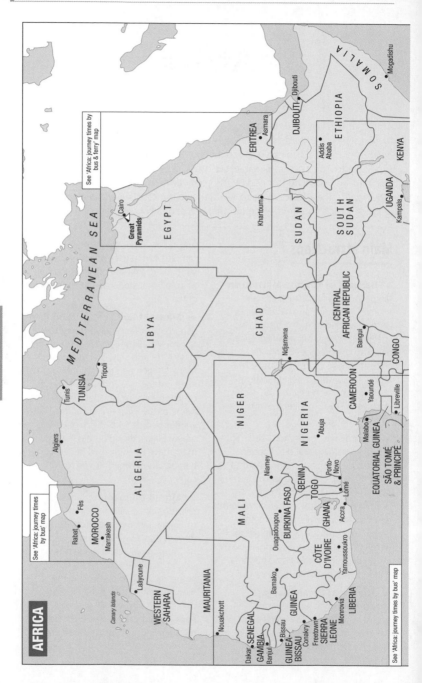

AFRICA

MEDITERRANEAN SEA

SOMALIA

Mogadishu

See 'Africa: journey times by bus & ferry' map

ERITREA
Asmara

DJIBOUTI· Djibouti

ETHIOPIA

Addis
Ababa

KENYA

UGANDA
Kampala

Cairo

Great
Pyramids

EGYPT

Khartoum

SUDAN

SOUTH
SUDAN

LIBYA

CHAD

Ndjamena

CENTRAL
AFRICAN REPUBLIC

Bangui

CONGO

Tripoli

CAMEROON

Yaoundé

Libreville

TUNISIA
Tunis

Algiers

NIGER

Niamey

NIGERIA

Abuja

Porto-
Novo

BENIN

Lomé

EQUATORIAL GUINEA

Malabo

SÃO TOMÉ
& PRINCIPE

See 'Africa: journey times by
bus' map

Fès

MOROCCO
Rabat

Marrakesh

ALGERIA

MALI

Ouagadougou

BURKINA FASO

TOGO

GHANA

Accra

CÔTE
D'IVOIRE

Yamoussoukro

Laâyoune

WESTERN
SAHARA

Canary Islands

MAURITANIA

Nouakchott

Bamako

Dakar
SENEGAL

GAMBIA
Banjul

GUINEA-
BISSAU
Bissau

Conakry

GUINEA

Freetown

SIERRA
LEONE

Monrovia

LIBERIA

See 'Africa: journey times by bus' map

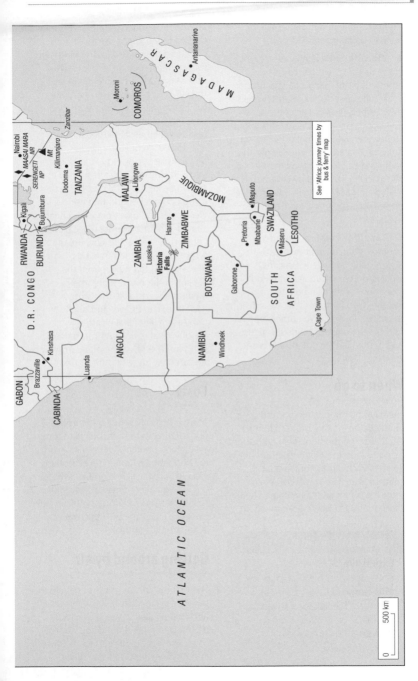

ATLANTIC OCEAN

GABON

CABINDA

Brazzaville

Kinshasa

D.R. CONGO

Luanda

ANGOLA

RWANDA
Kigali

BURUNDI
Bujumbura

Nairobi
MAASAI MARA
NR
Mt
Kilimanjaro
SERENGETI
NP

TANZANIA
Dodoma

Zanzibar

COMOROS
Moroni

MADAGASCAR
Antananarivo

MALAWI
Lilongwe

ZAMBIA
Lusaka

Victoria
Falls

ZIMBABWE
Harare

MOZAMBIQUE

Maputo

NAMIBIA
Windhoek

BOTSWANA
Gaborone

Pretoria
Mbabane
SWAZILAND
Maseru
LESOTHO

SOUTH
AFRICA

Cape Town

See Africa: journey times by
bus & ferry map

0   500 km

easier. Not to mention $800/£486 for permits, guiding and food.

● **Victoria Falls** Zimbabwe/Zambia. These days, Vic Falls has come to represent more than just a spectacular 1.7-kilometre-wide, 100-metre drop into the Zambezi River. It's an entire action-adventure park, with bungee-jumping, whitewater rafting, ultralite flying and horseback safaris. Not surprisingly, this is the largest crossroads on the African backpacker circuit. Keep in mind that from March to May the floodwaters kick up so much spray you can hardly see the falls.

● **Zanzibar** Tanzania. A former trading center, once populated with Phoenicians, Sumerians, Persians, Indians, Arabs, Portuguese and English. Stone Town, the main port, is an intricate web of streets that are a delight to get lost in. And, if you time your visit to avoid the crush of tourists, you just might. The beaches around the island are a big draw.

When to go

The daytime temperature in most of Africa doesn't vary more than ten degrees throughout the year (although it's not uncommon for it to drop twenty degrees each night). Your bigger concern is rainfall. In eastern Africa, there are "short" and "long" rains. The short ones (Oct–Nov) might mean an

afternoon thunderstorm that muddies the roads and keeps the roof hatch closed on the safari van. The long rains (March–May) may make the roads impassable. Most people prefer to travel to this eastern region in June to October, often trying to coincide with the Great Migration of over one million wildebeest, 300,000 gazelles and 150,000 zebras around July/August. Madagascar cyclones typically occur from November to March, and an eye should be kept on the weather reports if you do travel during that period. In western Africa, those put off by heat should aim for November/December. Otherwise, keep a lens cover ready for the dusty harmattan winds (Dec–March) that roll in from the Sahara. In the north, along the Mediterranean coast, the winter (Dec–Feb) can be wet and mildly unpleasant. For ideal weather conditions at various African game parks go to Ⓦ www.thesafaricompany .co.za/When_to_visit_Africa.htm.

Costs

There is certainly luxury accommoda-tion catering to the rich, but, with some exceptions – notably west Africa – Africa is a budget-travel zone. The exceptions include Botswana and Zambia, which are trying to go after upmarket, low-impact tourists; and Namibia. South African cities can get a little expensive but, overall, prices are still reasonable.

Getting around by air

This isn't the cheapest way to get around, but then flying rarely is. It can, however, help bridge gaps so you spend more time covering the ground you want to cover. The basic guidelines for air travel take on more importance in Africa,

Lowest daily budget
Expensive ($70/£42+): Botswana, South Africa, Namibia
Mid-range ($40–50/£24–30): Djibouti, Liberia, Libya, Rwanda, Zambia
Budget ($10–30/£7–18): Everywhere else

Security issues

It's always a good idea to check the current political conditions before visiting a country, but the following are worth a little extra research: Algeria, Angola, Burundi, Cameroon, Central African Republic, Chad, Congo (Democratic Republic), Côte d'Ivoire, Egypt, Eritrea, Ethiopia, Kenya, Liberia, Libya, Mali, Niger, Nigeria, Rwanda, Somalia (basically out of bounds no matter how adventurous you are), Sudan, South Sudan, Tunisia, Uganda, Western Sahara, Zambia and Zimbabwe.

particularly when you're not using major international carriers. This means you really ought to:

● Confirm your flight a couple of times (including on the day of the flight).

● Arrive early. You may end up winning a seat on an overbooked flight, even if you had a ticket and didn't think the seat

Recommended vaccinations

- Routine boosters for measles/ mumps/rubella (MMR), diphtheria/pertussis/tetanus (DPT) and polio
- Hepatitis A
- Hepatitis B
- Meningococcal meningitis (central Africa from Gambia to central Ethiopia)
- Rabies (optional)
- Typhoid
- Yellow fever (required in more than thirty countries, but not in far north or far south)

would require any winning. Plus, many flights have open seating, so you might even get a seat with some legroom.

● Some baggage inspectors may take their time rifling through your things, either out of curiosity or hope of financial payoff. If a bribe or "gift" is requested, and your belongings are in order, politely stand your ground. In a pinch, try handing over something that isn't hugely important to you.

● In South Africa, the budget airline Kulula (Ⓦwww.kulula.com) can also help arrange hotels and transport.

Air passes

● **Visit Africa** Ⓦwww.oneworld.com /flights/single-continent-fares. Allows access to a total of eight cities in Namibia, South Africa, Zimbabwe and Zambia. There's a minimum purchase of two flights. Prices are based on zones and are about 35 percent cheaper than standard fares.

● **Star Alliance Africa Airpass** Ⓦwww.staralliance.com. Connects thirty destinations in 23 countries on South African Airways and EgyptAir flights. Choose three to ten coupons, with fares based on the distance you fly, shaving about 30 percent off single tickets between the same cities.

Overland routes

The continent may stretch 7000km from north to south, but Africa's limited infrastructure has created surprisingly well-trodden overland routes. The most common is from Cape Town to Nairobi, which passes through Namibia, Botswana, Zimbabwe, Zambia, Malawi, Tanzania (often with a side trip to Zanzibar), then into Kenya. Most travelers now fly between Nairobi and Egypt due to the fighting in Sudan and near the

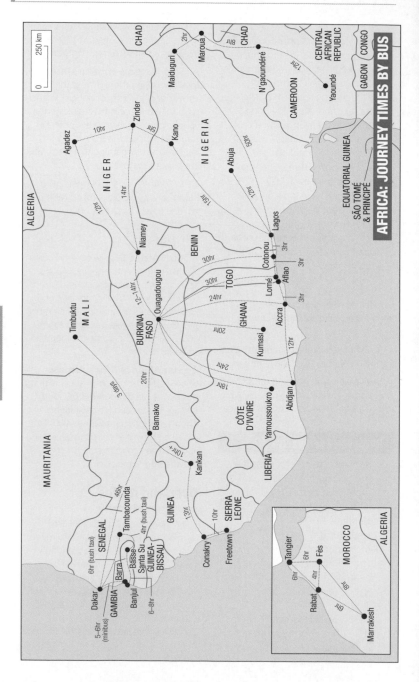

AFRICA: JOURNEY TIMES BY BUS

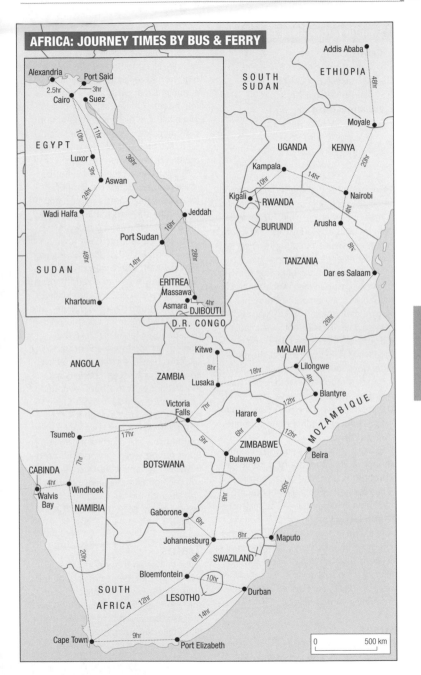

AFRICA: JOURNEY TIMES BY BUS & FERRY

Addis Ababa

ETHIOPIA

48hr

SOUTH
SUDAN

Moyale

Alexandria
Port Said
2.5hr   3hr
Cairo   Suez

UGANDA   KENYA

20hr

EGYPT

10hr   11hr

36hr

Kampala

10hr   14hr

Luxor

3hr

Kigali   Nairobi

24hr

Aswan

RWANDA   4hr

BURUNDI   Arusha

Wadi Halfa

Jeddah

8hr

Port Sudan

16hr   28hr

TANZANIA

Dar es Salaam

48hr   14hr

ERITREA
Massawa

SUDAN

Khartoum

Asmara   4hr
DJIBOUTI

26hr

D.R. CONGO

Kitwe

MALAWI

ANGOLA

8hr   18hr   Lilongwe

ZAMBIA

Lusaka

4hr   Blantyre

Victoria
Falls

7hr   12hr

MOZAMBIQUE

Tsumeb   17hr

Harare

5hr   6hr

12hr

Beira

7hr   BOTSWANA   ZIMBABWE

CABINDA

Bulawayo

4hr

Walvis   Windhoek

Bay   NAMIBIA   Gaborone   6hr

9hr   26hr

6hr

Johannesburg   8hr   Maputo

20hr   6hr   SWAZILAND

Bloemfontein   10hr

SOUTH   12hr   LESOTHO   Durban

AFRICA   14hr

Cape Town   9hr   Port Elizabeth

0   500 km

| **Sample return airfares** |
| **Cairo** to: |
| • Cape Town $600/£370 |
| • Marrakesh $400/£252 |
| • Nairobi $350/£220 |
| **Johannesburg** to: |
| • Dar es Salaam $400/£252 |
| • Marrakesh $500/£315 |
| • Windhoek $220/£139 |

Ethiopian/Eritrean border, but depending on political conditions, you may be able to make it all the way overland or catch a flight in Addis Ababa instead. Check with nearby embassies and other travelers for the most recent information.

The other primary route passes down the west coast between Tangier, Morocco and Yaounde in Cameroon. From the north, it makes the tricky crossing of the western Sahara, heads onto Mauritania and Senegal, then turns inland and traverses Mali. In Burkina Faso, the route either goes south to Accra on the coast or passes through Niger and Benin. The trails meet again in Nigeria and press on to Cameroon. From there, it's common to fly to Nairobi or Windhoek and continue south overland.

You can get nearly everywhere in Africa without your own transport – a combination of buses, trains and boats is going to be your best option, and your thumb may come in handy as well. You may not get to your destination exactly when you want to, but of course that's all part of the adventure. Because some of the routes are so poorly maintained, you'll probably have quite an adventure in your own vehicle as well. So long as you're armed with plenty of patience, you'll be fine.

Buses
Top-end buses, typically in South Africa and Namibia, are comfortable and will generally leave on schedule and adhere to the one-person-per-seat rule, but some drivers are a little overzealous with the air conditioning and, with a high-tech stereo system under their command, may simply bad-music you into a coma. Otherwise, buses depart when full or at the driver's whim, stop constantly, are driven wildly and cram up to five times the maximum allowable number of passengers on board.

In South Africa, there are a number of alternatives. There's the Baz Bus (Ⓦwww.bazbus.com), a hop-on hop-off minivan for travelers that moves along the main travel circuit. A one-way trip from Johannesburg to Cape Town on Baz will cost R2370/$290/£180. Intercape (Ⓦwww.intercape.co.za), Greyhound (Ⓦwww.greyhound.co.za) and Translux (Ⓦwww.translux.co.za) all run luxury bus services along the main routes and offer a direct trip from Johannesburg to Cape Town for $45–75/£28-47; Greyhound and Interscape both offer bus passes. Interscape's is a bit confusing, with separate tickets still required for each trip, but Greyhound's rates are: 7 days (R2376/$290/£180), 15 days (R4224/$516/£321) and 30 days (R580/$1048/£653) of unlimited travel. Granted, this isn't much of a bargain. Buses run between Johannesburg and Bulawayo in Zimbabwe. From there, you can connect to a train and arrive in Vic Falls 24 hours after leaving Jo'burg, assuming you don't get delayed at the border.

Trains
There will be ample opportunities to ride a train, but there's not enough track around Africa to make rail travel your sole mode of transport. Aside from South Africa's plush and outrageously priced Blue Train (Ⓦwww.rovosrail.co.za), spanning the scenic gap between Johannesburg and Cape Town (less

expensive trains on this route can be booked weeks in advance in June–July and Dec–Jan), there are the Mombassa–Nairobi, Cairo–Aswan and the Dakar–Bamako lines. These all offer a reasonably priced second-class service, some fitted with sleeper cars and über-cheap third-class compartments.

Cars

For years travelers have been driving around Africa, setting their own schedules and venturing off the main routes at the change of a breeze. For drivers, the overland route between Nairobi and Egypt is only sporadically open due to fighting in Sudan and near the Ethiopian/Eritrean border. Also, land mines litter the border region, so don't even think of crossing outside official border points. The only way to slip through safely is on the ferry from Wadi Halfa to Aswan. Check current conditions before heading that way. And South Sudan has a current chokehold on overland passage as well. But there's still plenty of driving to be had. There are four basic options: renting a car, renting a car and a driver, buying a car locally or shipping/driving a car from home. If you're traveling in countries that require an international driving permit (see box, p.61), pick one up before you leave. The Carnet de Passage is a must for most countries except Algeria, Morocco, Tunisia and Zambia, which issue temporary import permits for free upon entry or don't require one. But to pull off anything more than a rental, you'll need to do some homework. Try these books for starters: *Sahara Overland* by Chris Scott and *Africa by Road* by Bob Swain and Paula Snyder.

Rental

Of the four options, the least practical and economical for a cross-continent road trip is likely to be renting a car. The rental companies (such as Ⓦwww.aroundaboutcars.com) know the conditions of the roads and the toll they take on vehicles and will charge you accordingly. Many will not even allow you to drive across borders, or will limit you to Botswana, Namibia, Swaziland and Zimbabwe. However, in these countries you'll find quite decent roads – long highways that are actually easy to navigate – and you may find a two-wheel-drive rental is the best way to go. These start at around $31/£20 per day for an economy car. For $118/£74 you can hire a 4WD. Be sure to get recent information on carjacking so you know where to take precautions, and always take appropriate gear when heading off-road (extra water, petrol, sand ladders, exhaust-powered air jacks and so on). If you plan to rent with a major company like Hertz or Avis (to take advantage of frequent-flyer points or a business discount), you may be able to avoid distance limits by renting before you leave home.

Rental with chauffeur

This is an informal arrangement with a taxi driver or, preferably, the owner of a four-wheel-drive vehicle. And it will probably cost you less than a rental ($15–50/£9–30 per day), depending on the car, length of journey and your bargaining skills. Just make sure you negotiate a daily or weekly rate for the driver's services and pay the petrol separately. If the driver is paying for the petrol, they may do what they can to save it, even if it means driving very slowly, turning off the air-con and headlights (if they exist) and trying to refuse suggested detours. If there are any car problems, they're the driver's responsibility. Give yourself the option to bail out if the delays look serious and, in the first instance, try to sign up with a driver whose car looks roadworthy.

Visa and vaccination requirements for Africa

Algeria Visa required (90 days: $166/£105). No entrance if passport has stamps from Israel, Malawi or Taiwan.

Angola Visa required (90 days: $141/£89). Vaccinations against yellow fever and cholera required. Sufficient funds ($100/£63 a day) and copy of return ticket.

Benin Visa required (30 days: $140/£91). Vaccination against yellow fever required. Proof of sufficient funds and onward travel.

Botswana No visa (90 days). Proof of sufficient funds and onward travel required.

Burkina Faso Visa required (180 days: $100/£63; or 365 days: $150/£95).

Burundi Visa required (30 days: $90/£57; or 60 days: $180/£113). Vaccination against yellow fever required. Proof of hotel reservation and return/onward ticket.

Cameroon Visa required (30 days: $141/£89). Vaccination against yellow fever required. Proof of sufficient funds and onward ticket.

Central African Republic Visa required; 90 days: $150/£95. Proof of onward travel and yellow fever vaccination.

Chad Visa required (30 days: $100/£63). Extensions available on arrival.

Congo (Democratic Republic of) Visa required (30 days $115/£72; 60 days: $150/£95; 90 days: $200/£126; 180 days: $300/£189). Invitation from host and proof of yellow fever vaccination.

Congo (Republic of) Visa required (90 days: $120/£76). Proof of onward travel.

Côte d'Ivoire Visa required (90 days: $150/£95 for US citizens; $50/£32 for Canadians, Australians and New Zealanders). Proof of onward travel, hotel reservation and vaccination against yellow fever.

Djibouti Visa required (90 days: $60/£38). Copy of round-trip ticket.

Egypt Visas may be bought at airport on arrival (90 days: $15/£9). Make sure your hotel registers you with immigration within seven days. To be safe, overland travelers from Sudan should arrange a visa beforehand. No visa available at border with Israel or Libya (get beforehand or at embassy in Tel Aviv, Eilat or Tripoli); no visa required if you are only staying in Sinai between Sharm el-Sheikh and Taba (free 14-day stamp at border).

Equatorial Guinea No visa required for US citizens. All others must arrange visas before arrival (90 days: $100/£63). Proof of $2000/£1260 in funds, and records of yellow fever, smallpox and cholera vaccination required for all.

Eritrea Visa required (90 days: maximum stay 30 days: $50/£32), for all except Uganda and Kenya nationals. Copy of round-trip tickets or confirmed itinerary with entry and exit points, plus proof of sufficient funds ($40/£25 per day).

Ethiopia Visa required (30 days: $70/£44). Available on arrival at Bole airport for travelers from 33 countries, among them Australia, New Zealand, South Africa, the UK, the USA and most of western Europe. Onward travel required.

Gabon Visa required (90 days from day of issue: $140/£88). South Africans only need visas for stays longer than 30 days. Vaccination against yellow fever, round-trip ticket and hotel reservation required.

Gambia Visa required for citizens of the USA, France, eastern Europe (90 days: $140/£88). No visa required for nationals of Commonwealth and Scandinavian countries.

Ghana Visa required (30 days: $60/£38 single entry; $100/£63 multiple entry; visas are extendable). Proof of onward travel, sufficient funds and yellow fever immunization required.

Guinea Visa required (30 days: $100/£63). Vaccination against yellow fever and letter of invitation required.

Guinea-Bissau Visa required (30 days: $50/£32). Proof of onward travel, sufficient funds and yellow fever immunization.

Kenya Visa required (180 days: single entry $50/£32; multiple entry $100/£63; payable in US dollars only) for nationals of the USA, the UK, Australia and all European countries except Cyprus. New Zealanders and South Africans only need visas if staying more than 30 days. Getting a visa at the airport on arrival can involve delays.

Lesotho Visa not required for stays of up to 30 days. Proof of onward travel and cholera vaccination if traveling from a cholera-infected area.

Liberia Visa required (90 days: $131/£83 for US citizens, $70/£44 for other westerners). Apply for additional visitors' permit on entry. Letter from bank proving sufficient funds, letter from physician confirming health and yellow fever vaccination.

Libya At the time of writing, the new government was still in formation and the visa situation unclear. Check with your local Libyan embassy.

Malawi No visa required.

Mali Visa required. (90 days: $80/£50; US citizens pay $131/£83). All visas extendable. Proof of onward travel and yellow fever immunization required.

Mauritania Visas required (60 days: $116/£73). Vaccination against yellow fever, onward travel and proof of sufficient funds required.

Morocco No visa required for stays up to 90 days.

Mozambique Visa required (60 days: single entry $60/£38; 90 days: multiple entry $90/£57). Maximum stay 30 days. Proof of hotel reservation and onward ticket required.

Namibia No visa for up to 90 days' stay. Proof of onward travel required.

Niger Visa required (30 days; $100/£63). Onward travel, proof of sufficient funds ($500) and yellow fever vaccination required.

Nigeria Visa required (90 days: US citizens $160, UK citizens $144, Australians $141, Canadians $75, New Zealanders $2; all prices subject to

(continued...)

Visa and vaccination requirements for Africa (...continued)

$20/£13 processing fee). Apply online at ⓦwww.immigration.gov.ng. Letter of invitation, or evidence of sufficient funds required, as is certification of yellow fever vaccination.

Rwanda Visa not required for stays up to 90 days for citizens of Canada, the UK and the USA. Others pay $60/£38 for 90 days.

São Tomé and Principé Visa required (90 days: $65/£41). Available at airport (30 days for $50/£32).

Senegal Visa not required for stay up to 90 days for nationals of Canada, the USA and the UK. Citizens of Australia and New Zealand must have a visa (30 days: $45/£28), plus onward ticket, yellow fever vaccination and hotel reservation.

Sierra Leone Visa required (365 days, maximum stay 180 days: $160/£101 for citizens of the USA, Australia, New Zealand and the EU; $75/£47 for Canadians). Onward travel, sufficient funds and yellow fever vaccination required.

Somalia Travel really only possible in Somaliland (ⓦwww.visitsomaliland .com), which has a consular system of its own. Visas (required by all) available only at mission offices in London and Addis Ababa. Validity periods and fees are hazy, but hover around a reasonable $30/£19. Return ticket required.

South Africa Visa not required for stays up to 90 days. Onward travel ticket and sufficient funds required.

South Sudan At time of writing, it is not advisable to travel to this region.

Sudan Visa required (90 days: $151/£95). Letter of invitation, proof of onward travel (plus visa for next destination if needed), sufficient funds. Register with Ministry of Interior within three days. Health certificate that shows you are free of AIDS and ebola, plus yellow fever and cholera vaccinations if coming from an affected area. No visa will be issued for passports showing Israeli stamp.

Swaziland No visa required for stays of up to 60 days.

Tanzania Visas required, available at border (up to 365 days: $120/£76 for US citizens; 90 days: $70/£44 for everybody else). Proof of onward travel and sufficient funds required.

Togo Visa required (90 days: $140/£88 for US citizens; $32.50/£20 for everyone else). Proof of onward travel and yellow fever vaccination.

Tunisia Visa required for Australians and New Zealanders (30 days: $29/£18). No visa required for US and EU citizens staying up to 120 days, though proof of onward travel required.

Uganda Visa required, available at major borders and airports (90 days: $50/£32). Proof of yellow fever vaccination.

Zambia Visa required (180 days: $85/£54). Sufficient funds and proof of onward travel required.

Zimbabwe Visa required (90 days: $60/£38), issued on arrival. Proof of onward travel, sufficient funds.

Buying a car

Here's the classic decision: Land Cruiser or Range Rover. As more than one African overland aficionado will explain, Land Cruisers are reliable, but the spare parts aren't that easy to come by, while with a Range Rover, you can find the spare parts more easily, but you're going to need them. It's not a cheap option, but you should get your money back when you sell the car, if it's in reasonable shape. South Africa is a good place to pick up a vehicle. If you're buying secondhand, take the car to a mechanic for an independent inspection. If you're just driving on the well-surfaced roads around South Africa, Namibia and Botswana, you can skirt the 4x4 issue and pick up a cheaper travel-friendly VW minibus or sport wagon instead. Have your documents well organized and ready for presentation at each border. Keep your cool with the border guards and act like you're not in a hurry. In fact, just don't be in a hurry. That makes it even easier. For more tips, see the section in "How to get around the world" (p.59).

Bringing your own car

Typically, travelers take cars on the short ferry journey from Spain to Morocco. The cost for shipping a vehicle from Europe to sub-Saharan Africa is $800–2600/£485–1580, depending on the destination. Just be sure to lock down or remove anything that can be taken off with a screwdriver or it may not be there when your vehicle arrives. Again, you'll need a carnet (see box, p.61), and all the necessary permits and documents. If you plan to sell the vehicle in Africa, that should be prearranged when you get your carnet, so your deposit can be easily refunded. But you'll still have to pay the import duties in the country you're selling it in, so find out what that figure is beforehand.

Bikes

Pedalling is a fine way to see Africa. Rental cycles are available in most places you would want to ride a bike. And when they aren't, don't be afraid to ask ordinary people about renting their bikes, or go to a bike repair shop and make the same request. You'll find people quite flexible in this regard. For serious touring, bring a bike from home and make sure it can handle potholes and gravel with ease. Even if you stick to the main routes, you'll undoubtedly be stopping in places that most travelers speed by and leave choking in a cloud of dust. Of course, on a bike, you'll be eating a good deal of dust yourself, and you may want to bring a face mask. Also remember to plan your food and water carefully over long stretches; cycle early in the morning and in the late afternoon and rest in the shade during the heat of midday; try to coordinate your trip with the coolest months; get permission from villagers when camping near their settlements; and don't be afraid to use public transport. You can almost always toss your bike on a bus at a pinch. One more thing: you don't have the right of way on a bike… ever. Practice your emergency swerve.

Hitching

Hitching is part of the African way of life. In some towns you can actually hitch rides downtown. With an array of several modes of transport to choose from, it may still be your best choice. Other times, it may be your only choice. As a foreigner, you're a bit of an oddity on the side of the road and have a good chance of catching a quick ride, but you will invariably be expected to pay something. However, don't stand too close to large groups of hitchers, as the person who stops for you may not want to try to squeeze an entire group into the vehicle. See the section on hitching safety (p.143).

Boats

You may decide to float down the Nile on a felucca, starting in Aswan and ending just short of Luxor; cross Lake Victoria by ferry; or sail among the islands off the coast of Lamu. If you don't mind crocs, hippos and elephants within a paddle's length of your canoe, you might consider a trip down the Zambezi well below Victoria Falls or along Botswana's Okavango Delta. Few of these boats get you somewhere you couldn't otherwise access, but they do greatly enhance the "getting there".

Reading list

- Chinua Achebe *Things Fall Apart*
- Karen Blixen *Out of Africa*
- Shirley Deane *Talking Drums*
- Dian Fossey *Gorillas in the Mist*
- Kuki Gallman *I Dreamed of Africa*
- Barbara Kingsolver *The Poisonwood Bible*
- Nelson Mandela *Long Walk to Freedom*

- Rian Malan *My Traitor's Heart*
- V.S. Naipaul *A Bend in the River*
- Ben Okri *The Famished Road*
- Oona Strathern (ed.) *The Traveler's Literary Companion – Africa*
- Ngugi wa Thiong'o *A Grain of Wheat*

Visas

Many African countries require yellow fever and cholera immunizations, though these aren't the only immunizations you should have (see p.181), or even the most important. But without them, you could be turned away at the border, even with a visa. Enforcement of this varies from rigid to nonexistent, and often only applies to people coming from an infected area. Check with an embassy or the country's website for up-to-the-minute info.

"Onward travel" means officials want to see that you've got a ticket back home or on to someplace else and, thus, do not have aspirations to stay permanently. Again, this is rarely enforced, especially if you can demonstrate sufficient funds ($500/£315 per month or major credit card) and show your intended overland route. Country-by-country requirements vary (see pp.222–224).

Asia

To some travelers, Asia is the home of the most exhilarating natural landscapes on the planet: the soaring Himalayas. To others, it's a collection of frenzied cities and remote cultures connected by rough local transport through countless terraced rice paddies. Many see Asia as the epicenter of spiritual enlightenment. Some think of the geisha tea houses of Japan or the surfable breaks of Indonesia. And some travelers simply think: it's cheap.

The truth is that Asia has something for everyone. It's really just a matter of deciding what you're after. The low prices (outside Japan, Bhutan, Hong Kong and Singapore anyway) make most activities and journeys financially feasible for travelers on the lowest budgets. Surprisingly, though, much of Asia is still relatively untouched by the travel circuit, and if you're willing to forego the comforts of the backpacker infrastructure, it's yours to discover.

Main attractions

● **Angkor Wat** Siem Reap, Cambodia. This remarkable collection of one hundred temples and palaces (stretching over 60 square kilometres) was built by Khmer kings between the ninth and fourteenth centuries. It's only part of a much larger holy site that has been swallowed by the surrounding jungle over the last five hundred years.

● **The Great Wall** China. The unusual thing about this attraction is that you can't see it. You can, of course, see a tiny portion of it no matter where you stand – perhaps 20–40km in either direction – but precisely what makes it so incredible is the other 5960km out of view. Its appeal certainly isn't its defensive record – it was never effective at keeping invaders out. Most people just rode up, bribed the guards at one of the checkpoints and went on through. The Wall was, however, an example of China's forward thinking. Who else could have

imagined the publicity payoff of giving astronauts something to look at from outer space?

● **Nepal's Himalayas** Trekking is an activity that people come from around the world to try, yet it's almost never practiced by locals. Nepalese simply don't head out on trekking tours. Many walk on the same trails, but only when they need to get somewhere. The hair-raising vistas, sense of adventure and cheap guesthouses along the trails lure tens of thousands of travelers each year.

● **Taj Mahal** Agra, India. Bring your sunglasses. This white marble mausoleum has glacier-like reflective properties that your retinas won't forget in a hurry. Built in 1632–1653 by Emperor Shah Jahan in loving memory of his second wife, Mumtaz Mahal, who died prematurely from childbirth complications, the Taj is an architectural marvel that has been crafted down to the most minute detail.

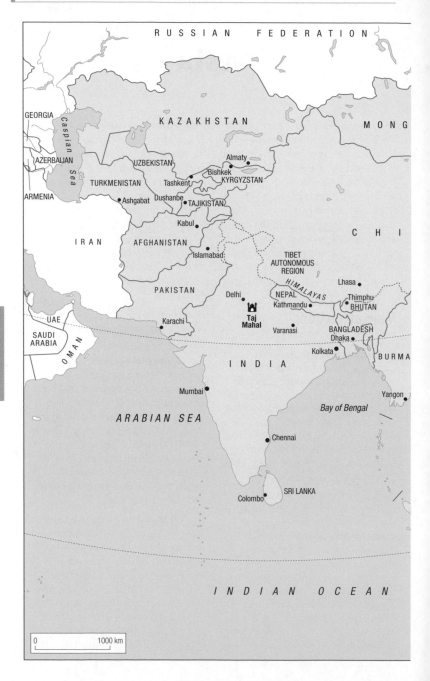

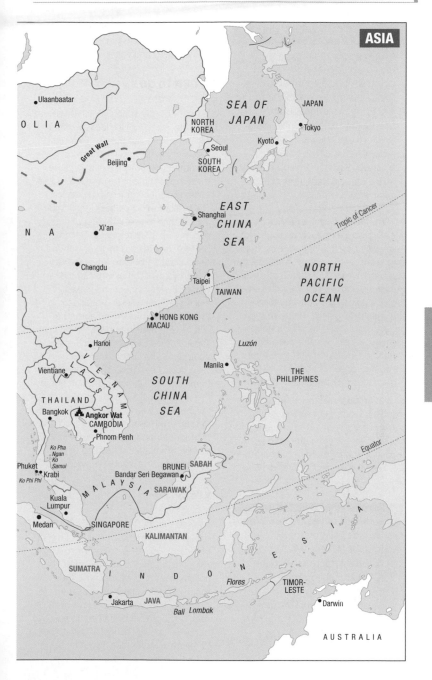

Security issues

It's always a good idea to check the current political conditions before visiting a country, but the following are worth a little extra research: Afghanistan, Azerbaijan, Bangladesh, Burma (Myanmar), Georgia, India, Indonesia, Iraq, Kyrgyzstan, Malaysia, Pakistan, Philippines, Sri Lanka, Tajikistan, Uzbekistan.

● **Thailand's beaches** Thailand doesn't have a monopoly on Southeast Asia's great beaches, but travelers simply can't seem to return home without an obligatory white-sand sizzle (both sides, extra crispy) on the eastern shores or the west coast (now protected by a tsunami-alarm system). There are still undeveloped stretches to be found, but as the word gets out, little palm-tufted islands and inlets are transformed from cheap backpacker hang-outs into fully fledged resorts right before your eyes.

● **Varanasi** India. The religious center of India is practically carved into the banks of the Ganges River just as it has been for over two thousand years. Those looking for eternal enlightenment are cremated on the ghats, and those seeking a less permanent fix bathe

Recommended vaccinations

* Routine boosters for measles/mumps /rubella (MMR), diphtheria/pertussis/tetanus (DPT) and polio virus
* Hepatitis A
* Japanese encephalitis (rural farming areas)
* Rabies (optional)
* Typhoid

not far away. Be especially respectful of religious customs regarding photography and conservative dress.

When to go

In northern Asia, spring (March–May) and autumn (Sept–Nov) are ideal, summer can get stifling, but the harsh winters (Dec–Feb) make traveling the most uncomfortable. Which is fine, because that's a great time to be in southern Asia, the Indian subcontinent in particular. The trickiest thing, perhaps, is planning a good time to trek, if that's your cup of chai. In Nepal, September to December is widely regarded as the best trekking season, but October to November is so popular that the crowds can easily disrupt the enjoyment and make it feel more like a weekend queue for the Louvre. Consider mid-September and early to mid-December, the brief shoulder seasons without the human traffic jams. The famous monsoon of India could keep you hot and drenched from June to September (though not in the northern hills), but it's not as severe in Cambodia, Laos, Thailand or Vietnam. In southern Thailand, Malaysia and parts of Indonesia, finding better weather can simply be a matter of heading to the opposite coast, a few hours away.

Costs

Asia has the cheapest and the most expensive countries in the world. Outside of the most expensive cities, where you can probably find dormitories, you'll be able to save funds by sharing a double room with someone. In the cheapest countries, the saving often isn't significant, but it can help when you're trying to get by on pocket change. Be sure to head for the markets for food if you're looking to save money. For those who travel

Lowest daily budget

Expensive ($60/£38):
Bhutan, Brunei, the east coast of China, Hong Kong, Japan, Mongolia, Singapore
Mid-range ($40–55/£25–35):
Mainland China, Malaysia, Philippines, South Korea, Taiwan, Thailand
Budget ($12–35/£8–22):
Bangladesh, Burma (Myanmar), India, Indonesia, Laos, Nepal, Pakistan, Vietnam

in relative luxury, prices don't fluctuate much by zone. People savvy enough to put up a multi-starred hotel know what their clientele are accustomed to paying, and charge accordingly.

Getting around by air

Some domestic flights are surprisingly cheap, so before you head off to a bus station for another twelve-hour journey, consider taking a peek at some local fares. You may decide it's worth the extra $20–70/£13–44 or whatever the difference may be. From Bangkok, you can fly nearly anywhere in Asia for $75–250/£47–158, with good timing, much less. Domestic one-way tickets in China cost $100–300/£63–189 and in India $50–150/£32–95.

Air passes

Most air passes must be purchased in advance, outside the country, and are probably best coordinated with your international ticket. If you've already arrived with an international carrier and you have a clever travel agent back home who has all the records from your trip, you may be able to work things out and have a ticket sent to you.

Asia

● **Visit Asia Airpass** ⓦwww .oneworld.com. The One World Alliance offers up fifty cities in eighteen countries on ten airlines. There's a minimum of two flights but no upper limit. The price is based on the geographic zone of each flight – South East Asia, North East Asia or South Asian Sub Continent – but expect to save up to thirty percent on normal fares.

● **Visit Asean Airpass** ⓦwww .aseanta.org/visitaseanpass.html. Travel between the ten countries of the Association of Southeast Asian Nations (which include Cambodia, Laos and Burma) on six different airlines. You buy a minimum of three coupons ($399/£251 for three) and no more than five ($525/£330), and itineraries must be set at the time of purchase. No domestic travel allowed inside Burma, Laos, Cambodia and Vietnam.

● **Cathay Pacific All Asia Pass** ⓦwww.cathayusa.com/offers/allasiapass /offer.asp. The All Asia Pass is valid for departures from Chicago, Los Angeles, New York or San Francisco and includes travel to Hong Kong and up to four other cities, with forty cities to chose from. The pass is valid for 21 days. The journey must be completed within 21 days but extensions of thirty or ninety days are available for additional fees ($300/£189 and $500/£315 respectively). Prices start from $1329/£837.

● **Sky Team Asia Pass** ⓦwww .skyteam.com/your-trip/Travel-Passes /Go-Asia/. Available if you fly to and from Asia with one of the fifteen Sky Team members, and covers 115 destinations in 23 countries in Asia and the Pacific in through one of four gateways – Beijing, Guangzhou, Seoul and Tokyo. There is a minimum of three coupons and maximum stay of sixty days. You have to book the first flight in advance, but the rest can be booked along the way. Expect to save up to 75 percent on normal fares.

- **Star Alliance Asia Airpass** Ⓦwww.staralliance.com. Fly to any ten of fifty available destinations in thirteen countries, with eight different airlines. Valid for three months. Dates and flights must be decided in advance. Save up to thirty percent on normal fares.

India

- **Jet Value Around IndiaPass** Ⓦwww.jetairways.com. Jet Airways offers four coupons for $440/£277, six for $600/£378 and eight for $720/£453, if your flight to and from India is Jet Airways, and four coupons for $480/£302, six for $660/£416 and eight for $800/£504 respectively if you arrive with any other carrier. Valid for 90 days (180 days if you buy eight coupons) on all domestic Jet Airways flights except to the Andaman Islands. Also available in Première Class for $1500/£945, $2160/£1360 or $2720/£1714 for four, six or eight coupons.

Japan

- **JAL Welcome to Japan** Ⓦwww .jal.co.jp/yokosojapan. Flights between sixty Japanese airports with prices based on a fixed sector rate of Y10,000 ($126/£79). Valid on up to five flights operated by JAL, JAL Express and Japan TransOcean Air.

Thailand

- **Discovery Airpass** Ⓦwww .bangkokair.com. Covers destinations in Southeast Asia serviced by Bangkok Airlines and Lao Airlines. The minimum purchase is three coupons ranging in price from $88/£55 for routes within a country to $120/£76 for international flights, $200/£126 for longer international flights. The maximum number of coupons you can buy is six, and the pass is valid for two months.

- **Thai Airlines Discover Thailand Pass** Ⓦwww.thaiair.com. Allows travel throughout Thailand. You must purchase a minimum of three coupons for $280/£176. Up to five additional coupons are available for $94/£59 each. You do not have to travel internationally on Thai airlines to purchase this pass, but you must buy it before arriving in Thailand.

Overland routes

Asia has several classic overland routes which can be avoided, adhered to or mixed and matched. One route connects Europe and Australia via the old hippie trail that cuts across Pakistan, India, Bangladesh, Burma, Thailand, Singapore, Malaysia and Indonesia.

From Moscow, you can take the Trans-Mongolian or Trans-Manchurian railways (see box, p.62) to Beijing – or vice versa. From Beijing, you've got a few options: the most expensive (based on per-day travel costs) is to head down the coast to Hong Kong or across the strait by ferry to South Korea and then on to Japan.

The four cheaper options are to head inland, then either:

- Through Tibet and into Nepal (check current visa info on this border crossing), then on to India, where you can pick up the trail going on to Australia.

- Along the old silk route, although the famous Khyber Pass between Afghanistan and Pakistan is closed to travelers at the moment. Instead, pick up the route to Australia via India, Thailand, Malaysia, Singapore and Indonesia.

- To Hanoi, then Laos and Bangkok.

- From Hanoi, going to Ho Chi Minh City to Phnom Penh and (possibly with a short flight here) on to Bangkok.

- Note that the classic Burma Road has recently opened for traffic, the first time since the end of World War II.

There's an incredible selection of transport available, from some of the world's least comfortable buses to high-speed trains with champagne service, and from colorful hand-decorated bicycle rickshaws to dusty grey elephants. Between most points, however, you'll be choosing among buses, trains, planes, boats and (if you're in a group) a taxi. In cities, public transport can be daunting. With the right frame of mind (relaxed, perhaps mildly hungover) you will eventually get the hang of it, even if you get lost once or twice in the process. Whether or not that's easier than learning to bargain and getting a feel for the local taxi and rickshaw prices is a tough call.

Buses

There are modern buses in Asia – the ones that run in Japan or around Thailand are especially stunning. But you'll invariably spend a good deal of time on the other kind. Despite what you may have heard, it's rarely the bus that's the problem. It's more likely just the chain-smokers, jammed-shut windows, screaming babies, crater-like potholes, un-policed roads and reckless drivers with an affinity for high-pitched synthesizer pop music played at conversation-halting decibels. Thus the mention of "bus" and "Asia" will often conjure up "bus ride from hell" stories, which is fine because – and here's what you need to remind yourself when hearing these – the person telling them obviously survived. Buses may not be the safest methods of transport, but they're often the cheapest, and sometimes the only way to get where you want to go.

Trains

Japan, China and India boast the most extensive rail networks in Asia, and they're a nice alternative to buses. That's not to say they'll offer the same level of escape. To even mention Japan's and India's trains in the same sentence requires a disclaimer: no two rail systems could be more different. The smooth, sterile, comfortable and climate-regulated high-speed trains in Japan arrive and depart on a schedule that many actually do set their watches by. Indian trains, provided you're not in first class, feature a cast of characters that ranges from hot-food sellers or relentlessly inquisitive businessmen looking for a joint-venture partner to the sweeper who brushes out the constantly accumulating layer of garbage on the floor. China's trains are somewhere in between, largely dependent upon what type of cabin you're in: "hard seats" (more people than seats), "soft seats" (same number of people as seats), "hard beds" (hard beds) or "soft beds" (fairly soft beds in a four-bed suite). China is pressing on fast with its high-speed rail network, aiming at 12,000 kilometers by 2020 and the magnetic levitation line from Shanghai airport already shoots passengers into town at the insane top cruising speed of 430kph.

While not cheap, Japan's rail passes (ⓦwww.japanrailpass.net) are at least good value – really the only way to afford the trains. With the bullet trains, you could easily travel half the length of Japan in a day and spend $300/£162 in the process. The passes come in three basic flavors: 7-day pass: $354/£223; 14-day pass: $564/£355; and 21-day pass: $721/£454.

Cars

Get a taste of what you're getting into before you rent a car. Sit in the front passenger seat of a taxi as you move about town for a few days and see if the high-speed chaos feels like something you'd be able to handle. If not, you can often hire a driver and pay even less, especially if you can find one or

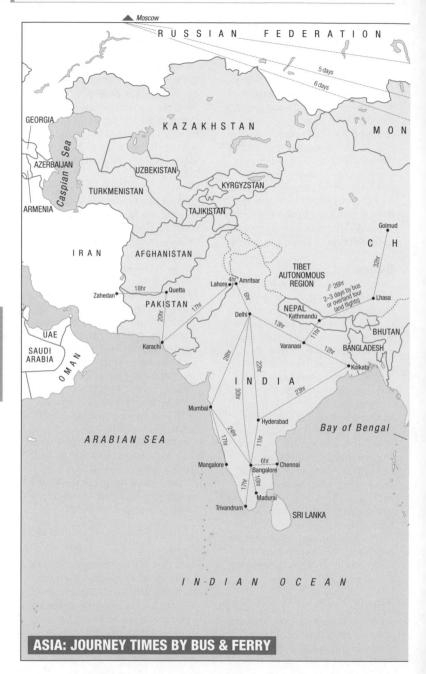

ASIA: JOURNEY TIMES BY BUS & FERRY

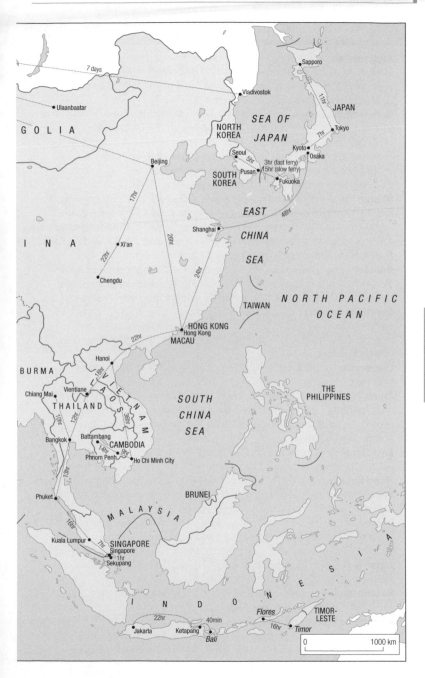

GOLIA

- Ulaanbaatar

7 days

- Vladivostok

• Sapporo

SEA OF
JAPAN

NORTH
KOREA

11hr

JAPAN

Seoul
5hr

• Tokyo

Kyoto

7hr

Osaka

3hr (fast ferry)
15hr (slow ferry)

Beijing

SOUTH
KOREA

Pusan

Fukuoka

17hr

48hr

EAST

INA

Xi'an

26hr

Shanghai

CHINA

22hr

24hr

SEA

Chengdu

NORTH PACIFIC

TAIWAN

OCEAN

HONG KONG
Hong Kong

22hr

MACAU

Hanoi

THE
PHILIPPINES

BURMA

18hr

V I E T N A M

Chiang Mai

Vientiane

L A O S

SOUTH

THAILAND

12hr

36hr

CHINA

Bangkok

Battambang
CAMBODIA

SEA

10hr

14hr

9hr

Phnom Penh

Ho Chi Minh City

13hr

Phuket

BRUNEI

M A L A Y S I A

18hr

Kuala Lumpur

7hr

SINGAPORE

Singapore
1hr
Sekupang

I N D O N E S I A

Flores

TIMOR-
LESTE

22hr

40min

16hr

Timor

Jakarta

Ketapang

Bali

0   1000 km

Visa requirements for Asia

Afghanistan Visas required (30 days: $100/£63 with two-week processing time). A 90-day visa is obtainable in Washington with 1–2 days processing time for $140/88, but may not be easy to get if you're not a journalist or aid worker. Letter of introduction required.

Bangladesh Visas required (30 days maximum stay; single-entry $32/£20 for Australians, $45/£28 for New Zealanders, $51/£32 for Canadians, $150/£95 for US citizens, $65/£41 for Brits and $9–78/£6–49 for citizens of other European countries). Double and multiple-entry visas also available, at equally haphazard rates and validity periods; check with your nearest embassy. Proof of onward travel required.

Bhutan Independent travel not permitted. All visitors must sign up for a pre-arranged itinerary with official tour company and pay a per-day fee based on season. Visa must be obtained before flight can be booked. Visitors pay $20/£13 on arrival when visa is stamped. Start applying for visas and booking accommodation at least 90 days before the start of the trip.

Brunei Visa not required for stays up to 14 days (Canadians), 30 days (New Zealanders and Brits) or 90 days (Americans). Australians need visas, but can pick up the 14-day kind on arrival. Proof of onward travel required.

Burma (Myanmar) Visa required for all visitors (28 days; $20/£13, but can be extended by 14 days); see ⓦwww.myanmarembassy.com/english /visa.htm. May need to coordinate with a tour company to arrange for an overland journey.

Cambodia Visa (30 days: $30/£19) required, available at some border crossings.

China Visa required, valid from date of issue (90 days: single entry $30/£19, double entry $45/£28). US citizens pay $140/£88 for both types. Special permits required for Tibet (see opposite) and Xinjiang. Onward travel. Maximum stay 30 days.

East Timor 30-day entry permit (renewable in 30-day increments) issued upon arrival. Proof of onward travel required.

Hong Kong No visa required for stays up to 90 days. Proof of onward travel.

India Visa required, valid from date of issue, not entry (6 months standard: $76/£48 for US citizens; $56/£38 for everyone else).

Indonesia Visa required (90 days: single entry $45/£28, multiple entry $100/£63). Transit visa available on arrival for seven or thirty days ($25/£16). Onward travel and proof of funds required.

Japan No visa required for stays up to 90 days. Proof of onward travel required.

Kazakhstan Visa required (30 days: single entry $40/£25; 60 days: double entry $60/£38). Maximum stay 30 days.

Kyrgyzstan Visa required (30 days: $100/£63).

Laos Visa required (60 days: $50/£32) Tourist version (15 days: $30/£19) available on arrival at International Airports and main board crossings.

Macau No visa required for stays up to 90 days for EU citizens, one year for Hong Kong nationals and 30 days for everyone else.

Malaysia No visa required for visit up to 90 days. Two-month extensions available after that.

Mongolia Visa not required for US citizens staying up to 90 days. Visa required for all others (90 days: single entry $55/£35).

Nepal Visa required, available on arrival at border and airport (15 days: $25/£16; 30 days: $40/£25; 90 days: $100/£63).

North Korea Visa required, lots of paperwork, no independent travel, no journalists get tourist visas, denials on whim. No tourist visa for US citizens unless for Arirang Festival on April 15.

Pakistan Visa required (90 days: $120/£76).

Philippines No visa required for stays up to 21 days. For an extension of up to 38 extra days, making a total of 59 days, you need a temporary visitor's visa, which costs $30/£19. For stays longer than 59 days, the fee is $90/£57 per month. Proof of onward travel required.

Singapore No visa required for stays of up to 30 days (extendable). Proof of funds, onward travel and yellow fever vaccination, if traveling from affected area within the last six days, required.

South Korea No visa required for stays of up to 90 days. Canadians can stay six months. Proof of onward travel required.

Sri Lanka No visa required for stays of up to 30 days (extendable for a fee). Proof of funds, onward travel required.

Taiwan No visa required for 90 days for UK passport holders, and 30 days for all others (no extensions if using the visa-waiver program) with onward ticket and no criminal record.

Tajikistan Visa required (30 days: $25/£16). Much red tape, few embassies.

Thailand No visa required for visits up to 30 days. Proof of $300/£189 in funds.

Tibet Chinese visa required plus a special Tibet permit (aka Tibet Travel Permit); obtainable on an organized tour, or via recognized travel agencies. Charges vary according to departure city and mode of transport (RMB400–1350). No Chinese visa necessary for air transit en route to Tibet, except for UK and US citizens. Make sure you get a multiple entry visa for Nepal if using it for transit in and out of Tibet.

Turkmenistan Visa required (10 days: $35/£22; 20 days: $45/£28; one month: $55/£35); maximum stay one year. Exact itinerary needed in advance, letter of invitation required. Visitors must register with travel agent.

Uzbekistan Visa required (30 days: $160/£101). Letter of invitation, travel itinerary.

Vietnam Visa required (30 days: $80/£50). Travelers from Denmark, Finland, Japan, Norway, South Korea and Sweden can stay for 15 days without a visa.

two other travelers to help share the cost. In more developed countries the traffic laws may not be as much of a problem, but navigating can be. In Tokyo, for example, directions are so complex most companies have resorted to printing small maps on the backs of their business cards.

If you're planning to buy a car or motorcycle, head into it with your eyes open. That means a full understanding of the paperwork and visas you'll need to cross any borders – which could take months to organize – and figuring out which countries require separate permits for each province. If you are handy with engines, make sure you buy a model you feel comfortable fixing, plus the tools and parts you'll need. If you don't have the know-how, make sure you have a model that can be fixed locally (ask about this on arrival). Better still, get a model that won't require fixing. But that's going to cost a lot more and it'll have a greater chance of getting stolen, scratched or broken into. If you want the flexibility and convenience of a car and you're not heading across the continent, the best bet may be to rent one with a driver included and make sure you both agree on the ground rules (in fact, put them on paper) before embarking on a long journey. For more on car travel, see "How to get around the world" (p.59).

Bikes

Asia is the home of the bicycle. Having said that, you're unlikely to come across any models with dual suspension, titanium frames and French derailleurs. Renting or buying a bike to ride in cities is recommended where cycling is widely practiced (such as Beijing) and inadvisable where it's not (Bangkok, for example).

Bike paths are almost nonexistent and there's very limited space on the shoulders of major roads, so long-haul cyclists should seriously consider a mountain bike with adequate shock-absorbers, and perhaps stick to secondary roads.

As a cyclist, you're at the bottom of the highway food-chain and cars and trucks will expect you to move out of the way. But, just in case, consider bringing ample visibility-enhancers (orange flags and Day-Glo strips) to help alert drivers who aren't accustomed to seeing cyclists and may be kind enough to swerve.

Bring all the spare parts you'll need for such a journey. Outside Japan, Singapore and Taiwan, you'll have a hard time locating anything that will work with your bike, including inner tubes.

Boats

In parts of Asia, river travel is not just a nice way to break up a trip or save some money, it's the only way to access certain destinations. Whether or not you head up Cambodia's Tonlé Sap to Angkor Wat, float your way along the Yangtze for days or skirt the traffic in Bangkok on the long-shaft-motor *khlong* boats, you'll have plenty of opportunities to ply inland waters.

Hitching

Hitching is not common in Asia, but it can be done. There's a larger chance of a communication gap, though – a raised thumb may be misunderstood as an offensive gesture. To stop a car, you'll have better luck waving your arm. A sign is very helpful for finding rides (have someone help you write it in the local language). Then, to be sure, use a map and point to the place you hope to go. It's polite to offer a token gift in exchange for your ride (a pack of cigarettes or little knickknack from home). Asian drivers have a habit of running errands on the way without much warning, so don't be too alarmed if the driver doesn't seem to be taking the most obvious route, but otherwise normal hitch precautions apply (see p.143).

Reading list

- Aravind Adiga *The White Tiger*
- Jung Chang *Wild Swans*
- Jung Chang and Jon Halliday *Mao: The Unknown Story*
- James Clavell *Shogun*
- Larry Collins and Dominique Lapierre *Freedom at Midnight*
- Clive Leatherdale *To Dream of Pigs*
- François Ponchaud *Cambodia Year Zero*
- Gregory David Roberts *Shantaram*
- Salman Rushdie *Midnight's Children*
- Mark Salzman *Iron and Silk*

Visas

Laos, the Philippines and Vietnam are the countries requiring most travelers to get a visa for a one-month stay or longer, but double-check with embassies. Sometimes this differs when arriving by air or overland. Nearly all countries require that your passport be valid for at least six months from your date of entry, and that you have proof of onward travel (plane ticket) and/or sufficient funds to finance your stay and your trip home. Usually, a major credit card will help demonstrate this.

Australia, New Zealand and the South Pacific

Australia is as diverse as it is overwhelmingly vast. With just under 20 million people in a space bigger than all of Europe, most of the country is as sparsely populated as an Icelandic beach in December. The reason is that the outback, however stunning, renders most of the country largely uninhabitable (by Western standards), and with world-famous diving, surfing and fishing, it's easy to understand why the vast majority of Aussies have decided to settle within 20km of the coast. New Zealand, while far smaller, seems to pack more diversity (not to mention sheep and rugby players) per square kilometre than just about any place on the planet, from fjords to volcanoes to some of the most gentle rolling green hills you've ever laid eyes on.

With developed infrastructures and politically stable climates, the concern is less on being able to get around in a scheduled or safe fashion, and more on how to cover the butt-flattening distances, try all the hair-raising activities and cope with the increased lager intake. Aussies and Kiwis are among the best-traveled humans on the planet. So, not only do they sympathize with the budget traveler, they cater for us so well that some people claim it has taken a good deal of the adventure out of the journey. Just the same, it would be a pity to miss the experience. People don't get much more welcoming – a slap on the back and a shared beer and you're practically related. Which means cultural immersion is within easy grasp.

Whether you're sailing or flying your way around the planet, you may have an excellent opportunity to visit one or more of the 3300 South Pacific Islands spread over 11 million square miles of ocean – home to some 6 million unfathomably friendly people (the Fijians were voted the "world's friendliest people" in *Condé Nast Traveller* magazine). Most arrive by yacht or plane (several RTW tickets offer stops) and Tonga, Vanuatu, Fiji, New Caledonia, Samoa, Tahiti, the Cook Islands and the Solomon Islands are among the most popular. Nearly all offer excellent diving, fishing and beaching and, for most, it's just a question of making time for more than a stopover (and saving some money) so the islands can be thoroughly explored.

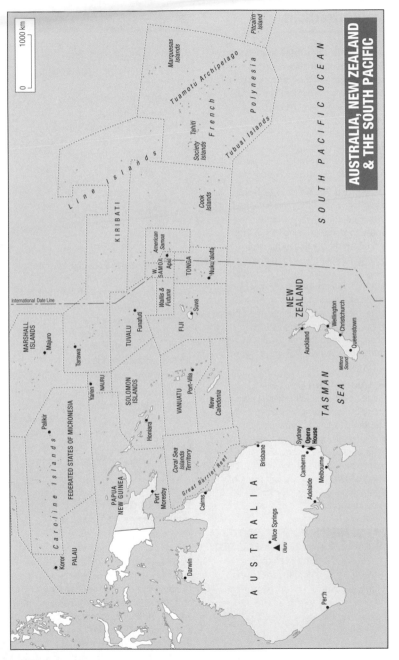

Main attractions

- **Great Barrier Reef** South Pacific. Beginning at Lady Elliot Island in the south and extending 2300km north to New Guinea, the Barrier Reef follows, in disconnected strips, the outer edge of Australia's continental plate, between 50 and 300km from the shoreline. Beneath the waves, it harbors some of the world's most diverse and spectacular marine life.

- **Milford Sound** New Zealand. A natural wonder that can be visited in a multitude of ways: whether you're trekking, kayaking or sipping a drink on the deck of a ship, this Southern-Hemisphere fjord is not likely to disappoint. Unless it's raining so much you can barely see it, which, unfortunately, is quite common, as it places among the top five rainiest places in the world (7–9m per year). More frequently, though, the rain simply adds stunning waterfalls, majestic mist and rainbows.

- **Queenstown** New Zealand. Credited with the commercial origins of the bungee-jump, this picturesque mountain town has expanded into other eyeball-ejecting ventures, from jet-boating down a narrow canyon river to parasailing to skydiving to flying gliders to… if you can think of something else, they're probably open to suggestions.

Recommended vaccinations

- Routine boosters for measles/mumps/rubella (MMR), diphtheria/pertussis/tetanus (DPT) and polio
- Hepatitis A (Papua New Guinea, islands)
- Hepatitis B (optional)
- Japanese encephalitis (Papua New Guinea, far northern Australia, islands of Torres Strait)
- Rabies (if you might be exposed to bats)
- Typhoid (southern and western Pacific)

- **Sydney Opera House** Australia. Tickets are readily available to many performances, although this Australian icon is best known for the view from the outside. The beautiful shell-inspired design came from a Dane – the late Jørn Utzon – who abandoned the project before completion due to political interference.

- **Uluru** Australia. Commonly known as Ayer's Rock, this mammoth rust-colored landmark is sacred to Aboriginal peoples and is the most-visited site in Australia. Familiarize yourself with the local debate before you decide whether or not to climb it.

When to go

There's never a wrong time to be in Australia/New Zealand, as long as you're flexible enough to migrate towards the weather you prefer. The main tourist season is the summer holiday, which runs from just before Christmas until the end of January. Expect resorts, buses and domestic flights to fill up during this time. The shoulder seasons are

October to Christmas and February to May. New Zealand gets a little cold and drizzly between June and September, but the far north is still balmy. Australia's outback season is October to November and March to May. Outside of that, you'll either sizzle during the day or freeze at night. If Melbourne gets too cold and wet in the winter, just head north until the temperature feels right. The South Pacific is fine so long as you miss the cyclone season around November to March, which can be escaped as close by as the Marshall Islands, just to the north.

Costs

Independent budget travelers can scrape by on $30/£18 a day with some effort, but $40/£24 a day is more realistic and $90/£54 if you like a little comfort, drink a lot of beer or enjoy a weekly gastronomic treat. Those not into the cut-throat savings common among students can figure on about $100/£61 per day. Again, for those who travel in relative luxury, prices don't fluctuate much. With scuba diving, bungee-jumping, crocodile tours and such, it's not difficult to top $100/£61 per day. The South Pacific islands are similarly priced, or slightly more expensive, mostly catering to high-end tourism, and just a few with budget accommodation. Tahiti may cost even the most budget-conscious traveler more than $75/£45 a day, so watch out that the week-long stopover on the way home doesn't burn a hole in your passport pouch. Fiji and the Cook Islands are more popular budget stopovers.

Hostels cost $20–40/£12–24 per person for a dorm or $40–60/£24–36 for a double – it's a paradise for quality backpacker hangouts. If you're staying at such places, consider picking up one of three cards (in addition to the ISIC): an International YHA card ($32/£20;

Lowest daily budget

Expensive ($75/£47+):
Marshall Islands, New Caledonia, Tahiti, Vanuatu
Mid-range ($50–70/£32–44):
Kiribati, New Zealand, Tonga
Budget ($20–45/£13–28):
Australia, Cook Islands, Fiji, Solomon Islands

Ⓦwww.hihostels.com); a VIP card ($37/£23; Ⓦwww.vipbackpackers .com); or a Nomads Mad card ($37/£23; Ⓦwww.nomadsworld.com) that gives you every seventh night free. The VIP- and Nomad-accepting hostels tend to be more centrally located than the International Youth Hostels, and both cards give about ten percent off room rates and a wide range of discounts on other goodies, from museums to telephone calls.

Getting around by air

In Australia, a plane is a decent way to connect some overland segments (it's four hours coast to coast). The shorter distances in New Zealand make it less appealing, but flights are cheap enough to prevent any unwanted backtracking. In the South Pacific, flying is the best way to visit the islands, and there are seemingly more air passes in this region than coconuts; see below, or check Ⓦwww.pacificislands.com/air-passes.

Air passes

● **Visit Australia and New Zealand** Ⓦwww.oneworld.com. Fifty destinations in the two countries serviced by LAN and Qantas and their affiliates. The minimum is two legs, but unlimited extra coupons can be bought after arrival. Fees are divided into five zones (depending on mileage). The deal is only available if you fly into Australia or New Zealand with a OneWorld alliance member airline, and must be booked before you leave home.

● **Circle Pacific** Ⓦ www.staralliance .com. Pricey pass for those in a hurry that offers destinations on four continents around the South Pacific. Prices vary according to where you start and how many miles you cover. Maximum of sixteen flight segments.

● **Circle Asia and Southwest Pacific** Ⓦ www.oneworld.com. Flights in northeast and southeast Asia and the southwest Pacific with British Airways, Cathay Pacific, JAL and Qantas. The fare is based on where your journey starts and finishes and the distance traveled: up to either 13,000 miles or 17,000 miles. Can only be bought in the region, and you must travel for between five days and one year.

Overland routes

Getting around down under is about as easy as it gets. And with no political conflicts to avoid and a reliable infra-structure, it's easy to design your own route. Both Australia and New Zealand offer excellent, outdoorsy packaged and unpackaged adventures.

Sample return airfares

Auckland to:
- Christchurch $50/£32
- Dunedin $80/£50
- Wellington $60/£38

Sydney to:
- Alice Springs $300/£189
- Cairns $150/£95
- Melbourne $50/£32
- Perth $160/£101

In Australia, the popular overland path forms a circle, starting in Melbourne or Sydney and going up the east coast, hitting the SPF 25 hangouts (Byron Bay, Airlie Beach, Whitsundays, Magnetic Island), then cutting inland and south to Uluru and finally looping back around to Melbourne and Sydney by way of the Great Ocean Road. If it's the same price on your RTW ticket to stop in Perth on the way in or out (even if it's a little more), a glimpse of Australia's barren west coast can be well worth the effort. Crossing the country can be done by bus, train and car. A less-traveled route will take you up the rugged north coast (unfortunately, you can't see the coast from the road for much of the journey) through Broome and on to Darwin, where you can see the nearby saltwater crocs first hand.

From Auckland in New Zealand, you can catch a ride south to Wellington, then take one of the frequent ferries across the channel to the South Island. You can make an overland circuit of South Island: go east and swim with dolphins on your way to Queenstown or make for the west-coast glaciers. Whatever you miss on the way down you can catch on the way back up.

Buses

Traditional bussing is, after hitchhiking and cycling, the cheapest way to move about. The main routes are followed by Greyhound (Ⓦ www.greyhound.com.au) in Australia, and Intercity (Ⓦ www .intercitycoach.co.nz) and Newmans Coachlines (Ⓦ www.newmanscoach .co.nz) in New Zealand. All but Newmans offer a range of passes with unlimited stops that are well worth looking into. Be warned, though: the two big catches with these tickets are that they are typically nonrefundable and don't allow backtracking.

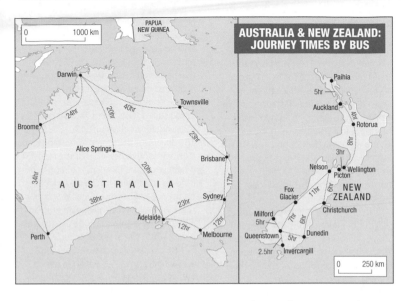

There are a number of bus companies such as the Kiwi Experience (Ⓦwww.kiwiexperience.com) and sister tour Oz Experience (Ⓦwww.ozexperience.com) that will shuttle you, at a very reasonable rate, from one pre-selected hostel to the next, stopping for all the important places (read: ones that give the company kickbacks) along the way so there's very little decision-making left for the traveler. It can be something of a party on wheels if you're looking for that sort of thing. Plus, the guides may be knowledgeable and they do take you to attractions that aren't easily accessed on other bus routes. In Australia, the classic "Knobs and Bells" pass ($2235/£1408) makes a loop that covers the east coast, cuts through the Outback and lasts twelve months with unlimited stops. With over thirty different itineraries to choose from (not including the flight combo passes), it's hard to find something you want to do that doesn't match up with one of their routes. The Kiwi Experience has nine bus passes to

choose from and trips average about $995/£627, though you can pay twice that for the "Full Monty" pass, which will allow you to cover the entire country in up to twelve months so you don't miss any of those *Lord of the Rings* filming locations.

Trains

In both countries, rail lines aren't nearly as extensive as bus routes (or quite as cheap), but for longer hauls, trains tend to be more comfortable and more scenic, offering a nice respite from bus travel and certainly worth at least one leg of the journey. Australia's Indian-Pacific line, between Sydney and Perth, is the world's second-longest (three full days of travel), with 478 continuous kilometres of completely unbending track (Ⓦwww.gsr.com.au). For other rail info, try the Country Link (Ⓦwww.countrylink.info). New Zealand's TranzAlpine line between Christchurch and Greymouth is particularly stunning, as is the Northern Explorer from Auckland to Wellington (Ⓦwww.tranzscenic.co.nz).

Cars

Driving is not a bad idea, especially if you have some specific off-road locations in mind or are hooked on back-road travel. You can rent (if you're 21), but at about $30/£19 a day for local rentals and $70/£44 for longer distances, it's a painfully quick way to lighten your money belt. If you plan to spend at least a month in the country, buying is a better way to go. You can pick up a used rust-bucket for about $1000/£630 and hopefully you'll be able to off-load it at the end of your trip.

A safer bet, and one that might keep you out of the repair shop, is to spend $2500–4000/£1575–2520 on a Holden Kingswood or Ford Falcon, the reliable (or at least fixable) road warrior of the traveler. For serious bushwhacking, check out a Toyota Land Cruiser. A road-weary model may set you back around $8000/£5040, but these things almost never give up. Depending on how much you fix it up and how clever you are at buying and selling, you could get anywhere from 65 to 110 percent back on your investment. If you're hopeless with mechanics, get the car checked out by a pro (🌐www.nrma.com.au) before you buy it, especially if you're buying from a fellow traveler – and don't take a clapped-out car into the outback, unless you're very well supplied with food and water. A buy-back plan is not a bad idea if you're arriving and leaving from the same place. You can find a dealer to offer you a price if you bring the car back in reasonable condition. If you're shopping for used motorcycles, consider the popular Yamaha XT600 Tenere (around $3500/£2200).

Whatever you buy, you'll have to get it registered (🌐www.rta.nsw.gov.au). But before you do, check with REVS, the Register of Encumbered Vehicles (🌐www.revs.nsw.gov.au), to make sure you're not buying a stolen vehicle. You'll also need to check to make sure there's no outstanding loan on the car, or you'll end up paying it or having the vehicle repossessed; for just $10/£6, REVS will issue a search certificate that will prevent repossession by a financier if the seller still owes money on the vehicle. If it's unregistered (also called "interstate" or "as is") you get to cough up $170–300/£103–181 dollars for the process. Try to pick up a car with the registration of the state where you hope to sell it. The registration requires third-party insurance, calculated on the type of car. If you realize you got stuck with a real rust-bucket, joining an auto club (with free roadside assistance) is well worth the $70/£42 or so.

Just so you're familiar with the terms (in Sydney, anyway – each state has its own rules): a Blue Slip is the registration, which you'll need to prove transferred ownership, and keep updated. The Pink Slip is a safety-check report, stating in rather vague terms that your car works, and also must be updated. The Green Slip is the obligatory third-party insurance.

Bikes

Cycles can be rented just about every-where, and are a great way to navigate the cities and venture a little further afield. If you don't have powerful tree-stump thighs and want to head between cities, the distances are a little more manageable in New Zealand. In northern Australia, pay particular attention to your water intake and sun exposure.

Boats

Ferries run from the North Island of New Zealand to the South Island (🌐www.interislandline.co.nz) and around several of the island groups in the South Pacific (🌐www.aranui.com), plus between Australia and Tasmania (🌐www.tt-line.com.au). They range from high-speed catamarans to rusting freighters to oversized dinghies.

Hitching

Hitching can be a good way to get around, although it's not officially endorsed anywhere (this book included; see p.143). The 1992 "backpacker murders" in Australia targeted women, men and couples, and changed the way people looked at hitching. In New Zealand, though, you'll often find there are so many people hitching in the prime spots, it'll feel more like you're standing in a queue.

With so many travelers owning vehicles, it's not difficult to post notices in the backpackers' hostels and catch a lift without wagging your thumb. You chip in for petrol (it's about 150 Australian cents a litre or $6/£3.80 a gallon), cram into the backseat and hope the driver didn't get stuck with a lemon.

In the South Pacific islands, the locals are so friendly it's not unheard of for taxi drivers to pick up hitchhikers and give them a lift for free. More likely, though, a shared taxi or minivan will pull over and pick you up for a small fee.

Reading list

- John Birmingham *The Tasmanian Babes Fiasco*
- Bill Bryson *Down Under*
- Peter Carey *The True History of the Kelly Gang*
- Bruce Chatwin *Songlines*
- Sean Condon *Sean and David's Long Drive*
- Alan Duff *Once Were Warriors*
- Robert Hughes *The Fatal Shore*
- Keri Hulme *The Bone People*
- Mark McCrum *No Worries*
- John Muk Muk *Burke Bridge of Triangles*
- Nevil Shute *A Town Like Alice*

Visas

Having a visa (Ⓦ www.immi.gov.au) is not an absolute guarantee that you'll

---

Visa requirements for Australia and New Zealand

EU Visa for Australia required, available free from Ⓦ www.immi.gov.au (click on "eVisitor") before arrival in Australia and valid for three months. To stay longer you need a proper visa; apply at least two weeks before your eVisitor expires.

USA and Canada Visa (called an ETA or Electronic Travel Authority) required, obtained at Ⓦ www.eta.immi.gov.au prior to arrival. It's issued free for three-month stays but you have to pay a A$20/$20/£13 service charge. Can be done through a travel agent, usually for a small fee. ETAs are valid for twelve months or the lifespan of your passport, whichever comes first, and cannot be extended. Unlike the eVisitor, the ETA allows you to study while in Australia.

If you have a criminal record, whatever your passport, your safest bet is to apply for a tourist visa (A$110/US$110/£69) when you apply outside the country.

be allowed into Australia – immigration officials may well check again that you have enough money to cover your expenses during your stay (around $500/£315 per month), and that you have a return or onward ticket. In extreme cases they may refuse entry, or more likely restrict your visit to a shorter period.

Twelve-month working-holiday visas are easily available to visitors aged 18–30 from most of western Europe and Canada, South Korea and Taiwan. Citizens of the USA, Chile, Malaysia, Thailand and Turkey and get roughly the same offer but with another name. Both types cost $270/£170. Visiting on a working visa is not normally a chance to further your career, since the stress is on casual employment: you are generally meant to work for no more than six months at any one job. Unfortunately, you must arrange the visa before you arrive in Australia, and several months in advance to avoid disappointment, as numbers are sometimes capped. Some travel agents, such as Trailfinders in the UK, can arrange working-holiday visas for you.

In New Zealand (ⓦwww.immigration .govt.nz), passport holders from Europe, the USA, Argentina, Brazil, Chile, Uruguay, Korea, Japan, Singapore and large parts of the Middle East don't need visas for visits of less than three months (six months for UK visitors). All visitors, however, need to provide evidence of sufficient funds to support yourself without working (NZ$1000/$766/£483 a month, or NZ$400/$306/£193 a month if your accommodation is prepaid), in the form of a bank draft, cash, travelers' checks, bank statement, one of the major credit cards or a friend or relative who is prepared to guarantee your accommodation and maintenance. You must also have a confirmed onward ticket and right of entry to your proposed destination.

Nearly all the South Pacific islands have the same visa requirements: an onward ticket and sufficient funds. On arrival, you get an automatic visa if needed, and permission to stay about a month. The island of Kiribati is one of the few exceptions, requiring visas from US and Australian passport-holders.

Central America and the Caribbean

The Mayans never realized they were laying the framework for a future travelers' trail. Much of Central America – the Ruta Maya (the Mayan route) – has become just that. Alongside spectacular ruins set against jungle backdrops are coasts that please divers and surfers alike, plus desertscapes, mountains, gorges, welcoming indigenous peoples and prices that are gentle on your pocket. Keep moving east (better get on a boat for good measure) and you arrive at the Caribbean, a string of island nations that stretch across vodka-clear waters from Florida to South America. Though many are rich with culture, the all-inclusive, tradition-free holiday is the major revenue source. Few people take the time to venture past the duty-free shops, meaning that travelers are left with plenty to explore.

Main attractions

- **Acapulco** Mexico. A *grand dame* of beach resorts that has been pulling in sun worshippers by the busload for well over half a century and lining them up under umbrellas on white sands. The pre-bungee cliff divers of La Quebrada are world renowned for their 45-metre plunges. Just inland, you'll encounter the often ignored darker side: garbage, poverty and traffic, though this real-life city is certainly worth a look.

- **Bay Islands** Honduras. Located 50km off the north coast of Honduras, these are the budget-travelers' Caribbean islands. Western Roatán and all of Utila are, anyway. Guanaja and eastern Roatán have gone upmarket. This paradise has one little drawback, though: insatiable sandflies.

- **Caribbean diving** The crystalline waters of the Caribbean make most people want to do one thing: jump in. With a snorkel or a basic scuba course, you can peek through the looking glass at the coral reefs, wrecks and phosphorescent fish on the other side.

- **Panama Canal** Panama. The 80-kilometre splitting of continents was completed in 1914 by the USA just before World War I. The engineering feats of this man-made wonder include a series of three sets of locks that raise and lower ships 26m, a dammed river creating Gatun Lake, and the Culebra Cut, a 14-kilometre-long, 192-metre-wide channel through a mountain. It takes the 13,000–14,000 ships that use the canal annually about nine hours to cross. A huge expansion is under way, expected to double capacity by 2014.

- **Tikal** Guatemala. Guatemala's ancient Mayan ceremonial center of temples, pyramids and plazas lies in the north of the country where it battles the ever-encroaching rainforest. Howler monkeys provide the soundtrack as you wander between the trees and ruins, feeling like you're lost in your own Tintin adventure.

Security issues

It's always a good idea to check the current political conditions before visiting a country, but the following are worth a little extra research: Guatemala, Haiti.

When to go

The chances of getting blasted by a Caribbean hurricane are slim at best, but it only takes one to toss your journey through a window or wrap it around a palm tree. With a close eye on the weather, these June to November storms can be avoided (most hit Aug–Oct), but it might mean an expensive last-minute flight. Also, because North American and European winter-sun worshippers get their tropical fix in the region, accommodation tends to fill up just after Christmas. Otherwise, with some minor highland-to-coast migration in certain spots to avoid rains or uncomfortably warm temperatures, it's good all year around.

Costs

Nicaragua, Honduras and El Salvador are the cheapest countries in the region, but even here prices can go up along the coast where surfers and sun worshippers gather. The all-inclusive resort areas, particularly in Mexico and around the Caribbean, are laughably expensive, especially considering how cheaply the locals live. You can find inexpensive eats, but there aren't always hostels, and camping is sometimes forbidden, so you may end up paying for the occasional $60/£38 room, which can be a budget-crippler. The only way to tackle some of these top-end destinations on a limited budget, therefore,

is going to be staying at informal family guesthouses and yachts in the marina with bunks for rent, or by Couchsurfing (see box, p.79). Such arrangements are not guaranteed, but can be found for $15–25/£9–16 when available, and you may also be able to negotiate cheap meals as part of the stay. Outside of Costa Rica, International Youth Hostel cards and ISIC cards will not be that useful. And with fewer dorm-style hostels, you're going to save money on accommodation if you travel with a partner or find a traveler on the way to help share costs.

Americans heading to Cuba will need to make sure they have ample US dollars or travelers' checks, as many places will not accept US credit cards. At the time of writing, efforts were under way to lift the US ban on letting its citizens visit Cuba, in the wake of which such rules will most likely change; check the current situation at Ⓦ www.travel.state.gov. For the time being, credit cards (even Visa and MasterCard) that are not tied to US banks are fine.

Getting around by air

International flight prices in Central America send a clear message to the budget traveler: take ground transport. Most of the Caribbean islands are within three hours of the southern USA, but

Recommended vaccinations

- Routine boosters for MMR, DPT and polio
- Hepatitis A
- Hepatitis B (optional)
- Rabies (optional)
- Typhoid
- Yellow fever (Panama, Trinidad and Tobago)

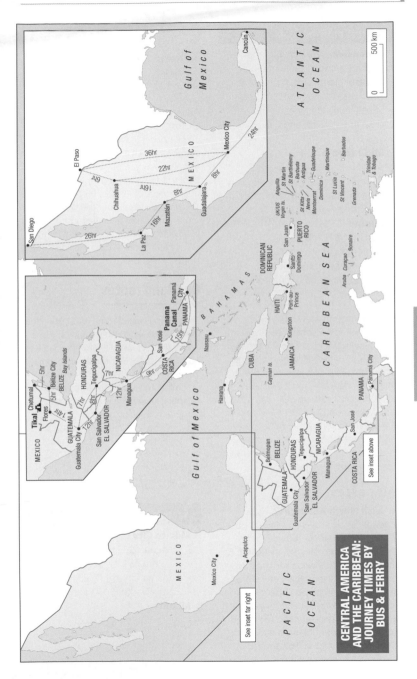

CENTRAL AMERICA AND THE CARIBBEAN: JOURNEY TIMES BY BUS & FERRY

Lowest daily budget

Expensive ($70/£44+):
Aruba, Barbados, Bahamas,
Bonaire, Martinique, Puerto
Rico, St Kitts and Nevis, St Lucia,
St Martin, St Vincent and the
Grenadines, Turks and Caicos,
Virgin Islands
Mid-range ($35–65/£22–41):
Antigua and Barbuda, Belize,
Cuba, Jamaica, Trinidad and
Tobago, coastal resorts of
Mexico
Budget ($18–30/£11–19):
Costa Rica, El Salvador,
Guatemala, Haiti, Honduras,
Mexico (except the coastal
resorts), Nicaragua, Panama

many flights stop a few times on the
way to the more southerly destinations. However, if you can put a group
together, a chartered flight among the
islands shouldn't cost you any more
than a standard fare, and it'll leave at
your convenience. Caribbean air passes
supply the most convenient way to see
the islands; the only other options are
hitching on yachts, using some of the
limited ferry services, or doing expensive
one-way hops.

Air passes

● **Visit North America** ⓦwww
.oneworld.com. Allows travel to up to
250 destinations in 25 countries with
One World Alliance airlines, including
the USA, Canada, Mexico and most of
the Caribbean islands. Buy between two
and ten coupons, priced depending
on the distance you fly, and saving you
as much as thirty percent on regular
fares. Travelers must be from outside
North America, and all flights must
be confirmed when you book. The

maximum stay in any one destination is
sixty days.

● **North America Airpass** ⓦwww
.staralliance.com. This Star Alliance pass
allows travel to 318 destinations in
twenty countries, including Bermuda,
Antigua, Trinidad and Tobago, Turks and
Caicos, Jamaica, the Caymans, Aruba
and Barbados. It's limited to three to ten
coupons, which are priced according
to how many you buy and where you
begin. It doesn't always represent a good
deal – check other fares before you buy.
You have to use all coupons within three
months, and your itinerary must be set
in advance, but can be changed for a
service fee. Not available to residents of
North America.

Overland routes

The major overland route runs between
the USA and South America, with a boat
ride or flight to avoid the Darién Gap (see
box, p.287), a lawless, roadless, guerrilla-
infested region between Panama and
Colombia. The route runs through either
Honduras or El Salvador and is most
commonly done by bus. Driving private
vehicles down from the US is also an
option, but one that may prove more
frustrating and come with more delays
than the local transport. See also "Ferries"
(opposite) and "Yachts" (p.55).

Sample return airfares

Mexico City to:
· Cancun: $272/£97
· Guatemala City: $358/£217
· Panama City: $437/£264
· San Salvador: $430/£260
Miami to:
· Martinique: $538/£325
· Puerto Rico: $314/£190
· St Thomas: $293/£177

Buses

In Central America, you've got everything from the chicken bus to the luxury bus, but mostly it's just chicken buses. When planning overland routes, consider that any more than two or three hours in a day on one of these, particularly if you wouldn't describe yourself as "petite", is going to be punishing. There are direct buses from the USA into Mexico and from Mexico to Belize and Guatemala. The relatively modern Tica buses (🌐www.ticabus.com) start in Tapachula in southern Mexico and connect the major cities all the way to Panama City (in 81hr and costing $132/£83 if you want to run the length of the line). In the Caribbean, most foreigners go by taxi or rental car, so the local buses, usually minibuses, are almost exclusively ridden by locals. The timing can be hard to calculate as most are privately operated, don't run to schedule and can stop innumerable times on the way or make detours at the driver's whim, which can mean plenty of delays by the time they arrive at their destination.

Trains

The Central American railway system is virtually nonexistent, due to jungle, lack of planning or government privatization. Mexico has kept a few scenic tourist lines alive, such as the Copper Canyon run from Chihuahua to Los Mochas (15hr; $153/£96; 🌐www.railsnw.com).

Ferries

Island-hopping ferry services in the Caribbean are simple in places and challenging in others. Between Martinique, Guadeloupe, Dominica and St Lucia there's a high-speed catamaran service called Lepers des Lies which runs six days a week (🌐www.express-des-iles.com) and costs $45–96/£28–60 for each hop. Ferries in the Virgin Islands run regularly and cost $6–50/£4–32

(🌐www.vinow.com/general_usvi/interisland_ferry). After that, it's just the odd connection here and there. French St Martin and Anguilla are connected by a link called, aptly enough, The Link (🌐www.link.ai), which leaves three times daily and costs $10/£6. Albury's Ferries service the Bahamas between Great Guana and Scotland Cay, Man-O-War Cay, Hope Town and Marsh Harbour for $17/£11 per crossing. There are also ferries linking Baja to mainland Mexico as well as between the Yucatán peninsula and the islands of Isla Mujeres and Cozumel.

Cars

Rentals in the Caribbean and Central America can cost as much or more than in the USA or Europe and, on top of that, some Caribbean countries like to make you buy a temporary visitors' licence unless you have an international driving permit. In Central America, an international permit will be useful if you plan to spend some time behind the wheel. You may want to take a few taxi rides first to get a firsthand look at driving conduct (or lack thereof).

Buying a car or motorcycle in the USA and driving overland is probably the best option for a long-term trip. To get a vehicle into Mexico, you don't need a Carnet de Passage, but you'll need a temporary import permit ($44/£28) online, at a Mexican consulate, or at a Centro de Internación Temporal de Vehículos (CITV) counter, which handles temporary vehicle entries at the customs office near border crossings). A $200–400/£126–252 deposit is also required, refundable when you leave the country. The price depends on the age of your vehicle. You might also pick up some Mexican auto insurance while you're there. The vehicle's certificate of ownership must be in your name, and you'll need a valid registration card and driving licence. Then you can't leave the country without the vehicle. If it's wrecked, or you have an emergency, you must seek permission at the Federal Registry of Vehicles in Mexico City or a treasury (*hacienda*) office elsewhere. Petrol prices in Mexico are higher than in the USA and there are very expensive toll roads ($33/£21 from Nuevo Laredo, on the Texas border, to San Miguel de Allende, north of Mexico City). You'll also be likely to encounter road blocks for drugs and weapons searches, so think twice (if it even requires that much thought) before you carry either in your car.

Bikes

Central American and Caribbean roads can be notoriously narrow, so you're going to be swerving or balancing on what's left of the road's shoulder. In the large cities, it's even more dangerous. So, while you're riding you'll want your bike to be as visible as possible. And when you're not riding make sure your bike is discreet, hidden and locked. On smaller roads, however, cycling is gaining popularity. From June to September, the rains may make cycling an uncomfortable and muddy affair, but the rest of the year is fine weather-wise.

Visa requirements for Central America

Belize No visa required for stays up to 30 days. Stays can be extended for up to 90 days. Sufficient funds ($60/£36 per day), return/onward ticket and a passport valid for three months after arrival.

Costa Rica No visa required for stays up to 30–90 days. Easier to leave the country for 72hr and re-enter than extend visa. Apply for extension first week of visit. Onward/return ticket required.

El Salvador No visa required for stays up to 90 days for most EU citizens and New Zealanders. Australians, Americans and Canadians only need a Tourist Card, bought on arrival for $10/£6. Passport must be valid for three months after arrival.

Guatemala No visa required for stays up to 90 days; 90-day extensions available in Guatemala City.

Honduras No visa required for stays up to 90 days; 30-day extensions can be obtained at local immigration office. Return/onward ticket required.

Mexico No visas required for stays up to 90 days for US citizens, or 30 days for nationals of Canada, Australia, New Zealand and most of Europe, but all need a tourist card ($23/£15), which is available on arrival and from travel agencies and most airlines serving Mexico. Proof of sufficient funds, and round-trip ticket.

Nicaragua Entry permit can be obtained on arrival for stays up to 90 days. Onward/return ticket required.

Panama Tourist card required for all non-EU nationals; available on arrival ($5/£3) from airlines serving Panama and valid for 90 days. Stay can be extended to 60 days. Visa needed for longer stays. Onward/return ticket required.

Hitching

Hitching is not a part of the Central American tradition, largely because the local buses are so cheap. In fact, you'll have a hard time to prevent the local buses from pulling over and offering a ride each time they pass. It can be done on less-frequented routes, though trucks (slow) and the back of pick-up trucks (unsafe) are the most common options. Your best bet is a posted note at a hostel or traveler café to share petrol costs with travelers who already have a vehicle.

Reading list

- Paula Burnett (ed) *The Penguin Book of Caribbean Poetry*
- Zee Edgell *Beka Lamb*
- Jamaica Kincaid *A Small Place*
- E.A. Markham (ed) *The Penguin Book of Caribbean Stories*
- V.S. Naipaul *A House for Mr Biswas*
- Charles Portis *Dog of the South*
- Jean Rhys *Wide Sargasso Sea*
- Salman Rushdie *The Jaguar Smile, a Nicaraguan Journey*
- Rosario Santos (ed) *And We Sold the Rain: Contemporary Fiction from Central America*
- Paul Theroux *The Mosquito Coast*
- Derek Walcott *Omeros*

Visas

US, Canada and EU passport-holders can stay between a few weeks and several months in all the Caribbean islands (except Cuba) without a visa. New Zealand and Australian passport-holders just need a visa for Trinidad and Tobago and Cuba; New Zealanders need a visa for the Dominican Republic. Americans need a license from the US Treasury Department to visit Cuba (typically given to journalists, aid workers or students studying in Cuba), though many have, at their own risk, visited illegally by traveling from Canada or Mexico. Most Central American and Caribbean countries require your passport to be valid for at least six months after you enter the country.

Europe and Russia

All roads don't actually lead to Rome. Swedes aren't all blondes. And the French don't tongue-kiss when they meet. However, none of these little disillusionments are reason enough to skip Europe on your trip. It offers the traveler more architecture, music, fashion, theatre and gastronomy per square kilometre than any other continent – which means heading off the main routes will still land you waist-deep in cultural treasures. The prevalence of the euro currency makes spending easier, and at least you're not giving away as much to the money-changers. What you do with this saving is quite limitless: climb an Austrian Alp, taste wine at an Italian palazzo, rent a surfboard in France, throw back a shot of Russian vodka, cool down with an icy Spanish gazpacho or soak your toes in the Adriatic on the Croatian coast.

Main attractions

● **Auschwitz Concentration Camp** Poland. A visit to Auschwitz (or Dachau, near Munich) may just be the most profound and enduring memory you take back from Europe. After a glimpse into the gas chambers, a view of the barracks and a walk around the compound, you begin to get a terrifying sense of what life here must have been like under Nazi control. It's impossible to leave unmoved.

● **The British Museum** England. Whatever Napoleon didn't manage to abscond with was snapped up by His or Her Majesty's far-flung forces – Egyptian mummies, Roman and Greek statues, Benin bronzes and exquisite Japanese prints are all (amazingly) under one roof. The current policy seems to be this: the rightful owners may not have their national treasures back but, like you, they're free to come and look at them in the British Museum and leave a donation on the way out to help finance the security system, lest they be stolen by someone else.

● **The Kremlin** Russia. It's not just a building, but an entire elevated citadel in the center of Moscow. About sixty percent is off limits to all but government personnel, but you can access the cathedrals, Patriarch's Palace and Armoury, which houses a fascinating collection of royal carriages, handmade weapons and Fabergé eggs.

● **The Louvre** France. This Paris museum could eat most sports stadiums for breakfast and still have plenty of room left over. It opened in 1793 and was immediately stuffed full of stolen goods pillaged by Napoleon's armies. Courtesy of architect I.M. Pei, it now sports a snazzy glass-pyramid entryway with a calming reflective pool that helps tranquillize the waiting crowds.

● **The Sistine Chapel** Italy. Michelangelo (without the aid of a chiropractor, mind you) painted the world's most famous ceiling fresco here in Rome. Beyond that, there's a vast collection of statues, frescos, maps and illuminated texts that leave visitors stunned.

Security issues

It's always a good idea to check the current political conditions before visiting a country, but the following are worth a little extra research: Albania, Armenia, Russian Federation.

● **Venice** Italy. The lovely canals and palaces of Venice are approached with more expectations than a George Lucas movie, yet never seem to disappoint. If you can see over the heads of all the tourists, the views are breathtaking at every step. Only after a visit can you finally understand the pains Marco Polo endured to return here.

● **Versailles** France. Louis Quatorze certainly knew how to live. There's the grand entrance, enough rooms to properly house all your party guests, endless gardens that require an army of trimmers and pruners, and a hall with more mirrors than a Las Vegas magic act. It's good to be the king.

When to go

There's no time when Europe should absolutely not be visited, but it can get rather cold and bleak in the winter (Nov–Feb), even in much of Turkey, and crowded in the summer (July–Aug). If

you're not a beach person, visiting in winter could actually work to your advantage, as you shouldn't have to queue for museums or reserve hostel beds. July and August are nice in northern Europe and the Alps, and a little too warm for comfort in the south. March to June and September to November are ideal for southern Europe, with perhaps a little overlap into the tourist season so you can appreciate what you're steering clear of.

Costs

Despite the high cost of living in many European countries and the large economic differences between some of them (Norway is the most expensive at nearly twice the average European costs, Bulgaria is the cheapest at just under half the average cost), budget-travel accommodation and supermarket food prices – the entire budget-travel infrastructure, really – are all fairly consistent. Once you start staying in nice hotels, eating in restaurants and hitting the bars, price differences become more pronounced (Norway, Sweden and Switzerland shoot up in the rankings). There are a few budget factors to consider. In Sweden, for example, you have the right to camp for free in many places. In Norway, no matter what your budget is, the $8/£5 beers are painful. And you could live for two weeks in Peru on the amount you'd have to spend to cross Monte Carlo in a taxi.

Lowest daily budget (excluding transport)

Expensive ($75–90/£47–57):
Britain, Finland, France, Germany, Norway, Sweden, Switzerland
Mid-range ($50–70/£32–44):
Austria, Belgium, Croatia, The Netherlands, Russia, Spain
Budget ($25–40/£16–25):
Bulgaria, Estonia, Greece, Latvia, Lithuania, Poland, Portugal, Romania, Slovakia, Turkey

EUROPE AND RUSSIA

0   500 km

S W E D E N

FINLAND

Helsinki

St Petersburg

Stockholm

Tallinn

ESTONIA

BALTIC SEA

LATVIA

Riga

R   U   S   S   I   A

Moscow
The Kremlin

LITHUANIA

KALININGRAD
(RUSSIA)

Vilnius

Minsk

BELARUS

Warsaw

P   O   L   A   N   D

Kiev

**Auschwitz
Concentration
Camp**

Kraków

U   K   R   A   I   N   E

SLOVAKIA

Bratislava

MOLDOVA

Chisinau

Budapest

HUNGARY

R   O   M   A   N   I   A

BOSNIA-
HERZEGOVINA

Belgrade

Bucharest

BLACK SEA

Sarajevo

SERBIA

BULGARIA

MONTENEGRO

KOSOVO

Sofia

ALBANIA

Skopje

MACEDONIA

Istanbul

Tirana

Ankara

GREECE

Aegean

T   U   R   K   E   Y

Sea

Athens

Crete

CYPRUS

Getting around by air

With cut-throat budget airlines battling it out in the skies, your biggest cost for flights within Europe is likely getting yourself out to the airport. Really. It's not uncommon to find flights for $15–35/ £9–22. Except for certain routes at certain times of the year when demand is particularly high. If you can find a great deal, it's not a bad idea to use it to augment your rail or bus pass, so you don't have to use several days of your pass (and your trip) to make a beeline across Europe.

Many of these start-up "no frills" carriers use minor airports located a little further from the city center, but you may even save time; some walks to the gate are only 100m. When they say no frills, they generally aren't kidding. But since the flights are almost never more than three hours, does it really matter that it feels more like a bus? Pack along a meal and you'll be fine. You might even pack some cheap, compact earphones so you don't need to buy the ones they try to flog you. No need to worry about safety. Whatever corners they need to cut to

streamline their company, there's no getting around the strict EU regulations that govern the industry.

Since every major European city and half the minor ones seem tapped into the budget routes and there's no single search engine (although Ⓦ www.skyscanner.net probably come the closest and Ⓦ www.cheapflights.co.uk will do the next best thing – scour the web for the best deals offered by other discount brokers and consolidators), the trick is figuring out which airlines cover which routes so you can visit their booking sites. To make a thorough search for the best airfare, visit Ⓦ www.attitudetravel.com/lowcostairlines and input where you're headed from to see where you can get on budget airlines.

Air passes

● **Visit Europe** Ⓦ www.oneworld .com. Offers 219 destinations in 52 countries (including Morocco and Tunisia) with member airlines of the One World Alliance; you have to fly into Europe with an Alliance carrier to qualify. Fares depend on the mileage you cover but often represent a fairly good saving on short routes. Buy the minimum two coupons before you leave for Europe; more can be purchased after you arrive. No upper limit.

● **Star Alliance Europe Airpass** Ⓦ www.staralliance.com. Flights to 280 destinations in 45 countries, with 13 Star Alliance airlines; available only if you fly to and from Europe on an Alliance carrier. Minimum three coupons, maximum ten, which have to be used within three months. Pricing is complicated, and taxes and surcharges are high – so keep a lookout for this when you compare prices.

● **EuropebyAir FlightPass** Ⓦ www .europebyair.com. Flights on twenty-plus airlines to more than five hundred cities in Europe and beyond for $99–199/ £62–125 per flight plus airport taxes, which break down into a service fee of

---

Recommended vaccinations

Western Europe

- Routine boosters for measles/ mumps/rubella (MMR), diphtheria/pertussis/tetanus (DPT) and polio
- Hepatitis A
- Hepatitis B (optional)

Eastern Europe

- Routine boosters for MMR and polio
- Hepatitis A
- Hepatitis B (optional)
- Rabies (optional)
- Typhoid

$42/£26 plus further charges for issuing and shipping paper tickets, which can be very high. All tickets except for Hamburg International are paper tickets, so you can change plans easier than with other passes. Non-refundable and only available to non-European residents.

Overland routes

Europe doesn't really have overland routes, it has an overland web. With open borders, an extensive infrastructure and travelers using bus and train passes like amusement-park tickets, there's more darting around on whims than specific A to B passage. The more socially inclined migrate like wildebeests to the major backpacker-endorsed festivals: Somerset's Glastonbury, Pamplona's Running of the Bulls and Munich's Oktoberfest. A railpass is your best bet (both for cultural reasons and leg room), although not quite as cheap as a bus pass. Biking and driving are viable options as well. Zipping around on flights, no matter how cheap, is probably not the best way to see Europe (hard to make inroads with the local community at 30,000 feet), but it offers a great chance to connect two or three spots that might otherwise be out of range. For example, you might want to spend the bulk of your trip in Spain and Portugal, but you can hop on a plane in Barcelona and get to Rome or Dublin for a long weekend without breaking your budget.

Buses

There are two bus passes worth looking into, and they both undercut the train fares: Eurolines (Ⓦwww.eurolines.com) and Busabout (Ⓦwww.busabout.com). Eurolines is cheaper while Busabout takes you right to a hostel (one they hope you'll stay at), and provides onboard movies and a guide. That gives you less reason to look out the window and less opportunity to meet locals, but it will save you time and the hassle of picking and finding a hostel. Eurolines and other local and national bus services are likely to be the cheapest option (after hitchhiking) for short-distance travel, particularly in the UK, where train prices are exorbitant. In the UK, consider the low-cost intercity service of Megabus (Ⓦwww.megabus.com).

Trains

Europe is train country. How else would you describe a rail network totalling 240,000 kilometres? (By comparison, there's 45,000km of rail in the USA and Canada, an area more than twice as large.) It's not necessarily the cheapest way to get around, it's simply the preferred way. And not because the rail routes are often more scenic, but the facing seats provide an opportunity to meet locals, the aisles allow you to stretch your legs, some carriages allow full reclining at night and the train's chug-chug adds an authentic travel beat to any conversation. There are several passes available at Ⓦwww.raileurope.com: see "Costs and savings" (p.76) to best take advantage of them.

In Turkey, the express trains and sleepers are worth looking into and provide a nice leg-stretching change from the bus rides, but the local (*yolcu* and *posta*) trains barely exceed the speed of rust.

Cars

Rental

For a longer road trip, rental is on the expensive side. To make it affordable, find a travel companion or group of them. If you're renting over 21 days, you can lease from Ⓦwww.kemwel.com, Ⓦwww.europebycar.com or Ⓦwww.renaultusa.com, all agencies that take advantage of tax loopholes by leasing out new cars then selling the practically new vehicles on the used market; a comfortable car for four is going to run

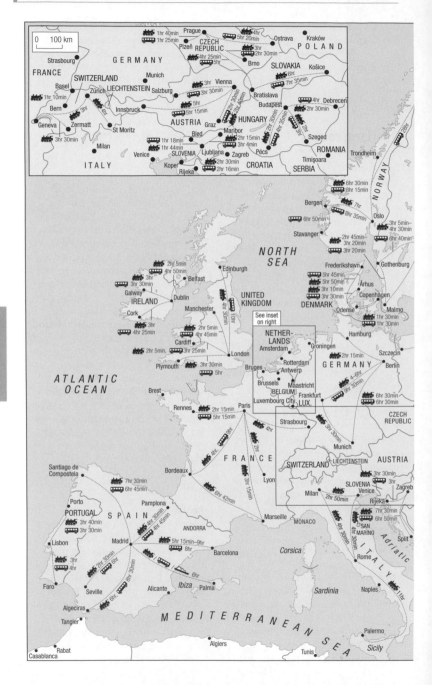

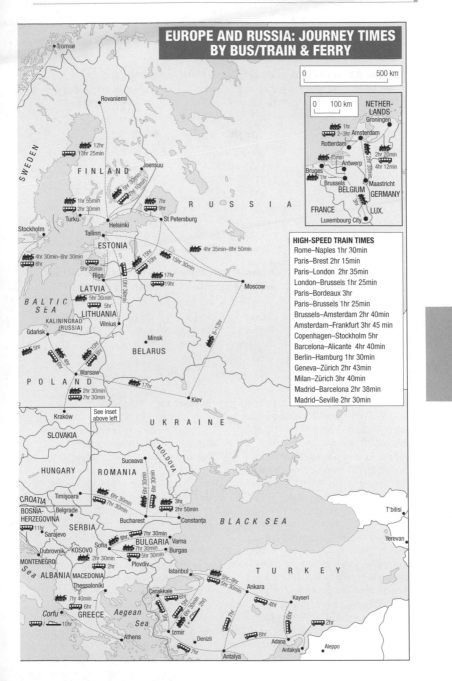

EUROPE AND RUSSIA: JOURNEY TIMES BY BUS/TRAIN & FERRY

0   500 km

0   100 km   NETHER-LANDS

HIGH-SPEED TRAIN TIMES
Rome–Naples 1hr 30min
Paris–Brest 2hr 15min
Paris–London 2hr 35min
London–Brussels 1hr 25min
Paris–Bordeaux 3hr
Paris–Brussels 1hr 25min
Brussels–Amsterdam 2hr 40min
Amsterdam–Frankfurt 3hr 45 min
Copenhagen–Stockholm 5hr
Barcelona–Alicante 4hr 40min
Berlin–Hamburg 1hr 30min
Geneva–Zürich 2hr 43min
Milan–Zürich 3hr 40min
Madrid–Barcelona 2hr 38min
Madrid–Seville 2hr 30min

Europe travel passes

Eurail

25 countries covered: Austria, Belgium, Bulgaria, Croatia, Czech Republic, Denmark, Finland, France, Germany, Greece, Hungary, Ireland, Italy, Luxembourg, Montenegro, Netherlands, Norway, Poland, Portugal, Romania, Serbia, Slovenia, Spain, Sweden, Switzerland

Global Pass	Adult	Youth
15 days	$763/£480	$497/£313
21 days	$985/£621	$642/£404
1 month	$1213/£764	$789/£497
2 months	$1711/£1077	$1113/£701
3 months	$2110/£1329	$1373/£865
10 days within 2 months	$900/£567	$586/£369
15 days within 2 months	$1181/£744	$770/£485

Eurail Select Pass

3 bordering countries within 2 months		4 bordering countries within 2 months		5 bordering countries within 2 months	
5 days	$483/£304	5 days	$540/£340	5 days	$594/£374
6 days	$533/£336	6 days	$590/£372	6 days	$644/£406
8 days	$631/£398	8 days	$688/£443	8 days	$743/£468
10 days	$731/£460	10 days	$786/£495	10 days	$839/£529

to about $350/£220 a week; a compact is $200/£126. And with petrol prices at over $1.50/£0.95 per litre ($6+/£3.80+ per gallon), plus tolls and parking fees, one month of travel – figuring on five hours' driving every other day – in a compact car for two is about $1000/£630 per person (that's $725/£456 per person if you drive every third day, $635/£400 if you drive every fourth day). With four people in a larger car, that's around $600/£378 per person driving five hours every other day, or $475/£300 driving every third day. Rental companies generally lease to those 18 and over, but some require drivers to be over 23. Rentals are best booked in advance, which can be done direct, via a travel agent or through the mainstream online flight-booking sites.

Buying a car

Buying a car in Europe is a fun alternative, provided you don't run into mechanical trouble or get stuck trying to off-load it before your flight leaves. For language reasons, the UK is a good starting point, though you'll want a left-hand drive if you'll be spending most of your time on the continent. To see what's available, look at the newspaper classifieds, as well as specialized magazines such as *Loot* (ⓦwww.loot.co.uk) and *Exchange and Mart* (ⓦwww.exchangeandmart.co.uk). At ⓦwww.gumtree.com and ⓦwww.tntmagazine.com/uk you'll find other travelers' cars and camper vans which, for high-mileage reasons, may not make the most sense (although, the seller may be able to help with all the paperwork as well as some great tips). Some of the

Eurail Select Pass Youth

3 bordering countries within 2 months		4 bordering countries within 2 months		5 bordering countries within 2 months	
5 days	$316/£199	5 days	$353/£222	5 days	$389/£245
6 days	$348/£219	6 days	$358/£226	6 days	$421/£265
8 days	$411/£259	8 days	$448/£282	8 days	$547/£344
10 days	$476/£300	10 days	$512/£284	10 days	$547/£344

Busabout

Nine countries covered: Austria, Belgium, Czech Republic, France, Germany, Italy, Netherlands, Spain, Switzerland
Northern Loop 11 cities $636/£399 (adults), $385/£385 (students)
Southern Loop 12 cities $636/£399 (adults), $614/£385 (students)
Western Loop 11 cities $636/£399 (adults), $614/£385 (students)
Flexitrip minimum 6 stops $556/£349 (adults), $534/£335 (students)

Eurolines Adult

	Low season	**Mid season**	**High season**
15 days	$267/£168	$311/£196	$445/£280
30 days	$400/£252	$426/£268	$585/£369

Eurolines Youth

15 days	$229/£144	$267/£168	$375/£236
30 days	$311/£196	$349/£220	$483/£304

vehicles are registered on the continent, and as long as you're not keeping the car in the UK for more than twelve months, you can get around the UK registration. In Germany, you might look into buying a Vorführwagen, a demo model which has been in the showroom and used for test drives, or a Jahreswagen, a low-mileage car in good condition that was bought at discount by a car-manufacturer employee and sold as soon as the law allows, which is one year.

The AA (ⓦwww.theaa.com) and RAC (ⓦwww.rac.co.uk) are the places to turn to for insurance; they have co-op arrangements throughout Europe for breakdowns. Once you cross into Asia or Africa, however, it's another story (see box, p.61). Bring extra copies of your documents and leave others with a trusted friend or relative, or in an online vault. They should include road tax, insurance and ownership papers. If you have a good driving record in your home country you may be able to get preferable rates with a European insurer. Get a letter from your insurance agent back home just in case.

EU driving licences are valid in all of Europe. Other foreign licences (US, Can, NZ and Aus) are accepted, but not in Italy, Austria, Spain and some East European countries, for which you should have an international permit, easily arranged in your home country (see box, p.61).

Bikes

This is a continent that deserves to be seen from a bike. The hamlets that tourbuses and cars roll past regularly are some of the greatest treasures. With the major bike races ripping by most places at some point or another (Giro d'Italia, Vuelta de España, Tour de France), you'll also find an unrivalled respect for cyclists. There's always a small pub that's happy to refill your water bottle or a château pleased to fill it with wine. On the other hand, Europe is crammed with narrow roads, high speed limits and no fewer than 20 million drivers who think they're Michael Schumacher. Denmark, the Netherlands, Belgium and Norway have some of the finest cycle-only touring trails for those who don't like to compete for space with motor vehicles or eat their exhaust.

Europe is also a great place to buy a bike, which will make a nice souvenir at the end of your trip. Or, if you can buy a popular international brand, you should have no trouble selling it in a hurry. All cities – and even many small towns – will have all the spare parts you'll need.

The larger cities all have bike rentals. In London, Paris and Rome they may be more likely to get you a bed at a nearby hospital than where you're going, but in cities like Amsterdam and Copenhagen they make city exploration a joy.

Hitching

Thumbing it in Europe is a little hit and miss, and don't think about it without reading the section on hitching safety (see box, p.143). In some countries, it's considered normal and drivers are sympathetic to your roadside plight (as many have done some hitching themselves). In others, such as parts of Scandinavia, you're something of a pariah. In places where it's not as accepted, take special care to dress well and get to service stations. Some countries have hitching organizations that will, for a fee, put you in touch with a driver heading in the same direction who wants to share the petrol costs. It takes away the thrill, but will likely get you where you want to go. A good place to get a grip on hitchhiking in Europe is ⓦwww.digihitch.com.

Visa requirements for Europe

Visas are only required for the following countries:
Russia notoriously complicated tourist visa required for all.
Turkey for citizens of the USA, UK, Australia and Canada (can be obtained at point of arrival $16/£10). Multi-entry visas valid for up to 90 days. Canada $197/£124, other countries $15–30/£9–18.

Visas

In general, Brits, Americans, Canadians, Australians and New Zealanders don't need a visa to visit European countries, but there are some exceptions (see box above). Russia requires a visa, and you'll need a transit visa to get there overland through Belarus. Australians and New Zealanders need one for Ukraine and Turkey also requires visas.

Reading list

- Julian Barnes *Letters from London*
- Bill Bryson *Neither Here Nor There: Travels in Europe*
- Charles Dickens *A Tale of Two Cities*
- Fyodor Dostoyevsky *Crime and Punishment*
- Anne Frank *The Diary of a Young Girl*
- Adam Gopnik *Paris to the Moon*
- Ernest Hemingway *Death in the Afternoon*
- Homer *The Odyssey*
- Peter Høeg *Miss Smilla's Feeling for Snow*
- Peter Mayle *A Year in Provence*

Middle East

Let's cut right to the chase: is the Middle East safe? Depends where you're going. From a travel perspective, the Arab Spring has caused a great deal of instability. Violence and protests can occur, but the fact that there are so many news bureaus covering such a small plot of land means that news of violence ricochets around the world. Often the countries are far safer than the media would have you believe, so it's good to check out the most recent political situation. When the region is plagued with headline-grabbing incidents that don't threaten general stability, the good news is that there's a chance you'll be visiting some of the world's greatest archeological sites in relative solitude. You'll also be able to enjoy the calming effect of walking barefoot over the hand-woven carpets of a mosque, tasting fresh-squeezed fruit juices, experiencing the hospitality and hummus of the Jordanians, and taking a desert safari in the United Arab Emirates.

Main attractions

● **Jerusalem** Israel. If you can see past the skirmishes that continue to mar this city, you'll find an architectural beauty forged from thousands of years of chaos. There's the Dome of the Rock, where Mohammed is believed to have ascended to heaven; the Church of the Holy Sepulchre, the last stop on the Via Dolorosa, where Christ was believed to have been crucified (the nearby Garden Tomb is also a possible site); and the Western (or Wailing) Wall, the closest piece of Israeli real estate to the ancient site of the Second Temple (where the Dome of the Rock now stands), before it was destroyed by the Romans in 70AD. As a traveler you're free to roam (after passing through metal detectors) to all three sites and pick up falafels, fresh dates and pistachio nuts along the way.

● **Palmyra** Syria. What remains today is the stone exoskeleton of a once magnificent city. The art and architecture of this oasis in the Syrian desert was a mixture of the Persian and Greco-Roman civilizations borrowed from traders heading from Baghdad and the Persian Gulf to Damascus and Jerusalem.

● **Petra** Jordan. This ancient Nabatean city, built into the rose-colored canyon walls in the Jordanian desert, had been lost to the outside world for over 1000 years when it was rediscovered in 1812 by Johann Burckhardt. The ruins are approached on foot via the Siq, a 1.2-kilometre canyon not much wider than a queen-sized mattress.

● **Red Sea diving and snorkelling** Israel and Jordan. One moment you're on the edge of a bleak desert, getting blasted by convection-oven-like winds. The next you're in an aquamarine paradise surrounded by schools of multihued fish. You pop your head up again to be sure the desert is still there. It is. The stark contrast simply adds to the experience of diving one of the world's great reefs.

When to go

Winter is the most likely obstacle you'll face, and that's only if you're trying to avoid the snow, which has been known to make many of the roads impassable. You might also want to try to sidestep the hot summer months if you're doing more than diving the Red Sea and swimming in the Med. Throughout the region, spring and autumn (April, May, Sept and Oct) are the optimum times to visit.

Costs

Fewer than half of the countries in the Middle East are easy on the money belt, and, by no coincidence, that's where you'll find nearly all the budget travelers. Israel, Jordan, and Egypt are the region's backpacker havens. Student cards are particularly useful, and can save you well over 25 percent at some museums and archaeology sites. Keep a pocketful of small change for baksheesh (tip) distribution; many of the irritating "services" that

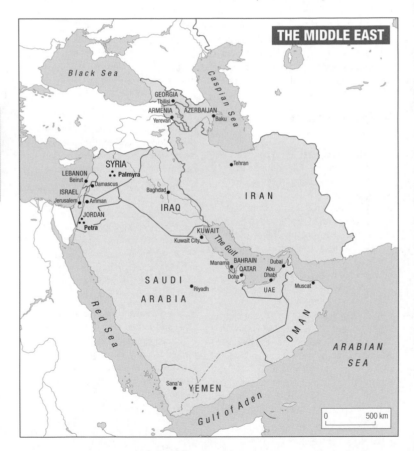

THE MIDDLE EAST

are done for you – such as pointing you in a direction you're already going – do not deserve baksheesh, but slightly more helpful services should be rewarded. This is simply part of the culture. You might want to keep coins separate from your bills so you don't have to flash your money and potentially draw more attention than you'd like. Diving trips around the Red Sea and some private tours of the archeological sites (often well worth it) are the most likely to dent your budget.

Getting around by air

Flying is the most reliable and speedy way to get around the Middle East, but it's also the most expensive. If your kidneys are tired from the long bus rides, you might try one longer hop, but without air passes available it's a quick way to drain your finances. There are no

flights available to Iraq, or between Israel and nearby countries, with the exceptions of Jordan and Egypt.

Overland routes

There's really just one classic overland route. It goes from Istanbul to Cairo, via Syria (which is, at time of writing, not advisable), Jordan, Israel and the Sinai Peninsula. Doing it in reverse makes things difficult if you allow the Israelis to stamp your passport, although they'll put it on a separate piece of paper if you ask. You could also pop over to Lebanon on the way, but the Lebanon–Israel border is still a little dodgy for crossings. Probably the best way to get around is on buses and trains, with hired taxis for harder-to-reach places outside of popular bus routes.

Buses
Outside of the rich, Sport Utility Vehicle-driving Gulf states, the bus is the most common mode of transport in the Middle East for locals and travelers alike. There are no bus package-deals for the region, but bus travel is so cheap that this isn't a problem. On some Arab buses, they like to collect passengers' ID cards. Hand over your least valuable photo ID. An old driving licence or ISIC card usually works fine. Some taxis function as buses as well. These shared taxis move a little more quickly, don't stop as long and cost a bit more. They don't have fixed times but run frequently on regular routes, and can often be flagged down from the side of the road if there's space available. (They usually leave from a regular departure spot when full, and places become available as they drop people off along the way.)

Trains
Trains are typically cheaper than buses, but they're also slower, less prevalent

Lowest daily budget

Expensive ($60-85/£38-54):
Oman, Kuwait, United Arab
Emirates
Mid-range ($30–50/£19–32):
Bahrain, Israel, Lebanon,
Qatar, Saudi Arabia
Budget ($15–30/£10–19):
Iran, Jordan, Syria, Yemen

and less frequent. One train runs weekly
between Istanbul and Aleppo (29hr;
$56/£34 including sleeper), while the
Hejaz railway between Damascus and
Amman (11hr; $6/£3), though note that
these services were suspended at the
time of writing; visit Ⓦwww.seat61.com
to see if they're back on track when you
want to go.

Cars

For more flexible travel, a long-term
taxi or rental car is going to be the best
option. Importing a car is unlikely to be
worth the effort and expense, unless you
plan to continue your trip across Africa or
on to Australia.

Bikes

Bicycle touring is uncommon in the
Middle East, but far from impossible.
The summer heat from June to August

Sample return airfares

Amman to:
• Cairo $200/£126
• Muscat $200/£126
Dubai to:
• Damascus $240/£151
• Riyadh $218/£137
Tel Aviv to:
• Amman $283/£178
• Istanbul $271/£170

can literally melt you into the pavement.
Keep a pair of lightweight trousers out
and available to quickly slip on when you
stop, as shorts are not likely to be a hit
with the locals.

Boats

There are a number of boats that can
bridge your overland travels in the
region, including a three-hour ride for
$60/£38 between Aqaba and Nuweiba in
the Sinai (1hr; $70/£44 for high-speed),
and an infrequent three-day ferry
between Jeddah and Suez ($105/£66).
Divers and others can catch a 1hour
30minute ferry from Sharm-el-Sheikh to
Hurghada for $45/£28.

Hitching

Hitching, defined as getting a lift for free,
doesn't really exist in the Middle East
outside of Israel. You'll see many people
standing along the road looking for a
ride, but they're either waiting for a bus
or a shared taxi or someone who will
give them a ride for the price of a bus or
shared taxi. In other words, you can hitch
(no thumbing, just extend your arm
palm down) but offer to pay for the ride.
In Israel, hitching is common but not
recommended, except for soldiers who
hitch in uniform with their guns slung
over their backs, and get rides immediately. Because of the tensions in the area,
Israelis are particularly wary of picking
up non-soldiers, so you might, if you're
male, try to befriend a soldier or two
waiting for a ride and see if they'll ask
the driver on your behalf for a ride. With
an armed soldier in the car, they usually
feel better about offering a lift.

Visas

For the Middle Eastern countries that
require visas, it's not a bad idea to try to
obtain them before leaving. Some visas

are easier to get from home and some are easier to get on the road while in neighboring countries. But even if you're turned down in your home country, there's nothing preventing you from trying again once you are in the area. Some visas may require a letter of recommendation from your embassy, which will have a standard

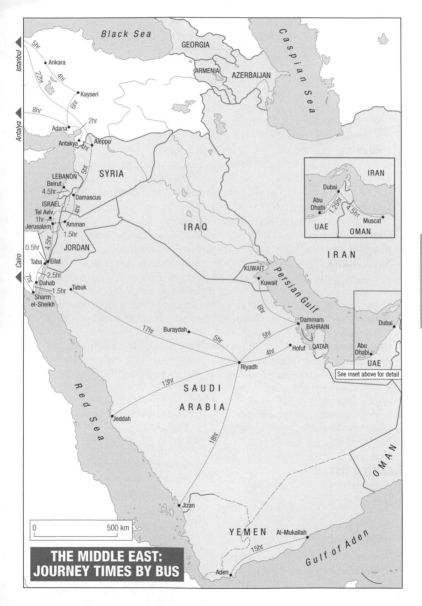

THE MIDDLE EAST: JOURNEY TIMES BY BUS

Visa requirements for the Middle East

Iran Visas required prior to arrival (up to 1 month: $128/£81). Because these can be tricky to get, it's easier to go with a tour operator. Visa will be refused if your passport has an Israeli stamp. Western Europeans, Australians and New Zealanders can get a 7-day tourist visa on arrival at airports in Tehran, Shiraz, Mashad, Isfahan and Tabriz.

Iraq Visa required (15 day tourist visa: $30/£19). Without press credentials, you might try at the embassy in Jordan, but the situation in the country is highly volatile at time of writing and a journey is probably not worth the risk.

Israel No visa required for stays of up to 90 days. $20/£13 entry fee may apply, depending on nationality. Can apply for additional 90-day extension. Proof of onward travel required. If you're traveling on to Arab countries, get the Israeli stamp on a separate piece of paper or you may not be allowed in.

Jordan Visa required (30 days: single entry $38/£24; 180 days multiple entry $98/£62); can be obtained on the spot at the border or airport, and extended for up to 3 months. No visa required if you arrive at Aqaba and stay less than a month. Departure tax of $28/£18 at all airports.

Lebanon Visa required (up to 1 month: $35/£22), available at airport on arrival. Visa refused with Israel stamp in passport.

Oman Visa required, valid for 3 months ($52/£33 for three weeks, extendable by one week); online application at ⓦwww.rop.gov.om.

Saudi Arabia Visa required; get a government Visit Visa application form at ⓦwww.saudiembassy.net. A no-charge three-day transit visa may be issued, but not to women unless accompanied by a male relative. Transits of less than 18 hours do not require visas. Proof of onward travel required.

Syria With the ongoing conflict in Syria the visa situation is unclear. Check with your local Syrian embassy.

United Arab Emirates Free visa on arrival for stays up to 60 days. Extension of 30 days costs $136/£86.

Yemen Tourist visa required (two months single entry; $40/£25.

letter for this purpose, but some embassies have been known to charge a small fee for issuing it.

Reading list

- Larry Collins and Dominique Lapierre *O Jerusalem!*
- William Dalrymple *The Holy Mountain*
- Nawal El-Saadsawi *The Hidden Face of Eve: Women in the Arab World*
- Thomas Friedman *From Beirut to Jerusalem*
- Tony Horwitz *Baghdad without a Map*
- T.E. Lawrence *The Seven Pillars of Wisdom*
- Naguib Mahfouz *Arabian Nights and Days*
- Peter Mansfield *The Arabs*
- Edward Said *Orientalism*
- Paul Theroux *Pillars of Hercules*

North America

Most people feel like they know the USA already, even if they've never set foot in the country. They know that American lifeguards can all afford plastic surgery; they know that American cars are often victims of high-speed police chases and have a tendency to blow up; and they know American bomb-defusers have been trained to wait until the last possible second before picking the right wire to cut. But you really can't judge the country through a TV set. In fact, much of what you see isn't even the USA at all. It's Canada, the down-to-earth, bilingual ice-hockey power to the north where many of the hit programs are filmed. Outdoor enthusiasts may find this land is especially worth a visit, with world-class hiking and skiing in the Canadian Rockies, pristine camping and paddling in the northern waterways, and the surging sixteen-metre-high tides in the Bay of Fundy.

What you may not learn about the USA by watching Canada is that there's delicious Cajun cooking and a rich culture along the Gulf of Mexico; some of the world's most dramatic rock formations in parks across Utah, Arizona and Colorado; a unique art community in New Mexico; and more warm hospitality than you can shake a pitcher of lemonade at.

Main attractions

● **Banff** Canada. This national park is Canada's top year-round resort, the home of the country's first wildlife sanctuary and the aquamarine Moraine Lake. You'll find everything from hikes to hot springs, camping to caving and glaciers to… well, more glaciers. The nearby Columbia Icefield has around thirty of them.

● **Grand Canyon** USA. This unfathomably stunning hole in the ground is still getting bigger. Scientists estimate that the Colorado River is deepening the bottom at the rate of 15m per million years. Three million visitors come here every year, some who hike down to the bottom and others who stay up on the rim and watch the IMAX film about hiking down to the bottom. The film, plus an array of postcards, may

be your only chance to see the canyon if you arrive on a day when it is completely cloaked by smog pumped out by the Navajo Generating Station upriver. There's no shortage of spectacular scenery in this region, and other (less crowded) national parks (such as Arches, Canyonlands and Zion) make for even better day-hikes and camping trips.

● **Las Vegas** USA. Vegas offers a smorgasbord of sin, some fantastic shows and exuberantly over-the-top casinos based on New York, Venice, Cairo and so on, that take ostentation to new levels.

● **New York City** USA. It was once, and arguably still is, the great gateway to the New World. These days, though, you have to take a special boat ride to float by the Statue of Liberty and land at Ellis Island (now a terrific museum of immigration). People-watching in Times

Square will keep you busy for a good half-hour. And the city's 150 museums, 900 art galleries, 18,000 restaurants and 2000 bars and nightclubs will keep you occupied a lot longer.

● **Niagara Falls** USA/Canada. This natural-wonder-cum-honeymoon retreat can be viewed from both the USA and Canada. You don't have to ride over in a barrel to appreciate the force of the three cascades: Bridal Falls, American Falls and Horseshoe/Canadian Falls. A total of three million litres per second make the fifty-plus-metre drop over the 1.2-kilometre-wide rim.

When to go

There are two things to try to miss: the winter weather in central USA and the north (Dec–Feb), unless you're skiing; and the crowded national parks in summer (July–Aug). In spring (March/April) the skiing is still good and the weather elsewhere is favorable. In the fall (Sept–Oct) the changing leaves paint the hills with wonderful Technicolor hues. If you're after the California surfin' safari beach scene, go from June until late August or September.

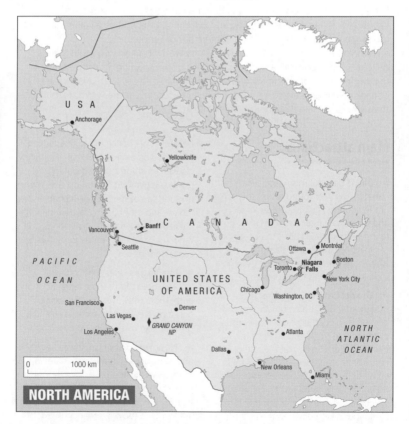

Costs

Grab a thick slice of pizza at a food stall, a bagel for breakfast or a burger at Mickey D's, and you shouldn't be spending more than $3/£2. If you're staying at hostels, you can get by on $40/£24 per day in the USA and $35/£21 in Canada, not including inter-city transportation.

Getting around by air

Americans love to drive, but they also like to get where they're going quickly, which explains why the enormous airport parking lots are usually full. Certain routes are cheaper than others, and there are a lot of competitive and seasonal price cuts. So as long as you don't attempt, as they do so often in the movies, to walk up to the counter and buy the next flight out, or book last-minute during peak seasons, you can get some great deals. This can be helpful if you're looking for an occasional hop and a jump to help get you around. Crossing continental USA in the air takes five and a half hours, and from the West Coast to Hawaii is a little over five hours.

The general deal available to those arriving from overseas by plane is to buy three to ten coupons. Three coupons cost around $400/£241 and ten will set you back around $1100/£664. Depending on the airline, special coupons must be purchased for the Caribbean, Hawaii and Alaska. Enquire with your travel agent, as coupons should be purchased when you buy your flight over.

Air passes

● **Visit North America** ⓦwww .oneworld.com. Allows travel to up to 250 destinations in 25 countries with One World Alliance airlines, including the USA, Canada, Mexico and most of the Caribbean islands. Buy between two and ten coupons, priced depending on the distance you fly, and saving you as much as thirty percent on regular fares. Travelers must be from outside North America, and all flights must be confirmed when booking. The maximum stay in any one destination is sixty days.

● **North America Airpass** ⓦwww .staralliance.com. This Star Alliance pass allows travel to 318 destinations in twenty countries, including Bermuda, Antigua, Trinidad and Tobago, Turks and Caicos, Jamaica, the Caymans, Aruba and Barbados. It's limited to three to ten coupons, which are priced according to how many you buy and where you begin. It doesn't always represent a good deal – check other fares before you buy. You have to use all coupons within three months, and your itinerary must be set in advance, but can be changed for a service fee. Not available to residents of North America.

Overland routes

North America's infrastructure allows for a range of routes. It's really more a matter of what type of transport you're using and connecting your favorite stops in some sort of mileage-friendly order.

Sample return airfares

New York to:
- Chicago $199/£120
- Las Vegas $238/£144
- LA $263/£159
- Miami $175/£106

San Francisco to:
- Boston $261/£158
- Hawaii $391/£236
- Seattle $129/£78

Vancouver to:
- Anchorage $507/£306
- Minneapolis $440/£265
- Toronto $516/£311

There's the New York to Key West drive; the route that leads down the eastern seaboard; and the classic from New York to LA via Chicago, picking up what's left of Route 66. Crossing Canada, you might head from Quebec to Vancouver via Montreal, Toronto and Lake Louise, then turn north and make your way to Anchorage along the Alaskan pipeline.

In terms of the best way to get around, it's a bit of a toss-up. Buying a car is a fine way to go – it's flexible, cheap and takes advantage of the zillions of miles of smooth highways (though you will, of course, be adding to the greenhouse gases the USA is internationally frowned on for producing). Trains are convenient where they exist, but don't provide much flexibility in routes, and the buses leave a great deal to be desired.

Buses

Greyhound (Ⓦwww.greyhound.com) isn't exactly the pride of America, but it works, linking all the major cities and some of the lesser ones. Often, in big cities, Greyhound stations are in the very seediest areas, so think twice about late-night arrivals. The Discovery Pass offers unlimited travel and unlimited stopovers on all Greyhound buses. It comes in a few flavors: 7 days for $253/£160, 15 days for $360/£226, 30 days for $461/£290 and 60 days for $564/£355. Greyhound also offers

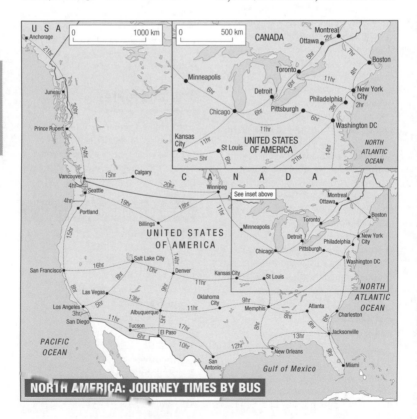

NORTH AMERICA: JOURNEY TIMES BY BUS

some web-only booking prices that are worth checking out. The alternative is the Green Tortoise (ⓦwww.greentortoise .com), a bus bedecked with cushions, bunks, a fridge and a good sound-system. It runs primarily on the West Coast between San Francisco and Seattle, but there's also a Boston–New Orleans route, and it makes summer crossings to New York and Alaska with many activity-oriented stops en route.

Trains

North America's rail network is not extensive by European standards, nor high speed (unless you count the Boston–New York–Philadelphia–Washington Acela train, which is only high-speed according to American speed limits), but it does cover most of the major stops. Students get fifteen percent off normal ticket prices.

With presentation of a non-US passport you can pick up the USA Rail Pass at any Amtrak station (ⓦwww .amtrak.com). The one-month national pass is priced at $429/£270 (15 days, 8 segments), $649/£408 (30 days, 12 segments) and $829/£522 (45 days, 18 segments). One segment is defined as getting on and then off a train, which means that a changeover will cost you an extra segment. Regional passes are about thirty percent cheaper (useful if you plan to just stay on one coast or the other). For west-coast explorations, the California Rail Pass gives you seven days of travel over 21 days for $159/£100.

Canada offers two types of passes (ⓦwww.viarail.ca). The Canrailpass System, where you get seven one-way trips anywhere in Canada during a 21-day period. And Canrailpass Corridor which offers the same thing, but limited to the Quebec City Windsor Corridor. Bookings must be made three or more days in advance. And fares vary according to season. Check out the online trip planner for the latest prices.

Cars

You needn't be jumping a convertible over washed-out bridges or driving full speed through police road blocks to enjoy an American road trip. The country is set up to be explored by car, and the low petrol prices make it economically feasible. Navigating city roads can be more than a little daunting, but the open highways, secondary roads and small towns are a breeze, and you'll have access to virtually any place you can find on a map.

Rental

To rent, you'll need to be over 25 and own a major credit card (or be prepared to leave a large cash deposit). At the cheaper end, you're looking at around $150/£91 per week, but check the websites of the major firms for regional or seasonal bargains. Insurance for other cars or people you may damage or injure is mandatory. For an extra $10–15/£6–9 per day you can get insurance for the car you're driving; some credit cards provide this if you use them to pay for the rental. If you're not covered, give it some serious thought, as otherwise you'll be liable for every scratch, scuff or dent the car returns with, whether you were in the car at the time or not.

If you're bringing the car back to the same place, you can often make a good

Sample train fares

New York to:
- Chicago $100/£63; 19hr
- Los Angeles $266/£167; 61hr ($1117/£703 with sleeping cabin)
- Miami $135/£85; 28hr
- Seattle $193/£121; 65hr ($1039/£655 with sleeping cabin)

Toronto to:
- Vancouver $464/£292; 87hr

leasing arrangement with local car dealerships, so call a few for price estimates. You might say you'll be doing some extensive touring in the region, probably going out of state at some point, but you may not want to mention that you're taking a cross-country road trip unless it's part of a legal document you're signing. However, it's generally best to go with the major rental firms (Ⓦwww.hertz.com, Ⓦwww.avis.com, Ⓦwww.thrifty.com or Ⓦwww.budget.com), since they're better able to handle out-of-state breakdowns and other problems that may arise. Other cost-savers to consider: if you don't bring the car back to the same spot, rental companies will charge you a fortune in drop-off charges, possibly more than a week's rental fee; and if you don't mind an unflattering set of wheels, you can save money with a company like Rent-a-Wreck (Ⓦwww.rent-a-wreck.com) that specializes in well-used vehicles. In well-populated areas, this should be fine, but it may not be great for the long desert crossings.

An alternative to rental is a "driveaway". Car owners who want to transport their vehicles long distances (typically from coast to coast) but don't want to do the driving themselves, leave their cars with a driveaway agency such as Ⓦwww.autodriveaway.com. For a fee, the agency guarantees delivery of the vehicle and finds drivers – drivers like you. You're expected to cover about 650km per day in the direction of your destination, but that does leave some room for small side-trips and adventures. Some agencies help out with pocket money, others don't (Autodriveaway chips in for a free tank of petrol). You'll probably be expected to cover the petrol charges, which add up to about $85/£54 a day for a fuel-efficient car and $100/£63 for a gas-guzzler on a cross-country trip (if you cover about five hundred miles a day). Check the phone book under Automobile Transporter for local agents and sign up a week to a month in advance.

Buying a car

Buying a car in the USA is relatively easy: check out Ⓦwww.autotrader.com and Ⓦwww.newspapers.com. You'll need cash, but you can pick up a rumbling rust-bucket for as little as $400/£252. A low-mileage, zippy car with air-con that you can sell for a good price will set you back $8000–10,000/£5040–6300. Whatever the state it's in, take the car to a mechanic to see which things need replacing to make it roadworthy, and pick up AAA membership ($55/£35; Ⓦwww.aaa.com) to assist with breakdowns – consider AAAplus ($80/£50) if you're taking an old car through remote areas, and you might want to buy a cheap cell phone so you can take advantage of your insurance. Watch out for cars that have been scrapped then salvaged from a junkyard and touched up to sell to an unsuspecting buyer. Ask for the Vehicle Identification Number and check online at Ⓦwww.vehicleidentificationnumber.com.

Don't forget about the fuel efficiency. Sure, it would be fun to drive down the road in a classic American houseboat-sized car with a set of old bull horns strapped to the front, but most of these drink preposterous amounts of fuel, and you'll be kicking yourself each time you head to the pump. Despite the continent's fascination with sport utility vehicles, you do not need four-wheel drive. But, if you're driving in the south or southwest in the summer, you will want air-con strong enough to deep-freeze a large steak.

Think in terms of resale when you buy. Study the online newspaper classified ads where you're selling and compare them to the prices where you're buying: Ⓦwww.kbb.com will give you the official value of a car, but that's just a starting point for negotiations. You can also use the site to calculate the depreciation of the mileage you'll be adding. Stay away from off-beat colors: silver metallic is always a safe bet. And consider buying a car somewhere like California or Florida, where the climate is gentle, and selling it someplace with tough winters, such as Minnesota or Boston, where they'll be impressed that the car is still in such good condition. Just keep in mind that northern buyers may not be as interested in peppy sports cars that can't handle snow.

Car camping

Sleeping in your car at rest stops is a dodgy plan. One idea, provided you arrive well after dark, is to look for nice residential areas and park among expensive cars. If the owners are willing to leave them on the street overnight, it's logical to assume it must be quite safe. Only problem here is that if police are patrolling the area, they may not like you camping there, so be discreet – arrive late, leave early and buy some little screens for the windows.

Bikes

North America is a reasonably good place to bike. The downside is that the distances are long, often with very little of interest in between the towns, and the bigger cities are rarely bike-friendly. There are, however, excellent places to mountain-bike and some exceptional stretches of road: think ski towns and areas in or near national parks. In many of the biking hubs, it's possible to rent a top-end set of wheels ($30–40/£19–25 per day). Cycling in June to August in the south will be extremely warm and, conversely, if you're going to the north in November to March, take your thermals.

Hitching

Beyond the standard warning against hitching in general, here's an added one for the USA: forgetaboutit! It's considered especially unwise, probably due to the amount of well-armed people out there who never quite made it on *The Jerry Springer Show*. Canada is safer. In both cases, hitchers not dissuaded by this warning should take heed of safety information (see box, p.143).

Visas

Under the US Visa Waiver Program no visa is required for a stay in the USA of up to 90 days for citizens of Andorra, Australia, Austria, the Baltic States, Belgium, Brunei, Czech Republic, Denmark, Finland, France, Germany, Hungary, Iceland, Ireland, Italy, Japan, Liechtenstein, Luxembourg, Malta, Monaco, The Netherlands, New Zealand, Norway, Portugal, San Marino, Singapore,

---

Stars, bars and maple leaves

Americans love to wear their stars and stripes T-shirts, sweatshirts and baseball caps, but tend to leave them at home when venturing abroad. Most Canadians, meanwhile, don't want much to do with the **national flag** in Canada, but plaster themselves with little red-and-white maple-leaf patches when traveling overseas to make perfectly clear they should not be confused with Americans, who, by the way, also often wear Canadian maple-leaf patches. If you're not sure which part of North America a traveler is from, guess Canada first. "Where in America are you from?" is still Canadian travelers' most dreaded question.

Slovakia, Slovenia, South Korea, Spain, Sweden, Switzerland and the UK, But don't forget to complete your online ESTA form at least three days in advance ($14/£9).

Visitors from Australia, New Zealand, USA, western Europe and the British Commonwealth don't need visas to enter Canada. For others a 180-day single entry visa costs $65/£39, and a multiple entry visa costs $130/£79.

Reading list

- Margaret Atwood *Surfacing*
- John Berendt *Midnight in the Garden of Good and Evil*
- Truman Capote *Breakfast at Tiffany's*
- Jack Kerouac *On the Road*
- Armistead Maupin *Tales of the City*
- Toni Morrison *Beloved*
- J.D. Salinger *Catcher in the Rye*
- Alexis de Tocqueville *Democracy in America*
- Mark Twain *The Adventures of Tom Sawyer*
- Tom Wolfe *The Bonfire of the Vanities*

South America

Botanists love South America, possibly the most geographically dynamic continent on the planet, with the world's largest rainforest and the world's driest desert (Chile's Atacama) a bus ride or two away from each other. Anthropologists and sociologists are still combing the rainforest, studying indigenous, isolated tribes. Climbers have a selection of scaleable peaks that stretch from Colombia to Patagonia. Amateur adventurers are lured by the challenges of overland travel as well as the stunning Inca ruins. For urbanites, the cities offer a combination of congestion, coastal vistas and fantastic salsa and samba clubs. And soccer-lovers are in for a real treat: some of the world's most acrobatic stylists come from these parts.

  The most common language is Spanish (many people elect to begin their trips with a short language course, which is a huge help), but from country to country the dialect can be as different as Australian and American, complete with unique words and expressions. On average, travelers here tend to be a little older and more experienced than the ones who visit Europe or Australia. They seem less in search of spiritual enlightenment than the ones in India and less tan-hungry than the ones in Thailand. Couple the scary diseases with even scarier political regimes and rebel groups, and it's easy to understand why the travel routes haven't turned into tourist superhighways.

Main attractions

● **Amazon rainforest** Often called the "lungs of the world", this impenetrable snarl of vegetation bigger than Western Europe produces twenty percent of the planet's oxygen. It accommodates the world's second-longest river (over 6300km), which carries twelve times more water than the Mississippi and discharges it upwards of 250km out into the Atlantic. Despite its ongoing destruction, it's the most biodiverse natural phenomenon going and can be best explored in Brazil, Bolivia, Peru and Ecuador.

● **Angel Falls (Salto Angel)** Venezuela. It can't be seen in one glance.

You need to start at the bottom and slowly tilt your head back to take in all 979 metres of the freefalling water. The world's highest waterfall isn't that easy (or cheap) to get to. This southern Venezuelan wonder is most commonly seen out the window of a plane, but it's possible to take a multi-day trip in a motorized dugout canoe.

● **Galápagos Islands** Ecuador. This barren, volcanic thirteen-island archipelago located 1000km off Ecuador's coast is best known for its unique wildlife, and the man who pointed out the process of natural selection that got them that way: Charles Darwin. The absence of natural predators affords humans an intimacy with the animals unheard of elsewhere. You can swim with sea lions,

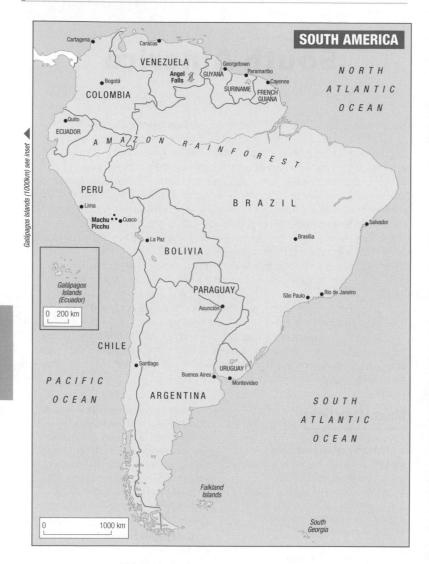

float alongside penguins, step over blue-footed boobies and pose for pictures next to marine iguanas.

● **Machu Picchu/Cuzco** Peru. Once the head of the Inca Empire, the town of Cuzco now serves as the springboard for trips to Machu Picchu, the mountainous "Lost City" (discovered by American historian Hiram Bingham in 1911). Most budget travelers prefer to arrive on foot by way of the Inca Trail, a sometimes-crowded four-day trek that takes in high-altitude passes, countless scenic overlooks and lush cloudforests.

- **Rio de Janeiro** Brazil. This city is easily one of the most breathtaking on the planet. A 27-metre-tall statue of Christ looms over the nine million *caipirinha*-drinking, samba-dancing, beach-football-playing Cariocas (inhabitants of Rio). Rio kicks into high gear during Carnaval, as everyone tries to rack up forty days' worth of eating, drinking and sinning before Lent arrives.

When to go

The weather in South America is welcoming year-round, especially if you're flexible. Often, that doesn't mean fleeing far. If it gets too steamy in the coastal lowlands, just head for the cooler surrounding hills. A few things to watch for: in the south of Patagonia, winter can get awfully cold, and shops and lodgings close; and the remote dirt roads near the Amazon basin get muddy and impassable during rainy season (Jan–April). That's also when the Inca Trail becomes wet and slippery and the Galápagos Islands are hot and drizzly. There are two peak seasons: South Americans tend to go on holiday from mid-December until Carnaval in February; and most foreigners arrive in July and August.

Costs

Argentina, Chile, Brazil, Uruguay and Venezuela are slightly more expensive than the rest of Latin America, but you

Security issues
It's always a good idea to check the current political conditions before visiting a country, but the following are worth a little extra research: Colombia, Ecuador, Venezuela.

Lowest daily budget
Expensive ($55–75/£35–47): Falkland Islands, French Guiana **Mid-range** ($30–50/£19–32): Argentina, Brazil, Chile, Uruguay, Venezuela **Budget** ($20–30/£13–19): Bolivia, Colombia, Ecuador, Paraguay

may be more likely to find larger price differences between cities and rural areas than between the countries themselves. Because South America has fewer hostels and more guesthouses (ie fewer dormitories), it's possible to make significant savings by traveling with another person.

Getting around by air

One look at the point-to-point air travel prices, and it's easy to understand why overland travel is so popular among budget travelers. As usual, domestic flights are often significantly cheaper, even over longer distances, so if it's just a matter of taking a little getting a smoother ride, that's a decent alternative.

Air passes

There are a variety of air passes you can turn to, but, unfortunately, most are for flights in a single country only and have to be purchased before you arrive. If you fly to the continent with a South American carrier, you can often get significant savings (up to $100/£63) on their air pass.

- **Visit Argentina** Ⓦwww.turismo .gov.ar/eng/menu.htm. Must be purchased in conjunction with an international ticket, minimum of three coupons ($399/£251), maximum of twelve ($1,049/£660).

Recommended vaccinations

- Routine boosters for measles/ mumps/rubella (MMR), diphtheria/pertussis/tetanus (DPT) and polio.
- Hepatitis A
- Hepatitis B (optional)
- Rabies (optional)
- Typhoid
- Yellow fever (tropical areas in all countries except Chile, Uruguay and southern Argentina)

● **TAM Brazil Airpass** ⓦ www.brol .com/brazilairpass.asp. Provides four to nine flights within thirty days. Prices start at $532/£335 plus taxes and fees for four flights.

● **Visit South America** ⓦ www .oneworld.com. This One World alliance pass covers up 34 cities in ten countries (Argentina, Bolivia, Brazil, Chile, Colombia, Ecuador, Paraguay, Peru, Uruguay and Venezuela), and offers savings of up to fifty percent, but always compare prices online before using up a coupon. Minimum of three flights. No upper limit. Coupons (one flight per coupon) are priced at $119–359/ £72–217 each depending on the length of your flight.

Overland routes

The classic South American overland route brought travelers down from Central America to Tierra del Fuego via the Panamerican Highway. Even Butch Cassidy and the Sundance Kid reportedly got as far as central Patagonia. Roads around the Amazon rainforest and the mountain highlands (Peru, Bolivia and Ecuador) are among the slowest going. The main routes in Argentina, Brazil,

Chile, Colombia and Venezuela are relatively well surfaced and allow traffic to move perhaps a little too fast for your own comfort level.

Buses

For short and mid-range distances, buses are the most common, conven- ient and usually the cheapest way to get around South America. Here's a general rule of thumb: the cheaper the bus is per hour, the slower you're going, the rougher the ride and the greater the chance that something can further delay your journey. In addition to the terrain, politics can slow things down. Major political disagreements usually find their way to the surface in the form of road blocks. Locals may drag a few trees across the road or go on strike, but generally if you wait for a few days the path clears.

Trains

There's no extensive rail network, but a number of classic train journeys are well worth the ride, such as the line from Salta to San Antonio de los Cobres (Train to the Clouds; ⓦ www .trenalasnubes.com.ar), which runs through the foothills of the Argentinean Andes. A one-day round-trip is $185/£117 including breakfast and

Sample return airfares

Caracas to:
- Bogotá $560/£352
- Lima $550/£346
- Quito $450/£283
- Santiago $800/£504

Rio de Janeiro to:
- Buenos Aires $330/£207
- La Paz $750/£478
- Quito $550/£346
- Santiago $400/£252

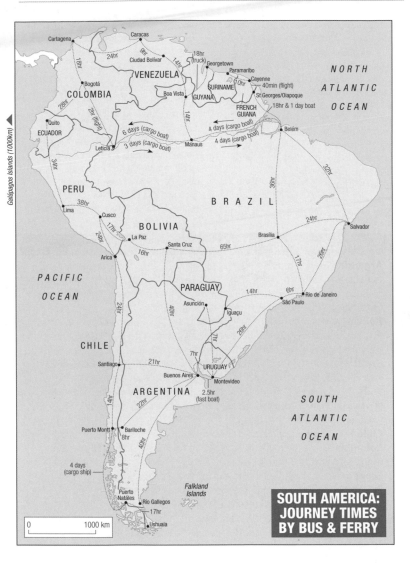

Galapagos Islands (1000km) ◄

SOUTH AMERICA:
JOURNEY TIMES
BY BUS & FERRY

---

afternoon snack. There's also the Bolivian eye-popper from Oruro to Villazon (Ⓦwww.fca.com.bo) via a seemingly bottomless gorge, which costs $10/£6 in "Popular" class and $38/£24 in "Ejecutivo."

Cars

Renting

Rental isn't such a great deal, but with a few travelers sharing the cost it can be an option. All you need to rent a car is a valid driving licence, major credit card or cash deposit and in some countries – Argentina, Bolivia, Colombia and Suriname (see box, p.61) – an international driving permit (Ⓦwww.theaa.co.uk). Driving is on the right-hand side, except for the daredevil passing that takes place on some roads. For longer-term rentals, look around for deals once you're in the city center. Make sure insurance is included with the quoted price of the vehicle, as it's usually mandatory. Also, watch out for sneaky offers, such as not having to pay for damage in the event of an accident. The catch? You have to pay seventy percent or so of the daily rate for as long as it takes to fix the vehicle. And you can guess how long it'll take to complete the repairs.

Buying a car

One of the best places to buy a car is Chile, specifically Iqueque, a duty-free port town well north of Santiago: customs officers there are reportedly accustomed to handling the international paperwork. Santiago also has a good reputation for car purchasing. With some luck you can even sell the vehicle for a profit in Peru, Bolivia or elsewhere. Asunción in Paraguay may be the best

Visa requirements for South America

Argentina No visa required for stays of up to 90 days for Americans, Canadians, Australians, New Zealanders, Latin Americans and citizens of most European countries. There is, however, an "entry request fee" for Canadians ($75/£47) and Australians ($100/£63).

Bolivia No visa required for stays up to 30 days for Europeans, Canadians, Australians and New Zealanders. Americans need visas ($135/£85). These are valid for five years, but the maximum stay is 30 days.

Brazil Visa required for citizens of the USA ($185/£117), Australia ($55/£35), Canada ($85/£54) and the Baltic States ($40/£25). Visas are valid for five years, but the maximum stay is 90 days. Travel must be started within 90 days of issue. Europeans are exempt from visas, but need sufficient funds and onward/return ticket.

Chile No visa required for stays of up to 90 days.

Colombia No visa required for stays of up to 180 days. Proof of sufficient funds and onward/return ticket required.

Ecuador No visa required for stays of up to 90 days.

French Guiana No visa required for stays of up to 90 days.

Guyana No visa required for stays of up to 30 days.

Paraguay Visa required prior to arrival, except for nationals of neighboring countries Cyprus, Ireland, Japan, Latvia, Lithuania, Malta, Poland, Slovakia, Slovenia and Venezuela.

Peru No visa required for stays of up to 90 days.

Suriname Visa required, plus onward/return ticket and vaccination against yellow fever if arriving from Brazil, French Guiana or Guyana. Visa issued in a few days at consulates in Guyana or French Guiana.

Uruguay No visa required for stays of up to 90 days.

Venezuela No visa required for stays of up to 90 days. Proof of sufficient funds and onward/return ticket.

place to sell if you can get there. The paperwork necessary for heading over borders can be gathered at embassies and consulates along the way, but it can be a hassle. You'll need a Carnet de Passage (see box, p.61), also known as a Libreta de Pasos por Aduana.

When it comes to choosing a car, you'd do well to pick up a Toyota Land Cruiser, especially if you've got some off-roading in mind. It's popular, attractive even with a few scratches and easy to sell. More important, it rarely breaks down. Tagging along behind buses after dusk is a good option, as there are scores of roads that become dangerous by night. But don't get too close on gravel roads as windscreens crack easily from stray flying pebbles. Petrol isn't that cheap, especially in the southern half of the continent and in difficult-to-reach areas, where it can rival European prices.

Bikes

Cyclists can find nicer, less chaotic roads, such as those in southern Argentina and Chile. The cyclist community is small, but it exists all over South America. For more on traveling by bike, see "How to get around the world" (p.62).

Hitching

The plausibility of hitching varies from region to region, but is sometimes the only means to reach out-of-the-way spots. In Chile, hitching is particularly popular, even among young Chilean travelers. Because traffic can be sparse along many routes, adequate food and water is a must. See the section on hitching tips and safety issues (see box, p.143).

Visas

Most travelers landing in South American countries will find visas are generally handed out on arrival (or can be purchased at that time). Brazil, Paraguay and Suriname are the typical exceptions, but check for overland entry requirements, which can differ from the rules for those who arrive by air. See below for more.

Some countries, most notably Brazil and Chile, have reciprocated US policy when it comes to visas, matching the heavy fees and paperwork that the USA demands of Brazilians and Chileans who want to visit America.

Avoiding the Darién Gap

To get from Central to South America (Panama to Colombia), there are a few options. There's the Darién Gap, a rough and lawless jungle between Colombia and Panama considered by many to be the most notorious overland stretch in the world. If you get robbed only once you're considered to have had excellent luck – some people get kidnapped for months, some never come out. This route should not be attempted.

Instead, take a flight to Puerto Obaldia, then a walk or boat to Capurgana, then a boat to Turbo (two hours), and from there a cargo boat (two days) to Cartagena. Option two is a flight from Panama City to Porvenir, then a sailing boat service (four to five days) to Cartagena via the San Blas Islands. From a budget perspective, however, neither of these is cheaper than flying: it costs $350/£220 to get from Panama City to Cartagena.

Reading list

- Isabel Allende *Eva Luna*
- Jorge Amado *Doña Flor and Her Two Husbands*
- Machado de Assis *Quinincas Borba*
- Bruce Chatwin *In Patagonia*
- Charles Darwin *On the Origin of Species by Means of Natural Selection*
- Peter Fleming *Brazilian Adventure*
- Ernesto "Che" Guevara *The Motorcycle Diaries: a Journey Around South America*
- Gabriel García Márquez *One Hundred Years of Solitude*
- Pablo Neruda *Selected Poems*
- Mario Vargas Llosa *The Notebooks of Don Rigoberto*

First-Time
Around the World

Directory

Offline apps

World Lens Can't read a sign in a foreign language? No problem. Point your phone's camera at it and this app will instantly translate words

JiWire Wi-Fi Finder The best way to avoid roaming charges is to get as much free wi-fi as possible. This app can find the closest source in 144 countries

iTriage Diagnose that weird illness with the free offline symptom checker

Travel Survival Rough Guides' practical $0.99 app has illustrations, up-to-date contacts for every embassy and emergency

services in the world, and can also store your personal emergent data

Jibbigo Speak into your phone and have your words spoken back in the language of your choice

Google Maps Lets you download a map areas for offline use. Sorry, Android only

MapPocket Not free, but cheap ($0.99) and iPhone friendly. This popular app lets you transfer maps between devices via Dropbox

OffMaps2 Also cheap ($0.99) and iPhone friendly. Lets you download the maps you want using OpenStreetMap and view offline

Online apps

Eventful It taps into your GPS and finds nearby events, concerts, shows wherever you may be and can be set up to send email alerts for events based on your interests

XE Currency Converter Converts currencies and calculates prices

Local Eats It searches the country's top-50 cities for local eateries by category, price, rank or neighborhood

WhereTraveler Provides "insider tips" on dining, shopping, entertainment and sightseeing. It even helps you convert currencies, calculate tips and translate languages. Still mostly for cities in the USA, but is spreading internationally

TripIt Consolidates all your travel bookings (flights, hotels, car rentals) into one easy-to-use app. Often works best to upload everything via computer first, then just access as need via the app

Camera apps

Camera+ Add controls to help turn your phone camera into an almost fully functional compact digital camera

Pano Turns up to sixteen photos into a stunning panoramic shot

360 Panorama As the name implies, it turns your photos into a single 36-degree panorama pic

Tripcolor A simple and easy to use photo-blog system that lets you – while off line

– take pics, mark the location on a map, add text and then have it upload automatically when you finally find a wi-fi connection

Instagam A photo filter and photo sharing app that has achieved almost cult status

Hipstamatic Another retro filter for your photos to give them that "I was there in the 60s" look

Snapseed A surprisingly powerful photo editing app

Transport

RTW flight specialists

Ⓦ **www.adventureworld.com.au** Australia-based with an office in New Zealand

Ⓦ **www.airtreks.com** A do-it-yourself RTW web planner

Ⓦ **www.bootsnall.com/rtw** Check for its latest on RTW round-up report

Ⓦ **www.flightcentre.com** Offices in Australia, Canada, New Zealand, South Africa, the UK and the USA

Ⓦ **www.roundtheworldflights.com** UK-based planner

Ⓦ **www.statravel.com** Student and budget travel experts with worldwide shops

Ⓦ **www.studentuniverse.com** USA-based and student oriented

Ⓦ **www.trailfinders.co.uk** Well-informed UK-based agents

Ⓦ **www.travelcuts.com** Canada-based with offices in the USA

Ⓦ **www.westernair.co.uk** RTW and budget trip specialists

RTW alliance sites

Ⓦ **www.oneworld.com** Ten-member alliance

Ⓦ **www.staralliance.com** The biggest alliance, with 21 members

Ⓦ **www.thegreatescapade.com** An alliance with a good online RTW planner

Flight booking engines

Ⓦ **www.edreams.com** Multi-language portal with cheap trains and hotels as well as flights

Ⓦ **www.expedia.com** Microsoft's online travel agency

Ⓦ **www.kayak.com** Finds you the best deal, then points you to the site where you make the actual booking

Ⓦ **www.opodo.com** Booking engine for flights, hotels, car rentals and package holidays, with versions in English, German, French, Italian, Spanish, Portuguese and the Nordic languages

Ⓦ **www.orbitz.com** The airlines' web project – a group booking engine with fares from 450 airlines

Ⓦ **www.travelocity.com** One of the early pioneers and still a leading booking site

Airlines and airports

Ⓦ **www.airlineandairportlinks.com** Links to all airports

Ⓦ **www.flightview.com** Allows you to check the status of any flight

Ⓦ **www.sleepinginairports.net** A budget traveler's guide to sleeping in airports

Budget airline travel

Ⓦ **www.cheapflights.co.uk** Search engine for other discount brokers and consolidators, though not comprehensive

Ⓦ **www.skyscanner.net** This simple-to-use site searches the budget carriers and finds the best prices

Trains

Ⓦ **www.eurail.com** Go direct for the daddy of all European rail passes

Ⓦ **www.raileurope.co.uk** Europe railpasses for Europeans

Ⓦ **www.raileurope.com** Europe railpasses for North Americans

Ⓦ **www.railplus.co.nz** Europe railpasses for Kiwis

Ⓦ **www.railplus.com.au** Europe railpasses for Australians

Ⓦ **www.railserve.com** Links to rail services around the world

Ⓦ **www.seat61.com** Excellent worldwide guide to travel by train

Cars and motorbikes

Ⓦ **www.aaa.com** American Automobile Association – your best friend after you buy the world's cheapest car in the USA

Ⓦ **www.caa.ca** Canadian Automobile Association – offers carnet information for Americans as well

Ⓦ www.driverabroad.com A one-stop-shop providing advice for self-drive travelers

Ⓦ www.europebycar.com Buys in bulk and offers discount deals with European rental companies on short-term (17 days or less) rentals and tax-free leases for longer rentals

Ⓦ www.horizonsunlimited.com Tips and tales on motorcycling around Europe

Ⓦ www.kemwel.com Another rental consolidator. Also offers motor homes

Ⓦ www.nationalautoclub.com America's long-established automobile association

Ⓦ www.nzaa.co.nz New Zealand's Automobile Association

Ⓦ www.rac.co.uk The Royal Automobile Club, which offers similar services to the AA

Ⓦ www.rac.com.au Australia's Royal Automobile Club

Ⓦ www.renaultusa.com Offers brand-new cars with unlimited mileage and comprehensive insurance with no deductibles

Ⓦ www.theaa.com The UK's Automobile Association, for all things automotive

Ⓦ www.viamichelin.com The Michelin Route Planner gives driving directions throughout Europe

Ⓦ www.wickedcampers.co.uk Cheap campervan hire from most European cities

Ferries and freighters

Ⓦ www.freightercruises.com UK-based freighter bookers

Ⓦ www.freightertravel.co.nz NZ-based freighter bookers

Ⓦ routesinternational.com/ships.htm Links to ferry services around the world

Accommodation

Collaborative travel

Ⓦ www.couchsurfing.com Well over 5 million members and continuing to climb, this is still the main game in town

Ⓦ www.tripping.com A newer interface and some other nice bells and whistles, but same basic concept as Couchsurfing

Ⓦ www.triptrotting.com Like Tripping, a newer start-up challenging the Couchsurfing market

Peer-to-peer rentals

Ⓦ www.airbnb.com This is the one that put this sort of rental system on the map, though it doesn't have the most properties

Ⓦ www.campinmygarden.com Private gardens as micro-campsites. Like Couchsurfing, but with tents

Ⓦ www.flipkey.com TripAdvisor's horse in this race

Ⓦ www.homeaway.com The largest list of properties (it runs several similar sites in several countries)

Ⓦ www.roomorama.com Probably the most stylish site of the pack

Ⓦ www.tripping.com In addition to providing a Couchsurfing-like service, it has also aggregated the peer-to-peer rentals in one easy search

Home exchanges

Ⓦ http://homeexchangeguru.com A good starting point before you jump in

Ⓦ www.Homeexchange.com Largest exchange company with over 18,000 listings worldwide (most listings of any agency in the USA, Canada, Mexico, France and Italy). Cost: $50 annually to browse other's listings, $100/63 to list your own home

Ⓦ www.Homeforexchange.com Third largest. Most listings of any agency in Australia/NZ. Cost: 18 months for $59/37

Ⓦ www.homelink.org Second largest in terms of listings. Cost: $110 for US residents, £115 for UK residents – the most expensive service. It has the most listings of any agency in Germany and Ireland, and is strong in the UK, the USA, Belgium, the Netherlands, Switzerland and Norway

Ⓦ**www.Intervac.com** Fourth largest. Cost: $95 for USA/Canada, £75 in UK. Most listings of any agency in Sweden and Finland

Hostels and B&Bs

Ⓦ**www.bandb.com** An international bed-and-breakfast directory

Ⓦ**www.hihostels.com** Hostelling International's main site

Ⓦ**www.hostels.com** Global hostel finder and booking engine

Ⓦ**www.hostelz.com** Hostel booking engine with reviews

Money

Currency exchange rates

Ⓦ**www.oanda.com** Quick conversions in 164 currencies

ATMs worldwide

Ⓦ**www.amextravelresources.com/#/specialist-by-destination** A list of AmEx offices worldwide, where you can also get cash advances against your card

Ⓦ**www.mastercard.us/cardholder-services/atm-locator.html** For MasterCard holders

Ⓦ**visa.via.infonow.net/locator/global** For Visa-card holders

Money transfer

Ⓦ**www.moneygram.com** Money transfers and bill payments at Thomas Cook, Amex and various banks and post offices

Ⓦ**www.westernunion.com** Another money transfer option

Discount cards

Ⓦ**www.hihostels.com** Hostelling International cards

Ⓦ**www.isic.org** International student identity cards, teacher cards and youth cards

Ⓦ**www.vipbackpackers.com** Discounts for select private hostels

Working and volunteering

Working

Ⓦ**www.anyworkanywhere.com** Find work in dozens of countries and get help with visa information

Ⓦ**www.iagora.com** An online community featuring entry-level jobs and internships around Europe

Ⓦ**www.jobmonkey.com** Search by job type, from skiing to teaching

Ⓦ**www.jobsabroad.com** This site allows searching by country or job type, and has links to study and volunteer programs

Ⓦ**www.liveworkplay.com.au** An Oz-based site with useful working-holiday information, including visa permits

Ⓦ**www.michaelpage.com** Professional work-placement agency

Ⓦ**www.monster.com** Jobs for skilled workers all over the world

Ⓦ**www.overseasjobcentre.co.uk** Guide to working and living abroad, working holidays and gap years

Ⓦ**www.wwoof.org** Directory of World Wide Opportunities on Organic Farms

Teaching English

Ⓦ**www.cambridgeesol.org** Home of Cambridge ESOL programs; allows you to find nearest location

Ⓦ**www.eslcafe.com** Dave's ESL Café is a TEFL forum with general job-searching and classroom-teaching tips and lessons

Ⓦ**www.teflinternational.com** For getting a cheaper TEFL certificate in Thailand or Egypt

Volunteering

Ⓦ **www.globeaware.org** Like MetoWe, it caters to those who want to volunteer on their vacation and will to pay handsomely for the short-term, well-planned experience

Ⓦ **www.goabroad.com/volunteer-abroad** Huge directory of international volunteer programs, which you can search by location

Ⓦ **www.idealist.org** Idealist works to connect people, organizations and resources with the aim of free and dignified lives for all

Ⓦ **www.metowe.com** Upper-end volunteer trips, but typically well put together. Can help place families as well

Ⓦ **www.takingitglobal.org** Online global community that helps point people towards current opportunities to take action

Ⓦ **www.vfp.org** Volunteers for Peace is a US-based organization with inexpensive international programs

Ⓦ **www.volunteerinternational.org** A regularly updated list of volunteer opportunities and internship exchanges provided by an alliance of non-profit organizations based in the USA

Travel tools

Online maps

Ⓦ **earth.google.com** The Big Kahuna of online maps, with tons of stuff you never dreamed was possible

Ⓦ **maps.google.com** Does all the things Google Earth doesn't

Conversions

Ⓦ **www.digitaldutch.com/unitconverter** This speedy site converts weights, measurements, distances and so on

Events

Ⓦ **www.festivals.com** Find out when and where the party is on, no matter where you go

Ⓦ **www.whatsonwhen.com** Every festival, museum exhibit, concert, major sporting event – you name it, you can find it here

Global adaptors

Ⓦ **www.kropla.com** For phone adaptors and line checkers – all the tools you'll need, and some you won't

Ⓦ **www.kropla.com/electric2.htm** The lowdown on how to plug in any electrical appliances you may be lugging with you

Language

Ⓦ **translate.google.com** The only translate tool you'll need. From phrases to websites. It'll even detect the language and provide the translations accordingly. For on-the-go translation, check out the offline apps section (see p.291)

World facts

Ⓦ **www.cia.gov/library/publications /the-world-factbook/index.html** No cloak-and-dagger stuff, just one of the best sources of information around

Ⓦ **www.countryreports.org** From flags to maps to national anthems, here's a good starting point for learning a little about the countries you're heading to

Ⓦ **www.nationalgeographic.com** The National Geographic Society offers a top-end presentation of the planet

Travel gear

Ⓦ **www.altrec.com** An online-only retailer with gear from all brands

Ⓦ **www.ems.com** Loads of gear with many web deals

Ⓦ **www.gear-zone.co.uk** A UK-based gear bonanza with easy-to-use layout

ⓦ**www.gogogear.com.au** A site for getting gear down under – it even has all the cheap stuff (ear plugs, sink plug, etc) for one-stop shopping

ⓦ**www.rei.com** The megastore US retailer has regular online specials

Weather

ⓦ**www.intellicast.com/global** Global ten-day forecasts

ⓦ**www.worldclimate.com** Average temperature and rainfall for a huge number of destinations

Communications

Phone services

ⓦ**www.skype.com** Call for free to other online devices and for about 2 cents a minute to landlines and cell/mobile phones anywhere in the world. Now integrated in Facebook so you can chat with friends online

ⓦ**www.google.com/talk** Another call-for-free-if-you-download-free-software deal. Many say it works better than Skype and if you've got enough friends using gmail, you can see when they're online without starting up Skype

ⓦ**messenger.yahoo.com** Yahoo's version of free video- and voice-chatting. Convenient if you're mostly in touch with Yahoo users

ⓦ**www.apple.com/mac/facetime** Apple's version of Skype for those with Macs, iPhones and iPads

ⓦ**www.onavo.com** Onavo Extend compresses your data and helps minimize the amount you are sending

Cell/mobile phones

ⓦ**www.telestial.com** Looking for a SIM card you can roam with? Compare rates between your local providers

ⓦ**www.onesimcard.com** Prepaid mobile service that greatly reduces the costs of calls when traveling

ⓦ**www.ipipi.com** SMS messaging world-wide including text to email service

ⓦ**www.which.co.uk/technology/phones/guides/using-mobile-phones-abroad/using-international-sim-cards** UK consumer magazine's guide to using mobile phones abroad

Satellite devices

ⓦ**www.delorme.com** Backcountry satellite device that sends emergency beacons, lets people follow you on a map, and pairs with your smartphone to text and update social media

ⓦ**www.findmespot.com** Backcountry satellite device that can send an emergency beacon and can update a list of friends/family with an "I'm okay" message. Also connects to your smartphone via an app for various media updating

Satellite phones

ⓦ**www.globalstar.com** Extensive, but not quite global

ⓦ**www.iridium.com** Provides the most complete global coverage

Free email

ⓦ**mail.google.com** 10 GB storage

ⓦ**www.hotmail.com** "Ever Growing" storage

ⓦ**www.yahoo.com** Unlimited storage

Country calling codes

ⓦ**www.countrycallingcodes.com** Get the dialling codes for every country, plus the ones you need to dial out of the country you're in

Health

Ⓦ **www.cdc.gov** The US Centers for Disease Control has the latest updated information on vaccinations and outbreaks

Ⓦ **www.who.org** Features a country-by-country health profile

Insurance

Ⓦ **www.insuremytrip.com** A good starting point for policy searches

Ⓦ **www.roughguides.com/shop** Rough Guides recommends World Nomads insurance packages which should cover most needs

Ⓦ **www.travelguard.com** A place to peek at a popular policy

Ⓦ **www.worldtravelcenter.com** An excellent spot for comparing different options

Travel advisory

Safety

Ⓦ **www.fco.gov.uk** The UK's Foreign Office is a good starting point

Ⓦ **www.smarttraveller.gov.au** The Australian government's advisory and consular assistance service doesn't pull any punches. Tips include what to do if you get arrested or sexually assaulted overseas

Ⓦ **travel.state.gov** The US State Department warnings can be a little imprecise – if one spot is potentially dangerous, they put the whole country on the list

Ⓦ **www.voyage.gc.ca** Canada's warning page offers all the basic plan-ahead info,

plus a surprising "Action Maze" game where you try to get yourself out of being wrongly imprisoned overseas. Big fun!

Embassies

Ⓦ **embassy.goabroad.com** Find an embassy anywhere in the world and get updated visa information

Customs

Ⓦ **www.cbp.gov** How to figure out what you can bring back into the USA

Tourist offices

Ⓦ **www.towd.com** Find a tourist bureau worldwide

Sights

World Heritage Sites

Ⓦ **whc.unesco.org** World Heritage Sites

Museums

Ⓦ **www.viator.com/museum-tickets** Skip the queues and buy museum tickets in advance worldwide

Ⓦ **www.tickitaly.com** Special site for purchasing tickets to Italian Museums, from the Uffizi to the Vatican

Responsible tourism

Ⓦ **www.responsibletravel.org** How to help minimize your impact while on the road

Ⓦ **www.sustainabletravelinternational. org** Helping travelers and tour organizers minimize their footprint on the environment and the cultures they visit

Ⓦ **www.tourismconcern.org.uk** Organization campaigning for smart, responsible tourism

Reading resources

Guidebook sites

Ⓦ **www.fodors.com** A very user-friendly site aimed at travelers with more pocket change than the average

Ⓦ **www.letsgo.com** Let's Go is an American classic for the college stomp in Europe, but its core audience is now expanding its horizons

Ⓦ **www.lonelyplanet.com** This site covers every country on the planet and has a much-subscribed travel-discussion site called The Thorn Tree

Ⓦ **www.roughguides.com** Set up for independent travelers of all budgets, with online chat boards, travel tips and in-depth country information

Ⓦ **www.travelerstales.com** Pushing the experiential side of guiding, Travelers Tales offers books full of true stories from people just like you

Budget travel

Ⓦ **www.budgettravel.com** Arthur Frommer's *Budget Travel* magazine is mostly focused on cheap holidays, but has good information for longer trips as well

Ⓦ **www.outpostmagazine.com** Shoestring globetrotting with a pleasing layout

Ⓦ **www.outsidemag.com** Excellent writing with an extreme sport and activity bias as well as eco and travel pieces

Ⓦ **www.tntmagazine.com** TNT magazine, with UK and Aus/NZ editions for work and flat finding

Ⓦ **www.transitionsabroad.com** Great information on working, studying and living overseas

Adventure travel

Ⓦ **adventure.nationalgeographic.com** National Geographic's award-winning adventure magazine: tight writing with an outdoor activity slant

Ⓦ **www.getaway.co.za** South African travel mag website offering inspiring travel writing with an African emphasis

Ⓦ **www.wanderlust.co.uk** *Wanderlust* magazine covers the classic travel destinations, plus reviews and interviews

Ⓦ **www.wendmag.com** New adventure mag for travelers without multi-million-dollar budgets. Has a serious green stamp, too

Upmarket travel

Ⓦ **www.concierge.com** Conde Nast's foray into the online travel world – reviews of "six-star" hotels and plenty of "must-see" items for those with ample money to spare

Ⓦ **www.islands.com** More cultural depth than you might expect, although you can practically get a tan flipping through the pages

Ⓦ **www.travelandleisure.com** Ranks everything from hotels to airlines and finds some room for interesting (albeit comfortable) travel in between

Ⓦ **traveler.nationalgeographic.com** A well-crafted travel magazine that's not afraid to show the effects of tourism – or the benefits of a comfortable room

Major newspaper/web travel pages

ⓦ **www.newspapers.com** Has links to newspapers all over the world.

The pick of the international bunch are:

ⓦ **www.theglobeandmail.com/travel** The Globe and Mail

ⓦ **www.guardian.co.uk/travel** The Guardian

ⓦ **travel.independent.co.uk** The Independent

ⓦ **www.latimes.com/travel** The Los Angeles Times

ⓦ **www.nytimes.com/travel** The New York Times

ⓦ **www.nzherald.co.nz/travel** The New Zealand Herald

ⓦ **www.smh.com.au/travel** The Sydney Morning Herald

ⓦ **www.telegraph.co.uk** The Telegraph

ⓦ **www.thestar.ca/travel** The Toronto Star

Online-only travel publications

ⓦ **www.bootsnall.com** A great travel resource with anecdotes that explain how to avoid some of the potholes on the road less travelled

ⓦ **www.connectedtraveler.com** Offers a refreshing perspective on cultural travel

ⓦ **www.gadling.com** Travel news and happenings around the world

ⓦ **www.igougo.com** Swap photos and travel writing, with mileage-type points accrued for your contributions

ⓦ **www.jaunted.com** News and pop-culture travel info

ⓦ **www.journeywoman.com** Highlights the female perspective and offers tips and tales

ⓦ **www.literarytraveler.com** Tracing steps of famous authors and learning about their inspirations are just part of the literary journey

ⓦ **www.matadornetwork.com** A site for travelers who are in touch with their feelings

ⓦ **www.tripso.com** Travel news and consumer advocate info. The oldest continuously published site of its kind

ⓦ **www.worldhum.com** A travel version of Arts and Letters Daily with original articles, interviews and reviews

Map specialists

ⓦ **www.mapworld.co.nz** NZ

ⓦ **www.randmcnally.com** USA

ⓦ **www.stanfords.co.uk** UK

ⓦ **www.worldofmaps.com** Canada

Small print and index

AUTHOR ACKNOWLEDGEMENTS

I want to start by thanking Peter Moore, a talented Australian travel writer and editor who helped me update websites and prices for this edition. He follows the latest developments of online travel news as closely as anyone and I was extremely happy to have him lend his expertise to this project. I also want to thank my editor, Eleanor Aldridge, for her patience and keen eye for detail. She has a particular talent for pointing out things that need to be fixed the most upbeat and positive way. Plus there's an entire fantastic team of designers, media, marketing and sales people at Rough Guides/Penguin, without whom this book would not ever even have a bar code. Thank you all.

Thanks too, to Lori Reich and Katie Morgans

A ROUGH GUIDE TO ROUGH GUIDES

Published in 1982, the first Rough Guide – to Greece – was a student scheme that became a publishing phenomenon. Mark Ellingham, a recent graduate in English from Bristol University, had been travelling in Greece the previous summer and couldn't find the right guidebook. With a small group of friends he wrote his own guide, combining a highly contemporary, journalistic style with a thoroughly practical approach to travellers' needs.

The immediate success of the book spawned a series that rapidly covered dozens of destinations. And, in addition to impecunious backpackers, Rough Guides soon acquired a much broader readership that relished the guides' wit and inquisitiveness as much as their enthusiastic, critical approach and value-for-money ethos.

These days, Rough Guides include recommendations from budget to luxury and cover more than 200 destinations around the globe, as well as producing an ever-growing range of eBooks and apps.

Visit **roughguides.com** to see our latest publications.

Rough Guide credits

Editor: Eleanor Aldridge
Layout: Jessica Subramanian
Cartography: Ashutosh Bharti
Picture editor: Natascha Sturny
Proofreader: Susannah Wight
Managing editor: Keith Drew
Assistant editor: Prema Dutta
Production: Gemma Sharpe
Cover design: Nicole Newman, Dan May, Jessica Subramanian

Editorial assistant: Olivia Rawes
Senior pre-press designer: Dan May
Design director: Scott Stickland
Travel publisher: Joanna Kirby
Digital travel publisher: Peter Buckley
Reference director: Andrew Lockett
Operations coordinator: Becky Doyle
Publishing director (Travel): Clare Currie
Commercial manager: Gino Magnotta
Managing director: John Duhigg

Publishing information

This fourth edition published February 2013 by
Rough Guides Ltd,
80 Strand, London WC2R 0RL
11, Community Centre, Panchsheel Park,
New Delhi 110017, India
Distributed by the Penguin Group
Penguin Books Ltd,
80 Strand, London WC2R 0RL
Penguin Group (USA)
375 Hudson Street, NY 10014, USA
Penguin Group (Australia)
250 Camberwell Road, Camberwell,
Victoria 3124, Australia
Penguin Group (NZ)
67 Apollo Drive, Mairangi Bay, Auckland 1310,
New Zealand
Penguin Group (South Africa)
Block D, Rosebank Office Park, 181 Jan Smuts Avenue,
Parktown North, Gauteng, South Africa 2193
Rough Guides is represented in Canada by Tourmaline
Editions Inc. 662 King Street West, Suite 304, Toronto,
Ontario M5V 1M7

Help us update

We've gone to a lot of effort to ensure that the 4th edition of **First-Time Around the World** is accurate and up-to-date. However, things change and if you feel we've got it wrong or left something out, we'd like to know.

Please send your comments with the subject line "**First-Time Around the World Update**" to @mail@uk.roughguides.com. We'll credit all contributions and send a copy of the next edition (or any other Rough Guide if you prefer) for the very best emails.

Find more travel information, connect with fellow travellers and book your trip on ⓦroughguides.com

Photo credits

Index

Maps are marked in grey